HAEGE'S
HOMESTYLE
ARTICLES
The Detroit News, 2000-01

Glenn Haege

Edited by Kathy Stief
Cover Photo by Edward R. Noble
Back Cover Photo by Ewald Stief

MASTER HANDYMAN PRESS, INC.

HAEGE'S
HOMESTYLE
ARTICLES
The Detroit News, 2000-01

Glenn Haege

Edited by Kathy Stief

Published by:
Master Handyman Press, Inc.
Post Office Box 1498
Royal Oak, MI 48068-1498 USA

First Printing April 2002

Printed in the United States of America

Library of Congress Card Number: 2002090496
Haege, Glenn
        Collected Detroit News Homestyle Magazine Handyman articles.
        Bibliography: h.

ISBN 1-880615-66-5

To all our "new editions"
at Master Handyman Press,
my new granddaughter Macy Kate
and her big sister Emily Diane,
my new grandson, Matthew Robert
and Kathleen's new granddaughter
Rosalie Pansy

Acknowledgments

The production of a large metropolitan daily newspaper is an incredible operation. How they seamlessly put together several editions of a huge newspaper day after day is awe-inspiring.

My relationship with the Detroit News is primarily with the Features section and Homestyle magazine. I don't know how Felicia Henderson, Rita Holt, Judy Diebolt, Marge Colburn and Sandy Silfven do what they do; but I am certainly glad that they include me as a small part of their team.

My Master Handyman Press crew is the other half of the team that makes my two weekly columns possible. In the sports world there's a saying that before you become a true professional you have to learn how to play through pain.

This year, my guys and gals proved themselves to be "true professionals." One member of the team lost his wife then went though a life threatening operation. Another had an automobile accident that would have been fatal if her Guardian Angel hadn't been working overtime.

In most organizations these folks would have been out for months. Not my crew. They kept coming in and "playing through pain". They are an inspiration to us all.

Big thanks also go to the WXYT crew who make my radio show a very enjoyable labor of love. My producer, Dave "King Pin" Riger, engineer, Tim "Short Order" Cook, are both unequalled anywhere. When Westwood One, the syndicator of the national "Ask the Handyman Show", decided to get out of the weekend talk show business, my executive producer, Rob David, took over the entire operation. The transition was seamless. I am sure Rob didn't sleep for a couple of months, but who's counting? See what I mean by being surrounded by professionals?

To all of you, my profound thanks. You make it seem so easy. My wife, Barbara, and I thank our lucky stars we have you all for co-workers and friends.

Glenn Haege
Royal Oak, Michigan

Table of Contents

Chapter 2 2001   **125**

December

Table of Subjects

INTERIOR

Introduction

This is the second book in my series of Detroit News Homestyle article reprints. The first book covered my first five years with the News, 1995 through 1999. This book covers 2000 and 2001.

The first book covered five years because I wanted readers to be able to access my News' articles from the very beginning. From now on I plan on bringing out reprint books every two years. From the readers point of view the stories will be fresher, containing more up to the minute information. Most home improvement books take so long to publish they are dated by the time they arrive in the stores. My Haege's Homestyle books come out a few months after the last article appears in the Detroit News.

From the writer's point of view, 104 articles are easier to work with than 500. The shorter format has allowed me to do things I could not do with the five-year book. Most important, I have been able to include a comprehensive, rather than a subject index. The first book subject index took 11 pages to cover five years. This book's comprehensive index takes 23 pages to cover 2 years.

In this book every subject and every expert I refer to in the articles, as well as every product and company I mention, is indexed. Hopefully, no matter how your mind works, you should be able to find the information you need. Cross-indexing alone took my staff 3 weeks.

I continued my practice of including both a traditional table of contents and a table of subjects. This way you can easily track all the articles on the subject area in which you are most interested. In most cases I carried over the subject headings from the first book. If you have the first book you can easily track the changes in the industry you are researching. I also used a multiple listing technique. If an article contains information on more than one subject area, I included it in every area.

In the last book I included a comprehensive phone listing at the end of the book. This year I settled for listing the phone numbers where they appear in the various articles. Barbara Andersen, with the able assistance of my office manager and her daughter, Kelly Boike, called every phone number in all the articles. Corrections where made whereever the area code or the number had changed. Regrettably, some companies have gone out of business. Where that happened we retained the reference but removed the telephone number.

Your home is your single most valuable investment. Your checkbook is the most powerful tool in your toolbox. My Detroit News Homestyle articles are designed to help you either make your new home the best it can be or to help you maintain and enhance your present investment. I do everything I can to put your checkbook on steroids and maximize the efficiency of every dime you spend.

My staff and I took the accumulated articles and did everything we could to make this book an enjoyable read and a state-of-the-art reference tool. If you want to get even more information on a particular subject check my web site, www.masterhandyman.com. You will find my latest Homestyle articles, all my weekly Detroit News Thursday Feature "Ask Glenn" articles, plus the complete listing of my most requested telephone numbers with direct links to the companies' web sites.

Enjoy the read. Use these articles to make your house the home of your dreams, then brag about the result.

WARNING - DISCLAIMER

This book is designed to provide information for the home handy man and woman. It is sold with the understanding that the publisher and author are not engaged in rendering legal, contractor, architectural, or other professional services. If expert assistance is required, the services of competent professionals should be sought.

Every effort has been made to make this text as complete and accurate as possible, and to assure proper credit is given to various contributors and manufacturers, etc.. However, there may be mistakes, both typographical and in content. Therefore, this text should be used only as a general guide and not as the ultimate source of information. Furthermore this book contains information only up to the printing date.

The purpose of this book is to educate and entertain. The author and Master Handyman Press shall have neither liability nor responsibility to any person or entity with respect to any loss or damage caused directly or indirectly by the information contained in this book.

WARNING - DISCLAIMER

Trademark Acknowledgments

Trademarked names, rather than confusion inducing, generic names, are used throughout this book so that readers can ask distributors, retailers, and contractors, about products that interest them. Rather than list the names and entities that own each trademark or insert a trademark symbol with each mention of the trademarked name, the publisher states that it is using the names only for editorial purposes and to the benefit of the trademark owner with no intent of infringing upon that trademark.

Trademark Acknowledgments

Chapter 1

2000 Articles reprinted from The Detroit News HOMESTYLE

Here are New Year's resolutions I'd like to see in building industry

by Glenn Haege,
America's Master Handyman

The nice thing about reading this article is that it means that the world did not end at 12:01 a.m. Eastern Standard Time. If you read the entire newspaper without being hit by a falling airliner you will probably make it through the rest of the day.

Making New Year's resolutions can be fun ... especially if you get to make them for other people. I decided to suggest some needed resolutions for the movers and shakers in the housing and home improvement industry. Here are five resolutions I'd like to see become reality in the next few years.

Resolution No. 1: Commit enough resources to residential building regulation, or get out of the business.

The governor of our fair state and our state legislators should decide once and for all whether the state should be in or out of the residential building regulation business.

If the state wants to regulate builders, there need to be enough inspectors and enforcement people to get the done job properly. For a start, Michigan should increase the number of state building inspectors by about 20 times the present number. This would put enough manpower on the job to get it done.

And why can't the state provide free 800 phone numbers so that taxpayers can call

and find out if the builder they want to hire is a legitimate businessman or a scumbag?

The Michigan State Commerce Department is not the Psychic Hotline. Taxpayers should not have to pay 900 phone line fees to get information they have a right to expect.

If the governor and legislature don't want to pay the bill for staffing properly, get the government out of the building regulation business. Pass legislation so that every job, or series of jobs totaling $2,000 or more, has to be bonded for triple the job cost (That's usually what it costs when a job has gone bad and has to be torn down and rebuilt).

If all the jobs were bonded, the bonding company would police builders and make sure customers got what they paid for. When a home owner was not pleased, he or she wouldn't have to go to court or swear out a complaint, they could look to the bonding company to make good on the job. After one or two bad bonds, the bonding companies would stop bonding a bad builder and he or she would be out of business. Simple.

Resolution No. 2: Compete on quality, not price.

I hate to hear that a builder is building to code. Building to code means that the builder is doing the minimum he can get away with and still pass inspection.

I'm sick to death of seeing $200,000 to $1,000,000 homes with cheap garbage disposers and builder's quality windows and garage doors that are only meant to last seven years. I hate the term builder quality. Builder quality should mean top quality. Instead it means the cheapest quality a builder, painter, plumber, roofer, or electrician can get away with.

Hey, it's the new millennium, fellows. You have more work than you can handle. If you're ever going to make the transition from cheap to quality, the time is now. Sure, you are going to lose some business if you don't have the lowest price. But right now, new customers, and customers who want quality, are relatively easy to come by. Why not all band together to give the public the good-quality housing and remodeling they need, and of which you can be proud?

Resolution No. 3: Get the greed for growth out of zoning.

Wouldn't it be wonderful if starting today every member of every zoning board resolved to remember that he or she works for his or her constituents, not the Chamber of Commerce or the megabuilders. Growth should not be approved for growth's sake.

It is the obligation of zoning boards to work to enhance the quality of life of the people they serve, not to increase the tax base at the expense of the citizens who already live there. Please, no more over-commercialization. No more new malls on over-burdened highways. No more building on unsettled land.

Resolution No. 4: Make building permits a guarantee of service.

Builders and buyers have a right to believe that when the building department grants a permit, that department has the necessary staff to provide the inspections and oversight required on a timely basis. Don't grant a building permit if you don't have enough building inspectors to do the job.

While you're at it, standardize your permit fee structure. According to state law, permit fees are not supposed to be income generators. When you make them too high, people tend to avoid applying for permits, creating the very hazards building that inspections were designed to eliminate.

Resolution No. 5: Be as straight-forward with the builder as you want him to be with you.

By and large builders are some of the hardest working, most honest people I know. They often put in 18- to 20-hour days trying to get the job done on time and on budget. Buyers should work with them, be straightforward with them and not try to nickel and dime them to death.

We've got ourselves a new millennium, folks. Let's all work together to make the most of it.

Do me a favor. Clip this article and pass it on to your grandkids or put it in a time capsule. Let's see if anything on my list becomes reality in the next 100 years.

Happy New Year!

Warm up to the various kinds of ice melters to get through winter

by Glenn Haege,
America's Master Handyman

Although it was warm enough to play golf or tennis this New Year's Day, we have only to look at last year's newspapers to be reminded about Michigan winters.

A headline on the front page of the Jan. 23 combined issue of The Detroit News and Free Press said, "Metro Detroit finds itself underwater. Sudden snowmelt, rain reveal crumbling roads while basements flood."

While we may have missed the Y2K Bug last week, there is no way we are going to dodge our annual war against winter, and it is up to us to be prepared.

The stores still have plenty of weapons for the Battle of the Blizzard. For those who like hand weapons, there are ergonomic snow shovels and roof rakes (long-handled, hoelike objects used to pull snow off roofs before it can cause damage). For those who prefer heavy artillery, there's still a fair assortment of all but the most popular-priced snow throwers. We are even blessed with plentiful supplies of rock salt, other ice melters and traction sand. But rest assured, as soon as we get our first big snowfall, they will disappear from retailer's shelves.

Ice melters are one of the best tools in our winter arsenal, but they are often misunderstood. I asked Steve Klocko, president of Gibraltar National Corp., which makes Quikrete, to review basic cold weather procedures. Gibraltar, (800) GIBRALTAR (442-7258), makes one of the largest selections of ice melters in the country.

Klocko's first words were: "Too many people use too much ice melter. The purpose of an ice melter is not to eliminate snow or ice, but to cut through and break the bond with the surface below. Once the bond is broken, ice and snow can be swept, shoveled or scraped away."

Ice melters should be spread like chicken feed. When distributed properly, ice melters do their job and disappear. When spread too thickly, they clump and can be tracked into the house or melt into a solution that can damage lawns and shrubs.

Not all ice melters are created equal. Klocko says that there are basically five types of ice melter, good old rock salt (which is technically sodium chloride), calcium chloride, potassium chloride, magnesium chloride and urea.

Rock salt (sodium chloride). This is the least expensive and the least effective of the five. It is only effective down to 20 degrees Fahrenheit. When it gets colder than that, it does nothing.

Calcium chloride. This is the fastest, most powerful and most expensive of ice melters and is 10 times more expensive than rock salt. It is produced from calcium chloride brine and formed into pellets or flakes. In the pellet form, it burrows down to the under-surface, creates its own heat and melts. It is effective to -25 degrees.

In its flake form, calcium chloride starts out being as effective as the pellet but

4

loses power rapidly and does not "burrow down." It does provide good traction for a limited period.

Magnesium chloride, potassium chloride and urea. Magnesium chloride is effective down to -13 degrees. Potassium chloride is effective to 12 degrees. Urea is effective to about 15 degrees. Their biggest benefit is that they are easier on the soil and surrounding vegetation than rock salt. Potassium chloride and urea are fertilizers, so they actually help heal the soil.

"When a person goes into a store to shop for ice melters, they can't just pick up any bag and expect them all to be the same," Klocko says. "They should read the bag just like they do when buying fertilizer. Reading the ingredients will tell you whether you have sodium, calcium, magnesium, potassium chloride or urea, or a combination of several of these.

"For instance the brand names Gibraltar makes are Quikrete Rock Salt, GNC Snow and Ice Melt Crystals (sodium chloride), Gibraltar Storm Front Calcium Chloride Pellets, Gibraltar DualFlake Calcium Chloride Flake, Mag Chloride Pellets (magnesium chloride) and Gibraltar Ice Devil Blended Deicer (sodium chloride, calcium chloride and potassium chloride).

Sodium chloride is the least expensive. Calcium chloride is the most expensive. The other products and blends are priced in between the two. All of these products are found in hardware, home center and even grocery stores.

A urea-based product called Anti Skid made by Suretrack Melt Inc., (717) 661-7179, also contains limestone chips. This is an excellent product for use on decks and walks or near delicate plants. It is so benign it can actually be dug into soil as a fertilizer when winter is over. In our market, Anti Skid is usually found at IGA supermarkets.

ICE MELTER EFFECTIVENESS CHART		
PRODUCT (DEGREES FAHRENHEIT)	TRADE NAME	EFFECTIVE TO
ROCK SALT	(Sodium Chloride)	PLUS 20 F
Sodium Chloride	GNC Snow & Ice Melt Crystals	PLUS 20 F
Urea	Sure Track Anti Skid	PLUS 15 F
Potassium Chloride		PLUS 12 F
Sodium Chloride, Calcium Chloride & Potassium Chloride Blend	Ice Devil	MINUS 10 F
Magnesium Chloride	Mag Chloride Pellets	MINUS 13 F
Calcium Chloride	Storm Front Pellets	MINUS 25 F
DualFlake Flakes		MINUS 25 F

Is the air in your house too dry? It isn't the heat, it's the humidity

by Glenn Haege,
America's Master Handyman

The desert is downright humid compared to our houses during the winter. For example, the Sahara Desert has a relative humidity of 25 percent, but the average heated home only hovers between 6 percent and 16 percent.

To solve the problem, most homes with forced air central heating systems have drum humidifiers, which look like foam-covered water wheels rotating in a tray of water.

Drum-style humidifiers are usually controlled by tiny humidistats located on or near the furnace. There are several problems with them: First, they need constant adjustment to provide more or less humidity every time the outside temperature changes, which few people do. Second, the drums become encrusted with minerals and are a breeding ground for bacteria and fungi. Third, there are now better systems available.

For cutting-edge technology, I asked three experts: Jim Williams of Williams Refrigeration and Heating, Warren, (888) 268-5445; Mark Ratliff of Hartford & Ratliff, Farmington, (800) 466-3110; and Mike Shorkey of Detroit Safety Furnace Co., Detroit, (800) 682-1538.

Williams Refrigeration and Heating is a residential and commercial heating company. Hartford & Ratliff specializes in hydronic and boiler type heating.

Detroit Safety Furnace is a major distributor of heating and cooling equipment.

Forced air heating systems

Natural gas, forced air central heating systems are the most common.

For these systems, Jim Williams favors the flow-through, powered humidifier made by companies such as Bryant, (800) 428-4326; Skuttle, (800) 848-9786; Research Products Aprilaire, (608) 257-8801; and Honeywell, (800) 345-6770.

In flow-through humidifiers, a broad trickle of water flows over an evaporative pad. Unused water drains out of the system. The two biggest benefits are far greater efficiency than drum-style humidifiers and continuous flushing. Bryant's Deluxe Fan-Powered Humidifier delivers up to 25 gallons of moisture a day. Aprilaire's Model 760 A has an evaporative capacity of .75 gallons an hour or 18 gallons a day.

A minor drawback is that $8 to $15 of water are wasted every year through drainage. I gladly pay this slight premium for increased health and comfort.

Williams estimates that replacing an old humidifier with the flow-through kind would cost between $325 and $500.

Mike Shorkey's favorite humidifier is the Humid-a-Mist Pulse Humidifier. This humidifier is an improvement upon

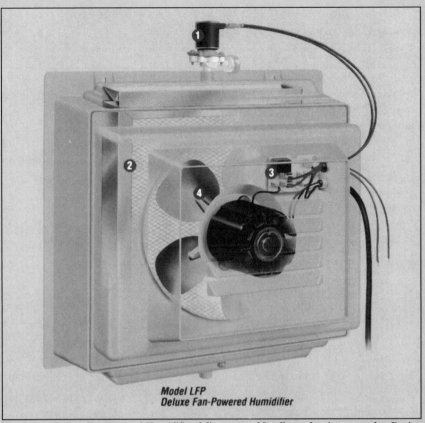

**Model LFP
Deluxe Fan-Powered Humidifier**

The Bryant Deluxe Fan-Powered Humidifier delivers up to 25 gallons of moisture per day. During operation, fresh water continuously flows over the evaporator pad, reducing mineral buildup and greatly prolonging service life.

the atomizing humidifier that sprays a fine mist into the hot air supply.

Usually, I am not in favor of this type of humidifier because a clogged misting nozzle can cause rusting.

Shorkey says the Humid-a-Mist solves this problem with a water filter that prevents clogging. In addition, the Humid-a-Mist is 100-percent effective, no water is wasted and no drain is needed. You can by-pass the heating system, permitting humidification with room temperature air.

The Humid-a-Mist is recommended for all forced air systems that do not have zoned heat. The installed cost should be in the $375 to $400 range.

All other heating systems

These include in-floor hydronic, electric or hot water baseboard, fireplaces or stoves, or any radiant heating system.

Folks without forced air thought they needed portable room humidifiers. According to Mark Ratliff, there are now two types of humidifiers available for hydronic, baseboard and other systems.

The first type uses hot water and includes Research Products' Aprilaire 350 and 360. The 350 is located underneath the floor, attached to the joists. Humidity is provided through a wall duct. The Aprilaire 360 is wall-mounted and distributes humidity through a wall grill. Both require 140-degree F water.

The second type includes high-capacity, steam-powered models such as the Skuttle 60 and the Honeywell HE 420/460. They are often used with heat pumps and Space Pak high-velocity forced air systems. Since humidification is created through internally produced steam, they can add humidity even at 70 degrees F.

According to Ratliff, both the hot water and steam systems have an average retail installed cost of $800.

Humidistat

No matter how good the humidifier, it will only produce the moisture needed if controlled by the proper humidistat. Furnace-mounted humidistats are ineffective because they are seldom adjusted properly.

Honeywell makes the H1008 Automatic Humidity Control and the PC8900

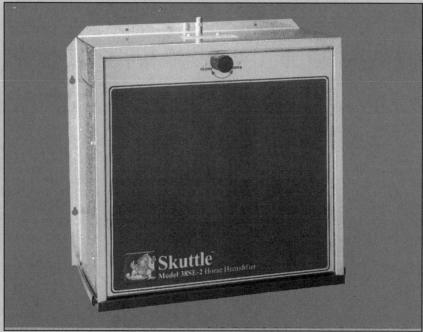

The Skuttle Model 38-SE2 By-Pass Flow-Thru Humidifier uses improved technology to reduce water consumption while maintaining an output capacity of 15.4 gallons of moisture per day at 120 degrees F. It can be mounted on either the return air or the warm air plenum.

Perfect Climate Control that calibrate both heat and humidity.

The Aprilaire Model 760A power humidifier features a truly automatic control that never needs to be set manually.

All humidifiers can have humidistats mounted next to the thermostat so that you never have to go downstairs to reset them when the weather changes.

Model 360

The Model 360 Aprilaire Humidifier is a wall mounted hot water humidifier. It can be used with any heating system but is especially useful in homes without forced air central heating. The 360 utilizes 140 degree F water to distribute up to 0.5 gallons of water per hour at 150 cubic feet per minute (cfm).

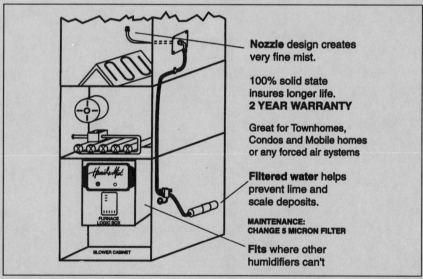

Nozzle design creates very fine mist.

100% solid state insures longer life. **2 YEAR WARRANTY**

Great for Townhomes, Condos and Mobile homes or any forced air systems

Filtered water helps prevent lime and scale deposits.

MAINTENANCE: CHANGE 5 MICRON FILTER

Fits where other humidifiers can't

The Humid-A-Mist Pulse Humidifier pulses a fine mist of moisture into the air stream of a forced air furnace system. The unit does not require heat to provide humidification and will deliver up to 14 gallons of moisture into the home's atmosphere. All water is pre-filtered. There is no standing water and no drainage is required.

9

Relative Humidity Conversion Chart

Outdoor Relative Humidity	-20	-10	-5	0	+5	+10	+15	+20	+25	+30	+35
100%	2	3	4	6	7	9	11	14	17	21	26
90%	2	2	4	5	6	8	10	12	15	19	23
80%	2	2	4	5	6	7	9	11	14	17	20
70%	1	2	3	4	5	6	8	10	12	15	18
60%	1	2	3	3	4	5	7	8	10	13	15
50%	1	1	2	3	4	4	6	7	9	10	13
40%	–	1	2	2	3	4	4	6	7	8	10
30%	–	1	1	2	2	3	3	4	5	6	8
20%	–	1	1	1	1	2	2	3	3	4	5
10%	–	–	–	1	1	1	1	1	2	2	3
0%	0	0	0	0	0	0	0	0	0	0	0

Outdoor Temperature

Courtesy of Skuttle Indoor Air Quality and ASI.

Impact of Relative Humidity on Air Quality

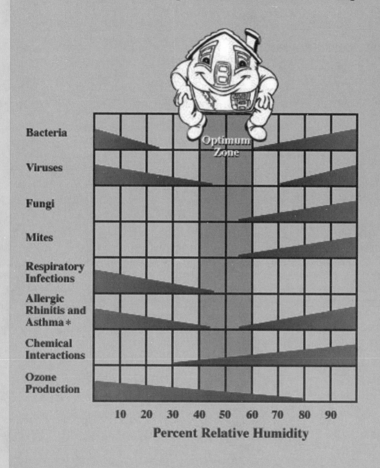

Courtesy of Skuttle Indoor Air Quality and
ASHRAE.

Latest in kitchen, laundry appliances rule national builders' show

by Glenn Haege,
America's Master Handyman

DALLAS

Last weekend, my staff and I joined an estimated 70,000 U.S. builders who had come to see 1,000 state-of-the-art exhibits from around the world at the Dallas Convention Center (more on the exhibits later).

The building industry enjoyed a boom year in 1999, so it's no surprise that everyone we talked to at the National Association of Home Builders International Builders show was confident that business would continue to be good in the new decade.

Even so, the American building industry has been experiencing almost too much of a good thing for the past several years. Operating at near-record levels has resulted in shortages in labor and key materials, said David F. Seiders, senior staff vice-president and chief economist of the Association. Seiders said he expects the Building Industry to experience a slight reduction in sales this year, which would allow builders and manufacturers to catch up with demand.

As far as new products were concerned, the biggest news was in kitchen and laundry appliances. Most other innovations were refinements or attempts to work around the industry-wide labor shortage.

Appliances and faucets

Some of the most exciting innovations are coming from appliance manufacturers.

GE, (800) 626-2000, soon will be introducing kitchen appliances that talk to each other and you via X10 technology. The futuristic refrigerator they had on display not only keeps food cold, it keeps a running inventory of the food used via a bar code scanner that logs the food in and out, then makes up a shopping list. GE's microwave will also set the cooking time of a product after it has scanned the bar code on the packaging. GE is partnering with Microsoft on this concept.

Maytag, (800) 688-9900, introduced refrigerators with ClimateZone, a new cold control feature that greatly extends the storage life of food. For example, a beef steak with a recommended storage time of one to two days will stay good for four to five days in a ClimateZone drawer set to Meats (31 degrees F). Fruit that would normally last two to three days will last seven to nine days in a ClimateZone drawer set to 'Produce' (34 degrees F).

Whirlpool, (800) 253-3977, introduced a new washing machine with Catalyst Cleaning Action. This new laundry cycle virtually eliminates the need to pretreat clothes. Kevin Madden, fabric care brand manager at Whirlpool, says Whirlpool considers this the company's biggest breakthrough since it invented the permanent press cycle more than 30 years ago.

Stainless steel was very prevalent with all the appliance makers. GE led the way in two directions. Its Monogram refrigerator had contoured, rather than flat, doors, and it has brought the price down to a more affordable level on some of its 2000 series stainless steel appliances.

Delta Faucet, (800) 345-3358, pioneered the pull out kitchen faucet/spray. Over the years, the company's market share has declined as more and more me too designs entered the market. Now Delta is poised to retake a commanding market share with an absolutely elegant Pull-Out Spray Faucet that reaches a full 60 inches for maximum versatility. It also has an ergonomic design that makes it easier to use.

Tools

Many of the displays were labor-saving devices. Stanley Works, (800) 782-6539, showcased lighter hammers and the Fat Max 25 tape rule that can stretch 11 feet without bending. Stanley's Bostich power tool unit exemplified the newer, faster and lighter nailers and screwguns now being introduced by most power tool manufacturers.

Bosch, (800) 866-2022, stressed increased power. One of the tools the company highlighted was a 24-volt, cordless reciprocating saw with a 30-percent longer run time than 18-volt battery models.

Home security

Almost every manufacturer in the door or lock business is now featuring keyless entry systems like those pioneered by Weiser Lock, (800) 677-5625. Kwikset's AccessOne key fob can open up the entry door and a Genie Intellicode garage door. Stanley's new door system includes a lit entry-way. Look for Stanley to partner soon with a major automobile manufacturer to have the same key fob open the car, garage and entry door.

More innovations

Weather Shield, (800) 477-6808, a leading window manufacturer, demonstrated the strength of its impact-resistant glass window by taking attendees into a three-dimensional exhibit that put them in the eye of a hurricane and showed that the new window would still protect homes even when hit by flying 2-by-4s.

Pella Window, (800) 54-PELLA, introduced an all-new casement window with a very stream-lined fold-away handle that almost disappears from view.

Heat-N-Glo Fireplaces, (888) 427-3973, displayed an innovative diamond-shaped fireplace that turns a fireplace into an almost magical design statement.

Most of the features these I've written about will not be available for 60 days to six months. I'll keep you posted.

JANUARY 29, 2000

Home products go high-tech Chicago Housewares Show lays out the new, the odd, the inventive

by Glenn Haege,
America's Master Handyman

CHICAGO

Every creature feathers its nest. When birds do it, they use pieces of twine and twigs. We use housewares to make a house a home. Housewares also make a heck of a big business. According to the National Housewares Manufacturers Association, housewares are a $63-billion industry.

Last week, the people who make the life-and-death decisions about what you and I put in our homes, the housewares buyers, had a look at what's new. They got together at the McCormick Center in Chicago for the International Housewares Show.

Buyers came from all over, Kmart, Target, JCPenney, Sears, Costco, Sam's Club, Wal-Mart, the department stores and cataloguers.

According to Jon Hauptman, senior associate at Willard Bishop Consulting Ltd., authors of the National Housewares Manufacturers Association's State of the Industry Report, three major trends will keep the housewares industry growing: Internet retailing, children's purchases and a booming seniors' market.

Seniors are the nation's most affluent buying group, and their numbers will double in the next 30 years, Hauptman says. From an ergonomic angle, that means almost every company is trying to make its products easier to use by older people. Softer, larger handles were everywhere. So were feel-good products such as aromatherapy, magnets and spas.

While looking at products in the kitchenwares section of the show, I

Photos by Ewald Stief

came across a very interesting saute pan by T-Fal Corp., (800) 395-8325. The center of each pan has a Thermospot that changes shape and color when the frying pan reaches the perfect temperature.

I asked Renee Paoletti, a buyer for the Damman Hardware chain in Madison Heights and one of eight people Damman sent to the show, what she thought of the saute pan. Paoletti was unimpressed. "Any cook who doesn't know when a frying pan is hot enough shouldn't be cooking," she said.

The biggest trend Paoletti noticed was that products are becoming more upscale. "The introduction of Krups into the upscale iron market is causing a lot of excitement. Damman, however, is sticking with Rowenta. When Rowenta's new $245 steam generator ironing system becomes available, we will definitely carry it in some of our bigger housewares departments," she says.

What makes the Housewares Show so exciting is that it's a monumental crap shoot. The market will decide the fate of the Thermospot saute pan and all the other new products. The show is extremely important to many small businesses. It's their one chance to demonstrate their products to the world. If they don't get orders, they may not be around next year.

One Michigan company did very well at the show.

 Pat Hanna of Hold-It Products in Walled Lake, (888) 766-4742, was showcasing the Easy Cleat Window Cord Keeper, a see-through plastic cleat that is attached to the window with suction cups allowing cords to be stored out of harm's way. Hanna and his brother, Bob, developed the product after Hanna read about an 18-month-old who was alone in his room and strangled to death while playing with a window blind cord.

Even before the Housewares Show, Easy Cleat already had been introduced in 1,000 Wal-Mart stores. "Buyers at the show got so excited that the Easy Cleat will be in all Meijer, Kroger and Home Depot stores in the next few months," Hanna says. "Big Canadian buyers are going to put it in almost all pharmacies and grocery stores in that country, too."

While most of the products at the show should be arriving in stores between April and June, Paoletti warns that manufacturers do not always live up to their promised shipment dates.

"One of the products I wanted to buy last year was just re-introduced at this year's show and I have no idea when it will actually be shipped," she says.

Housewares history

These facts about home products are courtesy of the National Housewares Manufacturers Association.

■ In 1864, Fred Walton created linoleum from oxidized linseed oil, cork powder and hessian.

■ A Bissell carpet sweeper cost $2.50 in 1900.

■ In 1908, inventive German housewife Melitta Benz lined a tin can with absorbent paper filters to strain coffee. The rest is history.

■ In 1930, Sunbeam sold 60,000 Mixmasters, the first stationary food mixer.

■ KitchenAid introduced the first electric coffee grinder designed by Egmont Arens in 1938.

■ Pyrex, used extensively in cookware, was developed for railroad signal lanterns.

■ The lint pickup was invented accidentally in 1956 by Nicholas McKay, when he forgot to dry-clean his suit.

■ In 1956, French engineer, Marc Gregoire affixed a thin layer of Teflon onto cookware. Voila! The first nonstick frying pan.

Glenn Haege picks out his favorite products from the show

Kitchens

 ***Dishwasher.*** The Countertop Dishwasher by Danby, (800) 26-DANBY, has microwave styling. It holds up to four place settings and hooks up to any sink faucet. Perfect for small apartments or dorms.

Blender. KitchenAid, (800) 541-6390, introduces the Professional Blender. It has a heavy-gauge, commercial-quality stainless-steel jar, powerful motor and stainless-steel blades. This powerful combination will allow you to crush ice at any speed.

 China. More than 100 chinaware companies had products on display. The most exciting thing to me was that the Home Lauglin China Co., (800) 452-4462, is introducing the first new Fiestaware in more than 40 years, called Fiestaware 2000.

Convection oven. Schaffield U.S. introduced a miniature, portable convection oven, Model AX- 737. It broils, bakes, barbecues, fries, roasts, boils without water, grills and steams. Imagine, all that and you can carry it from room to room.

Cutting board. Schaffield U.S. also has introduced two Cut & Slice Flexible Cutting Mats that let you slice or dice on the board, then use the mat like a scoop to pour the ingredients into a pan or bowl.

Pots & pans. Mirro/Wearever Division of Newell Rubbermaid, (800) 518-6245, has a new set of stainless steel pots and pans with Soft Grip handles that are stain-resistant, dishwasher-safe and oven-safe up to 400 degrees F.

Tea kettles. De Longhi, (800) 322-3848, continued its retro trend with a stainless steel, electric kettle that shuts off automatically when water reaches the boiling point. Joyce Chen, (800) 333-0208, introduced Splash porcelain teapots with a built-in strainer that keeps loose tea leaves in the pot.

Toaster oven. Toastmaster Inc., (800) 947-3744, makes upkeep a breeze with a toaster oven/broiler with a removable liner that pulls out and is dishwasher safe.

Glenn Haege picks out his favorite products from the show

Bedroom & bath

These innovations stress relaxation and indulgence.

Shower. DM Industries Ltd., (800) 848-2772, debuted the Shower Spa 3000D, which hooks up to your original shower mount and gives you a shower head, two top-loading soap dispensers, a body spray and towel bar, yet costs only $150. The deluxe full-body model gives eight showerheads and a shaving seat for only $1,100. If I got in, I might never leave.

Children's electric toothbrush. Oralgiene USA Inc., (800) 933-6725, has developed the perfect way to get kids to want to brush their teeth: the 60 Second Time Machine. This rechargeable toothbrush has lights, colorful gears and a special brush head that cleans the front, back and bottom of the teeth at the same time.

Remington Product's new spa therapy paraffin wax heat units soothe and soften the skin. Paraffin spa. Remington, (800) 736-4648, has added three Paraffin Wax Heat Treatment units to its Spa Therapy Collection. The machines can provide heat therapy, and soothe and soften the skin you love to touch.

Alarm clock. The Rise & Shine Natural Alarm Clock by Verilux Inc., (800) 786-6850, wakes you in the morning and puts you to sleep at night with natural light and sounds. There is also a back-up battery and snooze button.

Glenn Haege picks out his favorite products from the show

Laundry and storage

Compact washing machines. Haier America Trading LLC, (877) 337-3639, a $2-billion Chinese company, is introducing itself  to the United States with very compact three- and four-cycle, 3.3- and 8.8-pound top-loading washing machines. Danby, (800) 26-DANBY, offers a compact single unit, side-by-side washer/dryer. No apartment is now too small to have a drier of its own.

Iron. If you are looking for a heavy-duty steam iron, Rowenta Inc., (781) 396-0600, is the hands-down winner with its new Steam Generator, a powerful combination of a lightweight iron connected to a 33-ounce water tank. It produces enough steam for up to 1.5 hours of continuous operation.

Ironing board. Whitney Design, (800) 922-5524, has an ironing board that takes up almost no room. Just hook it up to the side of the dryer. It folds out of the way when not needed.

Storage bag. Presto Products Co., (800) 558-3525, has developed the Press Pack Reusable Storage Bag. Fill it with things you want to store, zip shut, then press or roll out the excess air. The air escapes through a patented one-way valve, creating compact, near-vacuum storage. Very convenient when traveling.

Glenn Haege picks out his favorite products from the show

Cleaning

Otres' kitchen sanitizer kills bacteria on sponges with activated oxygen. Anti-microbial products. These are the wave of the future. Almost every cleaning rag or sponge maker is touting some form of this technology. One company, however, stands out.

 *Web-Core,* (630) 961-4504, has developed two new products that use activated oxygen technology to sanitize kitchen sponges and toothbrushes. The Otres Kitchen Sponge Sanitizer replaces your current sponge holder. When you're finished cleaning, just put the sponge in the Sanitizer. Four hours later the sponge will be 99.9-percent germ free.

The Otress Toothbrush Sanitizer does the same thing for all your toothbrushes in three hours.

Cleaning cloth. Euroshine USA, (888) 441-1180, is introducing an ultrafine microfiber cleaning cloth. Just wipe with a dampened cloth and the microfiber easily eliminates dust and fingerprints. No chemicals are needed. The cloth is recommended for cleaning eyeglasses and optical lenses, furniture and flooring.

Cleaning mitt. When people do a lot of cleaning, they usually wear rubber gloves and hold a sponge or scouring pad. But Duramitt combines both functions. It's a work mitt to which a sponge or abrasive pad has been permanently bonded and is manufactured by Knight International Holdings, (312) 616-8888. Vacuum cleaner. Panasonic, (800) 211-7262, has eliminated drive belts in its new Beltless Drive Vacuum Cleaner. No more breaking belts! This breakthrough makes it a sure winner.

Steamer. Eureka Co., (800) 438-7352, has brought steam cleaning into the under-$100 price category with its HotShot Hand Steamer and Steam Mop. Both products deep-clean and sanitize with steam. No cleaning chemicals are necessary. The Hand Steamer solves a multitude of cleaning problems. The Steam Mop is the ultimate cleaning machine for vinyl, hardwood, tile, or marble. Eureka!

FEBRUARY 5, 2000

Readers have more questions about air cleaners and humidifiers

by Glenn Haege,
America's Master Handyman

Over the past two months I've written stories on air cleaners, humidifiers and ice melters. Because I've received so much mail on these subjects and we still have 30 to 60 days of winter left, I decided to do a summing up article.

Furnace filters

After my Nov. 20 article on the Dynamic Electronic Air Cleaner that combines electronic air cleaning technology with a replaceable filter mat you throw away every 90 days, I received questions from people with breathing conditions, wondering whether the Dynamic or an 'Air Bear' thick media filter was best.

Roger Ferguson of Environmental Dynamics, (800) 916-7873, said that in some sensitive medical situations a thick media filter in front of a Dynamic Electronic Air Cleaner would make the ultimate easy-maintenance air cleaning system. The majority of us do not need this much air quality. If you do, the combination should provide what you need.

Dynamic also makes a console version for use in apartments or homes without duct work.

Too little humidity

As I've pointed out, if the air in your house is too dry, it isn't the heat that's the problem, it's the humidity.

The furnace humidifier's humidistat (control) should be adjusted up and down with changes in the outside temperature. The chart at right may help. It shows the recommended humidity settings at various outdoor temperatures.

Jim Williams of Williams Refrigeration, (810) 758-2020, says, if your skin feels too dry, adjust the humidistat upward. If windows start fogging, lower the humidistat setting slightly.

Many people ask if they should keep their furnace fans running all the time in an effort to increase humidity. Actually, that is a fairly good idea because the only time that air is being filtered, cleaned or humidified is when the furnace blower motor is operating.

Many newer furnaces have a low-speed constant fan setting that makes this possible. If yours doesn't you may want to add a warm mist-style portable room humidifier.

Too much humidity

I also get a lot of letters from people who feel they have too much humidity in their house. Their windows are fogging up and water is draining onto the floor. The problem is usually not over-humidification but rather poor air ventilation. Not enough fresh air is coming into the house for proper air exchange.

We put a lot of moisture in the air through cooking, washing, even breathing. In a properly ventilated house, indoor air is exhausted while outdoor air is brought in. Poor ventilation causes stagnant, moisture-laden air. Humid, warm air hits cold windowpanes and turns into ice or condenses into water that drips onto the wall. So icy, foggy or wet windows are often a sign that your house is not getting enough air infiltration, which means you are not getting enough clean, oxygen-rich air.

The lack of proper ventilation also creates a partial vacuum that causes your air-starved house to suck air in through every available opening. You feel more cold drafts, but more importantly, the vacuum condition can cause air to be pulled in through the chimney. This can cause the carbon monoxide and other gases released through burning fuel in your furnace to be pulled into the house. This condition is called Negative Air. It could kill you.

To fix a Negative Air problem, you need to increase the amount of air infiltration. There are two inexpensive ways to do this. The first is to have your heating contractor add a nonelectronic air infil-tration device such as the Skuttle Model 216, (800) 848-9786. Another way is to go to your hardware store and purchase a do-it-yourself Equalize Air Kit by Xavier Enterprises, (734) 462-1033, that you attach to a basement window permitting a perfect air balance in your home.

Ice melters

Much of the snow has melted off the roofs, but we are only a storm away from a snow/ice emergency.

Since the Jan. 8 article, readers have been asking if they can spread salt or other ice melters on their roofs. Simple answer: No. Asphalt roofs were not made for ice melters of any kind.

If too much snow and ice starts to collect on the roof, use the proper tools for removal. The local hardware stores I checked with tell me that roof rakes are in short supply but they are trying to get more.

One more word about ice melters. Remember, they are just supposed to break the bond between the ice and the under surface. Don't expect them to shovel for you.

HUMIDISTAT SETTING	
Outside Temperature	Recommended Humidistat Setting
-20 F	15%
-10 F	20%
0 F	25%
+10	30%
+20	35%

No. 1 home improvement show will make your kitchen No. 1, too

by Glenn Haege,
America's Master Handyman

Nothing beats being No. 1. Last weekend's 2000 Home Improvement at the Novi Expo Center was the first local home improvement show of the new millennium. If you say the millennium doesn't start until 2001, not to worry, Novi will be the first show in 2001, too.

The first show of the year is always exciting, and there were some especially exciting new products at the show. Let's start in the kitchen.

This year I was amazed at how fast some manufacturers turned around their products from announcements to actual retail products going out the door.

The winner in this category has to be the new pull-out kitchen faucets from Delta Faucet, (800) 345-3358. At the beginning of January, Ray Kennedy Jr. introduced the new pull-out faucets to the world at the National Association of Home Builders (NAHB) Show in Dallas, and here they are ready to be sold.

The Delta faucets were a hit at last weekend's booth manned by Nu-Way Supply, (248) 889-9666. Not only were the faucets on display, the folks at the booth were already able to talk about the sales excitement the new faucets are creating. It seems shoppers are attracted to the faucet's high arch, ergonomically designed spray head and wide spray area.

A dual temperature refrigerated wine rack by the Sub-Zero Freezer Co., (800) 222-7820, was another item just introduced at the NAHB Show, that was on display at the Trevarrow Appliance exhibit, (800) 482-1948. The new refrigerated wine rack permits you to store red and white wines at different temperatures. The under counter model holds 46 bottles.

Trevarrow was also exhibiting the Flashbake 120 by Quadlux. The new oven uses eight 1,000-watt tungsten-halogen lamps to create 1,650 watts of cooking energy. It bakes, browns, broils, roasts and defrosts in about half the time of a regular stove.

When I said that this looked a great deal like GE's new Advantium, the Flashbake rep said it should since they are the people who make the Advantium for GE, (800) 626-2000. The biggest advantage the Flashbake has is that you can plug it into a normal kitchen outlet. Special 240 service is not necessary.

My last kitchen product is at least a couple of million years old. Booms Stone Co., (313) 531-3000, displayed a slab of Red Marinace multicolored granite. The orange, red, black, brown, you name it, stone comes from a Brazilian river bed. This exotic stone is available for countertops and islands at only about $80 a square foot installed.

Kurtis Kitchen's KraftMaid home office showed how easy it is to have an elegantly detailed home office created from semi-custom cabinetry.

Kurtis Kitchen, (734) 522-7600, had a display that showed that KraftMaid cabinets, (800) 571-1990, have come out of the kitchen and are now in every room. It seems like all home offices have sterile-looking shelves. Kurtis used KraftMaid units to create custom-looking office cabinets and shelves. What an elegant look, some shelf edges even had molding.

One of the most attractive ways to dress up a wall, fireplace or entrance way is to add stone. Williams Panel Brick, (313) 538-6633, had a gigantic display that demonstrated how easy it is to install cultured stone on any surface. The look is magnificent, the time needed is minimal and they even have free classes on Saturdays.

The Gingerbread Playhouses from Peters True Value Hardware of Highland won the Outstanding Display Award and were a hit with the small fry. Some even had ladders to upstairs lofts.

Peters True Value Hardware, (248) 887-7795, always displays fun play areas for children. This year its gingerbread cottage playhouses were a big hit with the little kids. Some of the playhouses even had ladders leading up to loft apartments. My granddaughter Emily would love one of these things.

Stained Glass Stepping Stones by Zelenka of Grand Rapids were a big hit at the Landscapesource.com display. Each stained glass figure is inset into a concrete stone.

If you have a landscaping problem, you just got a new internet resource. Landscapesource.com is a local internet company that will be selling on the internet and offering guaranteed 48-hour delivery throughout southeastern Michigan. If you are not a web head yet, you can call them at (877) 977-PLANT.

Landscapesource.com also showed 14-inch and 8-inch stained glass stepping-stones. Zelenka Nursery Inc. of Grand Haven, (800) 253-3743, crafts the stepping stones.

MARCH 4, 2000

Take a look at what's inside the American home of the new century

by Glenn Haege,
America's Master Handyman

If you are shopping for a new home, do you want a new, new house or an old, new house? Many people don't realize that housing styles change much like automobiles. The difference is that with houses it is more like changing the model decade than the model year.

That's why we have '40s-style bungalows and '50s-style ranches. It does not mean that the ranch style was superior to the bungalow. Many people prefer bungalows. It only means that in the '50s, the ranch house was king.

The National Association of Home Builders (NAHB) held seminars at the recent International Builders' Show in Dallas to inform builders about cutting-edge design. They also built a house called the New American Home 2000, sponsored by the National Council of the Housing Industry, Builder magazine and Ladies' Home Journal.

One of the seminars had five of the nation's leading residential designers talking about trends that will soon sweep the country. The speakers were Carol

Glenn Haege will answer your questions in new Thursday column

Every Thursday starting this coming week, Handyman Glenn Haege will answer your questions about home maintenance and do-it-yourself projects. Got a question? Write Ask Glenn, P.O. Box 1498, Royal Oak, MI 48068-1498; or e-mail editor@ole.net

Lavender, Lita Dirks, Jeffrey LaFerta and Steven Fuller. The Moderator was Sanford Steinberg. All are principals of their own firms. Steinberg, Fuller and LaFerta are AIA (American Institute of Architects) architects.

The New American Home 2000 implemented many of these trends. The house was designed by the Evans Group of Orlando, FL, and built by Custom Home Group, LLC, of Dallas. You can take a virtual tour of the home on Builder magazine's web site: www.builderonline.com.

The 4,495-square-foot home is located in Frisco, an exclusive Dallas suburb. At a mere $975,000, the house is way out of my price range, but many of the same cutting-edge design ideas can be carried out in $150,000 to $300,000 houses to which ordinary mortals can aspire.

OK, so what's new?

Old is in.

Not just old, but Mediterranean design. Name dropping words are Tuscan, Piedmontese, Italian Country and French Country Chateau looks. All those fancy stone work, pillars and curved arches have made it from being hidden treasures in Italian neighborhoods into the big-time architectural look.

Massive two-story exterior grand entrances are out; one-story, 8-foot-high door entrances are in. So are columns and turrets, also called rotundas. One sentence of clarification: Outside, the entrance is one-story. Inside, this still opens into a two-story vestibule/ entrance way.

The front of the house may not be at the front of the house.

Say what?

The way the designers have it figured, attractive single-story elements should project from the front and back of the double story main house. In the front it may be a single story living room or library that visitors pass on their way to the front door. In the back it could be a family room, garage or bedroom that combine to form an intimate L- or U-shaped courtyard.

Another in thing is to have several shallow-pitched roofing elements, rather than one main roof. Authentic clay tile and concrete tile looks are preferred roofing materials. The garage roof may be at a right angle to the rest of the house. Outcropping rooms may even have shed roofs to make them look as if they were added on over the centuries.

Roomy front and back porches and balconies are back. The consensus was that they should not just be design elements. They must provide comfortable, outdoor rooms.

Eclectic mixing and matching of materials for the exterior skin of the home is a big design feature.

For instance, a home's exterior may be a mix of stone, brick, stucco and wood. Easy-care vinyl and cementitious board, like Hardi-board, may stand in for wood.

The caveat is that all materials have to meld together. Colors must compliment each other.

Heavy materials, such as brick, stone and stucco should provide a base. Wood and shingle can cover the upper reaches.

Garages are pushed back and camouflaged with porte-cocheres wherever possible. The porte-cochere can be anything from a pillared arch to a trellis you drive through to reach the garage.

Finally, smaller lot sizes make private courtyards and landscaping that compliments the home's design more important than ever.

If you're house hunting, and having the newest of the new is important to you, look for the design elements I described here, then brag about it.

Guy's guide to grills gives him a chance to flex cooking skills

by Glenn Haege,
America's Master Handyman

As a lad, I used to love to burn rubber in my muscle cars. I don't mind telling you that I was close to being king of the hill. Nowadays, with a grandchild and everything, my wife, Barbara, won't let me drive my big Turbo Buick the way I used to.

Although muscle car days may be but a memory, I can still flex my muscles with my barbecue. New models debuting at the builder's shows are proof that I am not alone in my quest for the high testosterone grilling experience. Instead of horsepower, today's macho man brags about his grill's 16- or 18-gauge stainless steel and bigger, badder BTUs. Expect to see an independent authority come out with "sear" ratings that give performance criteria on the speed with which a given grill can crank out a medium rare steak.

I look at the new grills from the Olympian heights of an infrared gas griller. If Barb has the potatoes and salad ready, I can grill a steak, serve it to the family and be half finished eating it before ordinary gas grill guys have even flipped their steaks on the other side.

My TEC Infra-Red Gas Grill uses the same technology the automotive industry employs to flash dry paint. My grill's burners will sear a steak at up to 1,600 degrees F on high fire. I bought my TEC years ago at Michigan Fire Place & Bar-becue, (248) 689-2296. The new 2-burner TEC Patio II models start at about $1,600. If you need to feed an army, their 3-burner Sterling III runs about $3,500.

I like the TEC because it does an excellent job of searing in the meat's juices. Left unattended, it can turn a prime, 2-inch-thick New York strip into a cinder faster than you can answer the doorbell.

Haege adds new column

Now you can read Glenn Haege two times each week, on Thursday and Saturday in Homestyle. Write to him at Handyman, P.O. Box 1498, Royal Oak, MI 48068-1498, or e-mail: askglenn@ MasterHandyman.com. Include name and city.

Viking, the indoor oven company, came out with a state-of-the-art outdoor grill last year. Viking also went the infrared grill route. Two high-intensity burners put out 30,000 BTUs. Rotisserie models have an additional 15,000-BTU burner. Optional side burners are available. Base price for the heavy duty, stainless steel, 30-inch model is $2734. Add $400 for a rotisserie. Believe it or not, Viking's biggest problem is that they can't make them fast enough. Jimmies Rustics, (734) 522-9200, carry Viking and many other barbecues.

Two brand-new conventional grills have entered the high stakes, high-end competition. The Emberglow Outdoor Stainless Steel Grill by Sureheat, (800) 229-5647, is a 4-burner barbecue rated at 40,000 BTUs. The company claims a 1,000-degree searing temperature. Introductory priced at $1,199, the 16-gauge stainless steel grill carries a 98-year limited warranty. You can even take out two of the burners and cook with charcoal on one side to get a true charcoal taste. Emberglow is carried by William's Panel Brick, (800) 538-6650.

Patio Gourmet, the new barbecue by Heat-N-Glo, (800) 669-4328, the big fireplace people, is just being delivered. I first saw it at the company's research facility in December and have been waiting for it to appear on the scene before telling you about it.

The Patio Gourmet is built like a tank and carries a 10-year warranty. It uses stainless steel heat reflectors to provide even heat distribution. You can have cast iron or optional brass burners. Each is rated at 18,000 BTUs, giving the Patio Gourmet a drop dead 72,000-BTU capacity. Patio Gourmet is available with either a Jarrah wood or stainless steel cart. Prices range from $2,156 to $2,726. The new grill is at all Fireplace and Spa stores, (248) 353-0001.

Prices like these are enough to make most sane people forget about grilling and send out for pizza. There are many great grills made for rational people in the $200-to-$600 range. They include famous names such as Ducane, MHP, Broilmaster, Sunbeam and Weber.

They may grill as well as anything I've described today, but they will never turn your brother-in-law green with envy. I admit that it's a guy sort of thing. Muscle cars were never bargain priced.

Kitchen counters get sleek new surfaces

Granite, concrete, limestone and other durable materials offer stylish alternatives and are coming down in price, Glenn Haege says.

by Glenn Haege,
America's Master Handyman

Candise Waller of DeGiulio Kitchen & Bath in Birmingham says polished granite countertops add beauty to a home. Photos by Ricardo Thomas/The Detroit News

If your kitchen has polished granite kitchen countertops, you've come a long way from your mother's Formica or Wilsonart laminated surface, or even your older sister's Corian solid surface.

There is nothing wrong with laminated countertops. Bob O'Brien, general manager of Kurtis Kitchens and Bath Centers, estimates that about 85 percent of us still buy this very attractive and serviceable material when we remodel. It's the other 15 percent that is causing a kitchen frenzy.

On a "Wow Scale" of 1 to 10, polished granite is a 12. It has displaced Corian solid surface as the fashion leader. Honed stone is also coming on strong, along with concrete and stainless steel.

If you're considering a new look for your kitchen, remember that it's one of the best investments you can make. According to research by the National Association of Home Builders, the kitchen is the only room in the house that returns 111 percent on your investment.

Laminates are the obvious best choice if you are updating the kitchen but not replacing cabinets, if you are redoing your kitchen as a do-it-yourself project, or if you are concerned with getting the lowest out-the-door cost. Laminates are made from a plastic veneer glued to particle board. Formica, Nevamar and Wilsonart make the product in an almost inexhaustible number of colors. According to O'Brien, a laminated countertop lasts for about seven years.

Marsha DeSilva of West Bloomfield Township chose Corian solid surface countertops for her new kitchen. Her husband built the island countertop, at rear, from Brazilian cherry wood and granite. Photos by David Coates/The Detroit News

The American contemporary concrete countertop has been influenced by California designers. It is shown here with an overlapping movable cutting board.

Now, let's get to the high-fashion fun.

High gloss, polished granite is today's dominant high-end kitchen countertop material. Granite comes in an infinite variety of colors and patterns from all over the world. Architectural Stone of Troy carries a working inventory of 1,000 slabs in nearly 300 different colors, the popular Ubatuba is green, Violeta is beige, Blue Pearl is blue and there are dozens of blacks.

Kay Wisok of Beverly Hills is typical of the homeowners we talked to about why they chose granite. "It's just beautiful. I love the depth and brilliance of the look," she says.

Granite also combines beauty with strength and easy-care features.

Most granites have to be sealed with a penetrating sealer before being used as a countertop. But once sealed, you shouldn't have to worry about spills or scratches. Even so, you still shouldn't cut on it or put a pan on it that is hotter than 350 degrees (the bottom of a pan just off the stove can be 650 degrees).

As the popularity of granite increases it is becoming more affordable. Although some types of granite are rare, the high cost of granite is not usually caused by its scarcity but by labor costs. That's why stone from Europe and North America is expensive.

"Importing granite from India, China and Latin America combined with the introduction of labor-saving robotic shaping equipment has made granite a lot more affordable," says Garrett Van Horn of Architectural Stone. The installed cost on some polished granite has been reduced from $250-$350 per lineal foot to between $100-$150.

Scientists have been also hard at work trying to do Mother Nature one better, and cheaper. For example, Silestone is a man-made stone that is 95 percent natural quartz and recycled glass and granite, according to Ken Laymons of Ceramic Tile Sales in Southfield. "Silestone is like granite wishes it could be. It is harder than granite, doesn't stain or absorb moisture, so no maintenance is required, and it has a 10-year replacement warranty," Laymons says.

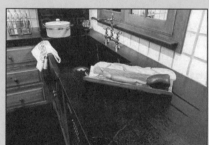

The countertop and sink have been handcrafted from soapstone. Grooves for a drainboard were routered into the stone.

Just as granite is becoming more affordable, honed limestone is starting to make a big impression. "The difference between polished and honed stone is the difference between bright and shiny and

29

old and comfortable," says Candise Waller, a designer at DeGiulio Kitchen & Bath in Birmingham. "Polished stone has a mirrorlike appearance that many of our customers love. Honed stone gives a weathered mat finish to limestone and granite that exudes relaxed Old World charm," she says.

Expect the growing popularity of Old World Mediterranean looks in exterior home design to make honed granite and limestone countertops popular and to bring about a resurgence in earth-toned and tumbled marble, ceramic tile and terrazzo.

Concrete is slowly making its way east from California. Designers like concrete because it can be tinted, stamped and inlaid with tile. Additionally, hand troweling the surface gives every concrete countertop a distinctive one-of-a kind appearance. On the down side, most local craftsmen still don't know how to work with concrete, and homeowners have to be willing to live with stress cracks. Presently DeGiulio Kitchen & Bath is the only local design center that features the product.

Stainless steel countertops are being used to compliment and extend the

The commercial influence of an easy-care stainless steel countertop is softened for the home with wood cabinetry.

clean, efficient lines of commercial-look stainless steel appliances. Although stainless steel scratches and shows fingerprints, it is very easy to clean, and it is impervious to hot pans, oils and stains. Wood cabinetry can be used to soften the look for use in the home.

There is still a lot to love with solid surface countertops. First introduced in the 1960s, DuPont Corian and newer solid surface materials made by Wilsonart and Swanstone are made from acrylic and polyester materials. They can be either shiny or have a matt finish. Because they are a solid surface, a router can be used to carve drain boards or make distinctive edges. They are also very easy to care for.

Since Corian and other solid surface materials have been nudged out of their high fashion slot, the industry has worked to make solid surface materials more price competitive to plastic laminates. DuPont has introduced the Corian Classic collection at a very competitive price. "This makes it possible for a large-volume distributor/installer, like Kurtis, to bring the installed cost of Corian down as low as $89 or $99 a lineal foot," O'Brien says.

Talon Industries has introduced Korstone, which is another lower cost, solid surface material. The Korstone kitchen countertop program is presently exclusively at Home Depot.

All of these surfaces are beautiful, but none of them are good cutting surfaces. For this reason, building in a section of butcher block countertop is becoming increasingly popular. The best butcher block material is considered to be secondary (second growth) sugar maple. This wood closes up after cutting and only needs an occasional application of mineral oil to stay looking beautiful.

Which leads us to another increasingly popular trend, the mixing of countertop materials. I call it eclectic, designers call it the unfitted look.

Here's how it works. When Dr. Stephen DeSilva and his wife, attorney Marsha DeSilva, of West Bloomfield Township, built their home with Robert R. Jones Associates, they chose Corian solid surface countertops, but they didn't stop there.

"In addition to being a hand surgeon, Steve's hobby is woodworking. We decided the wood left over from the construction of our Brazilian cherry wood floor was just too beautiful to waste. Steve designed and built our wood and granite island countertop," Marsha DeSilva says. The result was a countertop treasure that will always be a primary focus in their home.

You may not be as skilled as Dr. DeSilva, but by mixing and matching surface materials, you get a chance to express your personality and create a look that is uniquely your own. If you're on a budget, you can also use this trend to combine expensive and reasonably priced materials to bring down the overall cost.

In the final analysis, you should choose whatever goes best with your lifestyle and makes you and your family happy.

So enjoy yourself. Go for the gusto, then brag about it. You couldn't make a better investment.

Countertop cost comparison

Surface	Cost per lineal foot*	20-lineal foot countertop	Life expectancy
Polished granite	$100-$350	$2000-$7000	Lifetime
Corian and other solid surfaces	$89-$250	$1780-$5000	Lifetime
Concrete	$184-$368	$3680-$7360	Lifetime
Stainless Steel	$184-$368	$3680-$7360	Lifetime
Silestone	$130-$250	$2600-$5000	Lifetime
Laminate	$33-$50	$660-$1000	7 years

*Costs are for straight lineal feet. Special edge treatments, sinks and other modifications increase costs. Lineal feet are measured by the processed edges. A 2-foot by 3-foot island measures 10 lineal feet. A typical kitchen has 20 lineal feet of countertop.

Pros and cons of countertop materials

Surface	Heat resistance	Stain resistance	Scratch resistance
Concrete	Excellent	Fair	Good but no cutting
Polished and sealed granite	Good, nothing over 350 degrees	Excellent	Good but no cutting
Stainless steel	Excellent	Excellent	Good but no cutting
Corian and other solid surfaces	Not good, trivet suggested	Fair, most stains easily removed	Good but no cutting
Silestone	Excellent	Excellent	Good but no cutting
Tile	Excellent	Tile good, grout bad	Good but no cutting
Laminate	Not good, trivet suggested	Good but unrepairable	Good but unrepairable

Tips on buying

■ Where to get ideas: Look at all the builder and home magazines you can find. Visit kitchen and bath centers. Go to the big home shows, such as the one next weekend at Cobo Center.

■ Be practical: If you are just repainting or refacing your present kitchen cabinets, keep in mind that all cabinets have a 20-year service life. Redo the countertops with plastic laminate or simple tile that will only have a 7- to 10-year service life. Other countertop materials such as stone or solid surface will outlast the old cabinets and cannot be re-used.

■ Choosing a contractor: Kitchen remodeling is a work of art. Make sure the contractor has a good track record. Don't just look at pictures. Check out actual jobs and talk to former clients. Find out how fast the job was completed, how well the workers dealt with the family during the remodeling, how well they cleaned up after themselves and how prompt they were to make callbacks if something went wrong.

■ Can you do it yourself?: It's possible to install plastic laminate countertops yourself. Korstone has a special do-it-yourself program. And if you are meticulous, you can do simple tile work. However, professionals are needed to measure and install granite and other stones; Corian and other solid surface materials; concrete; stainless steel and Silestone.

■ Sources: For information, contact the following companies that helped with this article:
Architectural Stone, (248) 619-9900
Ceramic Tile Sales, (248) 356-6430
Dupont Corian, (800) 426-7426
Corian Distributor, (800) 444-7280
Formica Laminate, (800) 524-0159
Korstone, (877) 567-7866
Swan Corp., (800) 848-8707
Virginia Tile Co., (248) 649-4422
Wilsonart, (800) 433-3222
Kurtis Kitchens, (734) 522-7600
De Giulio Kitchens, (248) 258-6880
Home Depot, (248) 591-7520
– *Glenn Haege*

Kitchen shoppers can find lots of ideas at area home shows

by Glenn Haege
Special to The Detroit News

If you're kitchen or bath shopping, you are in luck. There are several home shows this weekend and next. Before you head out for a home show, here are some tips:

■ Make a list of the things you want to accomplish before you go to the show. If you've decided that this is the year to redo the kitchen or replace the windows, jot it down. If you're thinking about hardwood flooring or installing pavers, note that, too.

■ If you think you might need measurements, take them beforehand.

■ Wear comfortable shoes and go early. You'll have more energy, the crowds will be smaller, and salespeople are fresh early in the day.

■ Try to attend a talk about midway through the time you plan to be at the show. You'll not only learn something, you'll sit down for a half-hour and be revitalized for the rest of the day.

■ Don't just walk the show. As soon as you get your program, look up the must-see exhibits on your list and plan the most direct route. See everyone on your list first, then kick back and enjoy the show.

■ If you want to get a price quote from a particular company, ask if the owner or manager is there. Go over and introduce yourself. Ask if you sign up for an appointment today, when can you expect to be contacted? Then ask if you place an order within the next three weeks, when will the job be completed? By doing this, you'll be on a first-name basis with the boss, and you'll have a fairly good idea whether or not the firm can handle your business.

Go to the shows

Fourth annual WXYT Spring Home Expo, co-sponsored by Glenn Haege, who will be on hand to answer questions. 8 a.m.-6 p.m. today and Sun. Admission and parking free. Macomb Community College Center Campus, M-59 at Garfield, Clinton Township.

Lansing Home & Garden Show, 10 a.m.-9 p.m. today and 10 a.m.-6 p.m. Sun. Adults, $4. Children 6-14, $2. Children under 6, free. Michigan State University Pavilion, East Lansing.

82nd Annual GMC Builders Home and Detroit Flower Show, 2-10 p.m. Thurs. and Fri., 10 a.m.-10 p.m. March 25 and 10 a.m.-6 p.m. March 26. There is a mini-Kitchen and Bath Show inside this gigantic show, plus Kurtis Kitchen is bringing in top designer Jim Kringel to talk about new kitchen trends. Adults, $6.50. Seniors, $4.50. Children 6-12, $4. Children younger than 6, free. Cobo Conference-Exhibition Center, 1 Washington, Detroit.

Remodeling older homes ups lead risk

by Glenn Haege,
America's Master Handyman

Every so often we read newspaper stories about children in poor communities who have tested positive for lead poisoning. We think it's terrible that such a thing could still be happening, but we think it couldn't happen to us.

We fail to realize, however, that anyone living in a house built before 1978 could be in danger, too. It doesn't matter if your house has a value of $30,000 or $300,000.

Much of the housing stock, not just in big cities like Detroit, but also in hot suburbs such as Royal Oak, Troy, Rochester, Livonia and the Grosse Pointes, is pre-1978. During good economic times, homeowners cannot seem to remodel these homes fast enough. This very positive action could put these homeowners at risk.

The year 1978 is the cutoff because that's when the federal government banned the use of lead-based paint in residential housing. Before starting to panic, remember that the government says there is nothing wrong with lead-based paint as long as it stays on the wall. The Environmental Protection Agency pamphlet "Protect Your Family from Lead in Your Home" states, "Lead-based paint that is in good condition is usually not a hazard."

The danger comes from peeling, chipping, chalking or cracking lead-based paint. Your house has probably been repainted five times in the past 20 years and doesn't have any of those problems.

If your home was built before 1978, this EPA pamphlet, "Protect Your Family From Lead in Your Home," has vital information. Call the National Lead Information Clearinghouse, (800) 424-LEAD, for a free copy.

Unfortunately, according to the EPA, you can create a problem where none existed by remodeling. The hazard comes when electrical work, plumbing, carpentry, painting or window replacement disturbs a painted surface area over two square feet.

If you are having any of the work done professionally, or are living in a rental unit that is undergoing repairs, federal law states that the contractor must provide you with a copy of the "Protect Your Family" pamphlet before work begins.

The EPA is so serious about this that the booklet is published in both Spanish and English. Contractors are supposed to get a confirmation in writing from the owner and occupants that they have received the pamphlet.

Next to campaign finance laws, this is probably the most broken federal law on the books. The law does not apply to remodeling jobs or maintenance that you do yourself. But no matter who does the job, you should know about the potential dangers.

Removing or even cutting a wall puts a lot of dust into the air. If the wall was ever painted with lead-based paint, that dust could do you and your family damage. Lead dust can also form whenever lead-based paint is dry scraped, sanded or heated. Once the dust has settled, the vacuuming or sweeping can recirculate the lead dust in the air.

Work outside the house can spread lead dust onto the ground around the house. Children playing outside can absorb it. Just tracking dirt with lead dust into the house can redistribute the dust.

We all know that lead poisoning in children is dangerous. Growing bodies absorb lead more readily, and lead can damage children's hearing, brain and nervous systems.

Lead poisoning can create difficulties during pregnancy and cause other reproductive problems in both men and women. According to the EPA, it also promotes high blood pressure, digestive problems, nerve disorders and memory and concentration problems.

There are lead-testing kits, but the EPA says that they are not reliable. If you think that your home has a serious lead problem, you can call in a professional remediation contractor such as George Riegel's Healthy Homes, (248) 358-3311.

Lead is dangerous, but it can be handled. If you are going to remodel a home that has lead-based paint, take precautions to limit the risk. Workers should wear respirators and protective clothing while areas that have been painted with lead-based paint are removed.

Residue should be cleaned up and double bagged, then taken to a hazardous waste dump. The entire area should be washed with TSP (Trisodium Phosphate) and warm water. The mops and sponges used in cleaning must themselves be completely clean before they are re-used. Workers should shower on site and their clothing washed immediately.

Children and pregnant women should not be in the area while the work or cleanup is performed.

For information, call the National Lead Information Center, (800) LEAD-FYI or (800) 424-LEAD. Don't let the possibility that your home has lead-based paint stop you from remodeling. But this is definitely one time when learning all you can before you do so is the most important part of the job.

APRIL 1, 2000

These cleaning supplies, and a lot of elbow grease, will do the trick

by Glenn Haege,
America's Master Handyman

April Fool's Day, and if the Census wasn't bad enough, my wife, Barbara, handed me a draft notice from the SCC (Spring Cleaning Corps). This is no joke. After 31 years of married bliss, I know that life will be hell until the battle is over.

Spring cleaning is not something that can be postponed. All those billboards with the two big eyes on them are really pictures of America's mothers-in-law getting ready for their annual white glove inspections.

Not even Barbara, the official Ms. Clean of Metro Detroit, is close to being ready. There is so much happening in our lives, that we never quite get down to the in-depth cleaning that was standard in less hectic days.

I went looking for effortless answers to deep-cleaning questions. The first person I called was Mark Adams, the owner of Mr. Scrubs, (248) 548-0045, a Berkley janitorial service that specializes in cleaning big restaurants such as Applebee's, Merriweathers and the Outback Steak House.

If anyone should know the fast and easy way to handle grease and grime, Adams is the man. His secret weapon, elbow grease! "The best way to handle grease buildup is a good degreaser, hot water and plenty of elbow grease," he says.

OK, Mark, but is there a special degreaser that just cuts away all the grease and grime?

"All the professional degreasers at janitorial supply companies are basically the same. Most homeowners don't need anything that strong. My favorite product for in-home use is Spic & Span. Tell your readers to follow the directions. Most people use twice as much chemical as they should, and it doesn't do any good," Adams says.

The next person on my secret cleaning weapons list was Stuart Borman, one of the owners of Scrubs, Greenfield at 1012 Mile, (out of business). Scrubs is an entire supermarket-sized store devoted to everything in cleaning products.

He and Garrett Morris, Scrubs' cleaning expert, took me over to the sanitizer aisle. Garrett pulled out a gallon of Arrow Chemical Products' Fresh & Clean Neutraquat.

> *"My favorite product for in-home use is Spic & Span. Tell your readers to follow the directions. Most people use twice as much chemical as they should, and it doesn't do any good."*
> **Mark Adams**
> **Owner, Mr. Scrubs**

"If your readers are really serious about spring cleaning, this is the stuff," Morris says. "Arrow Fresh & Clean Neutraquat, (800) 482-0664, is designed for nonporous surfaces like tile, glazed porcelain, plastic laminate and stainless steel. It only costs $6.44 a gallon, but is a combination detergent, deodorizer, disinfectant, fungicide and mildewstat. It smells good, yet it is so strong that it will kill most any germ out there," he says.

According to Borman, the only problem is that the product is so concentrated you only need 2 ounces in a gallon of water to clean all the nonporous surfaces in your house. What do you do with the other 126 ounces of concentrate?

Any other cleaning secrets?

"Gleme Glass Cleaner by Claire Manufacturing may be the stealth cleaning product of the year," Borman says. "Gleme is a foaming glass spray cleaner that doesn't run, streak or leave any film. Priced at $2.15 a can, it is our best-selling window cleaner, and we don't know why. We've never advertised it. It just walks off the shelves."

On my way out of the store, Borman showed me a lamb skin duster on a bendable pole priced at $10.47. "Feather dusters spread dust. Lamb skin pulls dust off the surface being dusted. The bendable pole lets you get the duster into any nook or cranny," Borman says.

Julie Knaffla, a buyer at Damman Hardware, told me that she believes electrostatic sweepers and disposable dust cloths and pivoting brooms, mops and dusters are this year's big advances in cleaning products.

"Electrostatic sweepers like the Pledge Grab-It, Swiffer and O Cedar Static Sweeper make daily cleaning of hardwood floors, furniture, ceiling fans and high places easy. Their static charge enables the cloths to grab on to dust, dirt or hair. When dirty, you just throw the cloth away," Knaffla says.

"The other big cleaning breakthroughs are pivoting brooms and mops like the SpaceInvader line. Priced at just $8.99 to $13.99, they make cleaning a lot easier. The Pivot Broom can be changed from a straight sweeping broom to a push broom. The Butterfly Mop rotates from a traditional T-shape to an I-shape so you can clean very small places. The Swivel Dust Mop actually bends to get under chairs or other hard-to-clean areas," Knaffla says.

All these products sound good, but as I loaded up my car with the latest and greatest, I couldn't help thinking that Mark Adams of Mr. Scrubs was right. When you get right down to it, the most needed spring cleaning product is good old elbow grease. Aside from time, it is the ingredient most of us have in shortest supply. Use both wisely.

Even when maintained correctly, wood decks are stacked against you

by Glenn Haege,
America's Master Handyman

It's D Day for decks. Too cold to start working, but the perfect time to decide what to do. The following is from Linda Salazar of Plymouth outlines many people's deck-care dilemmas.

"Hi! I'm thinking about the annual chore of getting the deck powerwashed and stained. I am really tired of having to get this done every year. Last year I cleaned the deck instead with Olympic Deck Cleaner and did not stain.

"Is there a product that lasts? The deck really only looks nice the first year. The oil in the stain tracks into the house and collects dirt like a blotter. I hate to think of all the years that we have to keep doing this.

"If I were to move, I would build a deck that was vinyl or synthetic boards. This deck is very labor-intensive and costly. I wish I could rip it down.

"Do you have any suggestions on products or materials to consider for the future?" – *Linda Salazar*

Dear Linda: Now you know why, although I have written three books on deck care, I have a paver patio.

If you have a wood deck, constant maintenance comes with the territory. A good stain or sealing job lasts 18 months. To assure maximum life of the coating, you should clean the deck every 90 days during the deck season.

Major manufacturers have come out with heavy-duty deck sealers. Some of them are:
■ Penofin Ultra Red Label by Performance Coating, (800) 736-736-6346.
■ Natural Deck Oil by Bio-Wash, (800) 858-5011.
■ Olympic Maximum Waterproofing Sealant by PPG Industries, (800) 441-9695.
■ Wolman Non-Graying, Long-Lasting Acrylic Wood Finish by Wolman Products, (800) 556-7737.
■ Behr Deck Plus by Behr, (800) 854-0133.

These coatings are as close to armor plate as you are going to get from a stain or sealer. They have greatly increased solids for maximum Ultra Violet protection and superior performance. Still, most manufacturers only claim they will protect your deck for two or three years.

Consumers want deck stains to last as long as house paint. Do a good job painting the exterior of a house, and the surface will look good for seven, 10, maybe even 15 or 20 years. This longevity is not only due to product quality. It's also due to the fact that walls are vertical surfaces protected by roofs.

A vertical surface means that rain and snow drain off, leaving the wall dry, and the roof protects the surface from the elements.

Since a deck is a horizontal surface, it is at the mercy of the elements. Rain and snow soak the surface. People walk over it. Birds, well you know what bird do on it. Homeowners don't clean it properly.

On top of everything, most decks are usually not properly stained or sealed. When deck stain is tracked into a house, it usually means that an exterior stain, not a deck stain, was used, or that the stain was applied improperly. For instance, the instructions for Olympic Maximum say that all previous stains or seals must have been completely removed from the wood, and that the deck should be clean, dry and sanded smooth.

Decks usually do not have to be power washed. If you decided to restain your dining room table, you would not dump it in the back yard and tear off the old surface with a power washer. The biggest difference between your deck and your dining room table is that deck wood is usually softer and more delicate.

Behr, Bio-Wash, Penofin, Olympic and Wolman have developed stripping and deck wood preparation systems designed to work perfectly with their premium deck sealers. For optimum results, use the company's entire system.

If you decide that you just don't want to do this any more, look into a vinyl deck resurfacing product such as Durable Deck by Anchor Decking Systems, (888) 898-4990. Durable Deck strips can be fastened directly over an existing deck surface eliminating staining and sealing.

The product is distributed by Biewer Lumber in the Midwest, (800) 482-5717, and is found locally at Dillman & Upton, (248) 651-9411, and N.A. Mans, (734) 981-5800.

If the deck surface is in bad shape but the under structure is good, consider replacing the deck boards with composite materials such as TimberTech, (800) 307-7780; Smart Deck, (888) 7DECK-ING; Carefree Decking, (800)-653-2784; TREX, (800) 289-8739; or Fiberon Decking, (704) 463-7120, from Home Depot. These products don't look like wood but they never have to be stained or sealed.

So many people have deck questions that I put my entire deck book online so you can access all the information free on my web site, masterhandyman.com. If you are going to make a major change, better decide now, or you may not be able to find anyone good to work on your deck when the weather warms.

Remodeling fever hits the showers, faucet and other areas of bathroom

by Glenn Haege,
America's Master Handyman

CHICAGO

I've decided to come clean about this year's Kitchen/Bath Industry Show held in Chicago last week. That's because most of the innovations were in the shower.

That does not mean designers flocking in from all over the country did not find new kitchen items. It's just that I have already reported most of them while covering the National Association of Home Builders' and International Housewares' shows earlier this year.

Besides, bath remodeling is a definitely big business. The National Kitchen & Bath Association estimates that 10.59 million bathrooms will be built or remodeled this year. More than 7 percent of America's 102.6 million households will remodel their bath while less than 5 percent will remodel the kitchen.

So what made the biggest splash at the show?

Let's start with decorative glass block showers, which have been around for a long time but have been plagued with leaking problems. A salesperson at the Pittsburgh Corning Glass Block display explained that the trouble with these showers is that builders usually jury-rig glass block to fit shower pans of the wrong size. When they don't match exactly, the showers leak.

Glenn Haege takes a look at one of Pittsburgh Corning's glass block shower kits. The kits come in three different designs with made to measure acrylic shower bases that eliminate leaking.

Pittsburgh Corning, (800) 624-2120, solved the problem by creating three different kits containing specially designed acrylic shower bases and all the materials needed for three different glass block shower configurations.

Contractors can use the kits to create standard, walk-in and angle designs. While this would make a great do-it-yourself item, it is only for the trade for now. Nevertheless, it is a big step in the right direction.

A bathtub is wonderful, but as we get older many find it hard to get in and out. Add a wheelchair and they are a disaster. The Swan Corp., (800) 325-7008, has developed a Retrofit Shower System that makes it easy to yank out the tub and install a barrier-free, wheelchair-friendly shower.

Most showers, and therefore most shower bases, are square. Swan's new retrofit base fits the full 30-inch by 60-inch standard bath dimensions. The back panel extends the full width, eliminating butting panels together. The shower drain is not centered, but located at the extreme right or left, in line with the old bathtub drain. This may not sound important, but it will save hundreds of dollars in installation costs.

If you are over 40 and redoing your bath, at least think about this design option. Doesn't a big shower, with a seat and optional hand held shower sound luxurious? It also could be a lifesaver for you or someone you love. And the Retrofit Shower System comes in Swanstone's complete palette of colors.

Once you're in the shower, the shower head is all important. The European influence is being felt with extra large 6-inch sizes such as the Tropical Rain Shower Head by Alson's, (800) 421-0001, that lists for $500 plus.

These showerheads comply with U.S. guidelines because they have restrictors that cut back the flow rate to the government required 2.5 gallons per minute. If a nefarious person were to take the restrictor out, they could be drenched with more than six gallons of water a minute.

At the opposite extreme, Melard Manufacturing, (800) 635-2731, is introducing the Tidal Wave Self Cleaning showerhead for people in a hurry. The Tidal Wave mixes air and water 7 to 1 to create an explosive charge of water that keeps the head from ever clogging. It also creates extremely small water droplets that clean faster and enable you to get out of the shower quicker and cleaner. The Tidal Wave comes in overhead and hand-held models and costs about $15.

Not everyone wants to get out of the shower fast. For those who want to ease back and relax, Sussman Lifestyle Group, (800) 76STEAM, has created Mr. Steam, a small, electric-powered personal shower-sized steam unit. Turn on Mr. Steam and in about 5 minutes you'll have a shower filled with 120-degree steam. The unit only uses about 2 gallons of cold water an hour, but creates 15 gallons of steam, more than enough to soothe away all those aches and pains. The Mr. Steam unit costs about $1,000 plus $600 for installation.

If you like the idea of steam, but would prefer a free-standing unit, Axoma Spa by Vaxiel Health International, (800) 800-7222, has a one-person unit that sets up in 15 min-

Alsons' Tropical Rain shower head is 6 inches wide to give bathers an immediate drenching.

utes, and requires no plumbing or wiring. The cost of the Axoma Spa is only $1,495 plus $50 shipping and handling.

Water pressure balancing is not a new idea, but a good thing to consider if you are remodeling the bath. Pressure balancing keeps the shower taker from being flash frozen or scalded when other folks use hot or cold water. The Mixet Master by the Mixet Division of Alsons Corp., lets you set the temperature once, then keeps the temperature constant to within two degrees anytime you turn on the shower.

After spring home check-up, it's surprising how long To-Do list is

by Glenn Haege,
America's Master Handyman

Two weeks ago, the TV weathercasters had us convinced that we would be using our snow blower again. Now it's time to think spring.

Of course, you'll want to start by putting away your snow blower, snow shovels and ice chippers.

Have you emptied the fuel from the snow blower or at least put in a couple ounces per gallon of gas stabilizer? Once the fuel situation is taken care of, be sure to get the snow blower cleaned, oiled and ready for its long summer nap. If your snow blower is a few years old, take it into the service department for proper servicing. Many dealers will store it until fall for free if they service it for you.

Snow shovels and ice chippers should also be cleaned, oiled if necessary, and stored out of the way. Rock salt and other ice melters should be stored above ground level in airtight containers if possible.

To begin getting your house ready for spring, it's a good idea to grab a pencil and paper and walk around the house three times. First, look at the roof and gutters. Second, look at the windows and siding. Third, look at the ground, deck and any equipment such as barbecues and lawn furniture that has been stored outside.

By the time you have circumnavigated the house three times you will have a To Do list that will keep you occupied for a weekend or two. More than that, you will have taken the time to really look at your house, analyze the state of affairs and start thinking about long-term projects.

Even if the roof looks good, it makes sense to climb a ladder and make certain the gutters are secure and free of debris.

Are the window and door screens in good shape? If not, get them fixed now, before the summer rush.

Almost everyone's windows are dirty. You can make exterior windows dazzle by cleaning them with a solution of a teaspoon of a good liquid hand dishwashing detergent like Palmolive or Joy and 4 ounces of white vinegar to a gallon of water. Apply with a sponge, squeegee off, and wipe off the drips with a cotton towel, not paper.

If you want to wash the windows inside, use the same technique but change the cleaning solution to 4 ounces of house-hold ammonia and a teaspoon of liquid hand dishwashing detergent to a gallon of water.

There is nothing like washing the windows to give you a good opportunity to inspect your home's vinyl or aluminum siding. If the siding and gutters look dirty, make a note to wash them when it gets a little warmer. Armor-All, Alumin-Nu and Krud Cutter all make good aluminum and/or vinyl siding cleaners. You'll find at least one of these products at your local hardware store.

Is the ground starting to sink into bird bath-like depressions around the house? This is the biggest cause of leaky basements, so it should be monitored every spring and fall. The ground should slope away from the house, 1 inch per foot, for a distance of 5 feet around the entire perimeter. If the bird-bath effect is just starting, you may be able to get by with a couple bags of topsoil, mulch or gravel.

If the slope has flattened or reversed for a considerable area, it is time to remove the sod; trench down 24 inches deep by 24 inches wide; and re-build the slope. This is a major To Do item. Put in 6 inches of coarse gravel on the bottom, then 6 inches of pea gravel, followed by 6 inches of sand. Top off with 6 inches of topsoil and replace the sod. The final result should keep rain water draining away from your house, keeping your basement dry for years to come.

The deck can be washed now, but intensive deck care should be put off until it has had a chance to dry out and nighttime temperatures do not drop below 50 degrees Fahrenheit.

If it has been a couple of years since you had your central air conditioner checked, call for an appointment. The technician can add Freon or other cooling agent if the temperature is over 60 degrees.

If the lawn furniture is dirty, you can clean most of it with a 30-to-one (12 cup per gallon) solution of Simple Green and water. This solution will work on wood, metal, plastic, even really dirty padded outdoor furniture. There are also many special vinyl lawn furniture cleaners on the market. If plastic furniture still looks a little dirty, go to the automotive section and get Meguiar's Mirror Glaze Professional Plastic Cleaner No. 17. Meguiars also makes a sealer, but it will make the surface very slippery.

I don't know about you, but I'm getting tired just thinking about all this.

Life's little problems don't have to cause big headaches at home

by Glenn Haege,
America's Master Handyman

Even in the greatest country in the world we are surrounded by vexing little problems. Maybe they are more annoying here because our lives are filled with so much bounty that little things take on a magnified importance.

I'm not talking about the house burning down or the basement flooding. I'm talking about little things like a dull bathtub; grout that won't come clean; an irreplaceable broken tile; a small tear in vinyl flooring or a mirror that is beginning to go black around the edges.

The products that can solve these little problems are out there, but usually they are made by small companies that do not have the marketing clout to get in the stores where you can find them. That's where I come in. If it's OK with you, I'll leave the big problems like war and peace to the prognosticators and take of these lesser problems right now.

Brian Smith, the developer of Bath Brite, had been in the bathtub reglazing business for years. He found that many people were having their bathtubs reglazed unnecessarily. All that was wrong with the porcelain surface of their tubs was that it needed a deep cleaning that would remove the years of built-up soap scum and chemicals that had been absorbed into the tub surface.

Smith's solution is the three step Bath Brite system that uses a Phosphoric Acid based cleaner to deep clean and remove stains. After cleaning, a special Bath Brite Sealer is applied that restores and rebuilds the worn porcelain or fiberglass surface. The third step is a Gloss Enhancer that restores the tub's natural shine.

Bath Brite kits are produced by the Super Jet Co. of Dearborn Heights and cost $39.95. Each kit contains enough product to restore two tubs. In Metro Detroit, you can find the kits at Damman Hardware. You can also order directly from the developer by calling (877) 739-0990 or visiting the web site at www.superjetco.com.

It's almost never too late to save a bathtub. This is an old, cast iron bathtub the makers of Bath Brite salvaged from a garbage dump. It was completely stained and rusted.

This is the same tub after its porcelain finish was deep cleaned and restored with Bath Brite.

When I talked to Smith about this article, he asked me to please tell people to read and follow the directions. 'Bathtubs are easy to renew, but you can't expect the product to work unless you read and follow the directions,' he said.

If you have grout work that is dull and discolored and just won't come clean, Smith has also developed a heavy-duty grout cleaning kit called Grout Brite. The product is also made by Super Jet Co. and costs $39.95.

If the bath is chipped or the surface has been worn though, the surface has to be repaired before it can be deep cleaned and sealed. A company called Porcelain Plus has developed a product that can fix chips or worn spots in porcelain or fiberglass tubs. The same product works on repairing chipped surfaces on stoves, refrigerators and washing machines.

The multicolor Porcelain Plus Tub, Sink & Appliance Repair Kit costs $14.95. If you just need white, they have a one-color kit for $12.95. You can order the kit by phone at (800) 475-3708 or on the Internet at www.porcelainplus.com.

Invariably, if a ceramic tile breaks, it will likely be at least 20 years old and impossible to replace. Porcelain Plus also makes a Marble, Tile & Solid Surface repair kit that you can use to invisibly seal a cracked ceramic tile surface. The kit comes complete with cleaner, putty, hardener, six colors you can mix to get the exact surface color you need, plus all the tools necessary to do the job. All for just $14.95.

Linoleum and vinyl flooring are comfortable, attractive and an excellent value for your flooring dollar. Nobody wants to be around when you burn or cut a hole in either of these surfaces. R Crew Inc. has developed the Floor Saver Linoleum Repair Kit that enables you to turn an unsightly hole into an almost invisible bonded patch that mimics the surrounding surface. The entire seven-step procedure only takes about 15 minutes from start to finish.

Currently, Floor Saver is only available directly from the manufacturer. One kit contains enough product to patch three quarter-size holes and costs $29.95. You can place an order by calling (800) 490-2001 or order on the Internet at www.floorrepair.com.

Sooner or later almost every mirror starts to turn black along the edges. This is because the silver nitrate reflective surface has become corroded or otherwise dissipated. Usually you have to either live with the problem or get the mirror 'resilvered,' a very expensive procedure.

Millennium International Development Corp. has solved the problem with Mirr.Edge. This is a mirrored acrylic bevel strip which you can paste on the edge of your present mirror. This hides the black edge and looks like very expensive beveled glass. The cost for this fix is 25 cents a lineal inch. Fixing an average 3 foot by 4 foot mirror would cost $42. Order direct from the manufacturer at (800) 757-2990, or check out their web site at www.mirredge.com.

Hey, this was so much fun, maybe I should make my next book, Saving the World, Fix It Fast & Easy III.

MAY 6, 2000

Using the best deck cleaner gets results you want: Less maintenance

by Glenn Haege,
America's Master Handyman

 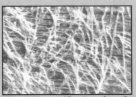 

This 43 X magnification of heavily weathered cedar shows how dirt, mold and wood cells damaged by ultra violet rays have severely damaged the outer layer of the wood.

This 43 X magnification of weathered cedar shows brightened wood using a bleach-based cleaner. Lignin, the natural wood bonding agent, has been destroyed, leaving loose wood fibers.

This 43 X magnification of weathered cedar brightened by Bio-Wash Wood Wash restorer shows a far smoother surface that will offer a good foundation for staining or sealing.

It's deck cleaning time. Time to rush out to your local hardware store or home center and pick up the deck cleaner of your choice. All things being equal, many people make their buying decision based solely upon price. After all, a deck cleaner is a deck cleaner is a deck cleaner, and you've got more important things on which to spend your hard-earned money.

Unfortunately, all deck cleaners are not created equal. The cheaper deck cleaner/brighteners usually include some form of chlorine (household) bleach as their brightening agent. Quite often, the ingredient list does not say bleach, it uses the chemical term, sodium hypochlorite. Using a product with this ingredient on your deck can be a problem.

Years ago, I used to recommend cleaning and brightening decks with a solution of TSP and household bleach in water. I stopped doing this when I learned how hard the bleach was on the wood. The bleach took away the gray and killed the mold spores, but at the same time it mangled the wood fibers and left a residue that kept stains and sealers from penetrating the wood properly.

I first learned of this phenomenon when the owners of Bio-Wash Products showed me photographs of microscopic blowups of cedar decking taken by an independent Canadian chemical testing company. The magnification was 43X.

The first slide was of weathered cedar. You could see how a combination of dirt, mold and dead wood cells had turned the surface black/gray. This jumbled, blackened surface was not only unattractive, the cell structure was so clogged that not even penetrating stains could be absorbed by the wood properly.

The second slide showed how a bleach-based cleaner lightened the wood but destroyed the lignin, the natural glue that bonds wood fibers together. When the wood fibers were no longer bonded, they became a loose mass to which stains and sealers could not adhere properly.

This is the reason why so many hard-working homeowners only get a single season out of their deck stains and sealers. They do all the work, but the cheap cleaner/brightener used makes it impossible for the stain or sealer to stick.

The final slide showed weathered cedar brightened with Bio-Wash WoodWash restorer. The citric acid used in the cleaner gets rid of the dead wood fibers but does not affect the natural bonding agent in the wood.

This is not a commercial for Bio-Wash WoodWash, (800) 858-5011. It is very good, but it is only one of many different cleaner/brighteners that do a great job. Others are Behr Wood Cleaner Brightener/Conditioner, (800) 854-0133; Cabot Stain's Problem Solver Wood Brightener, (800) 877-8246; Flood Dekswood/Natural Wood Brightener, (800) 321-3444; Penofin Weather Blaster, (800) 736-6346, and Wolman Fence & Deck Brighteners, (800) 556-7737.

The only problem with these excellent products is that they cost a little more than the cut-rate stuff. But you know what? You work too hard. You and your deck are worth the good stuff. So use the very best, get a great-looking deck, then brag about it.

MAY 13, 2000

Remodeling job may take longer than expected, so get started now

by Glenn Haege,
America's Master Handyman

I don't know about you, but when I look at the calendar I don't see the date, I see Memorial Day, July, August, Labor Day and Thanksgiving stretched out in front of me.

Whether we like it or not, June 21 is the longest day of the year. Everything after that is downhill. If you have a major home project to do this year and haven't started yet, you better start yesterday.

If you think I'm overreacting, take a look at the numbers.

To find out how long a major remodeling job should take, I consulted with Adam Helfman of Fairway Construction, (800) 354-9310, and Joe Aielo of Pine Building Co., (888) 500-7463. Both firms had banner years last year and could easily increase their business by 50 percent, if they could find crews that could live up to their high quality standards.

If you wanted to start a major project like a room addition, today, and were able to sit down with a contractor or his representative Monday, you might not be able to use that room until well after Labor Day.

Maybe you would still be rushing with last-minute changes to get ready to show off the room to the in-laws at Thanksgiving.

Here's the math for remodeling time frame, showing the event and estimated number of days.

■ First meeting with salesman/designer: one.
■ Days to final design: seven to 14.
■ Blue prints from architect: 7 to 14.
■ Request for building permit: 14 to 28.
■ Time to start date: 28 to 42.
■ Actual construction: 7 to 35.
■ Total minimum time frame: 54 to 134.

The total adds up to between two days and 412 months.

If you started calling around today, the job would be completed between the end of July and the middle of October. If the contractor is booked and can't start until the beginning of August, you could be talking a December completion date. Or, if you run into snags, delays are inevitable.

For instance, your plan may call for the back wall of your room addition to be a little too close to the lot line according to city code. If your plan is against code, you and the builder have to apply for a code variance. This procedure could easily add another couple of months, especially during the good old summer time when people go on vacation.

Or you may have fallen in love with a certain kind of tile, or magnificent custom cabinetwork. Special orders can easily add another two to six weeks.

Guess what, folks? We are now talking an April completion date. And that is with a good contractor working his darndest to make you happy.

There are a number of ways you can shorten the time frame. The two most important are to know what you want and to not build accidental roadblocks.

A couple that knows that they want a 20-by-30 family room added to the back of the house off the kitchen will use the salesman/designer's time a lot more efficiently than the couple who just wants more space for the family to get together.

If the first couple has done some shopping and knows that they want a Heat and Glo direct vent fireplace, Model No. XYZ, and three sets of Andersen sliding glass door walls like "the ones in this ad," so much the better. That couple will get exactly what they want, using the minimum amount of time for design and blue prints.

The second couple may take two or three weeks to get an approximation of a design they like. And they will get what the salesman thinks they should have, rather than what they may really need.

There are also a wide variety of roadblocks well-meaning homeowners put in the path of modernization contractors. The most common is not having every family member that will have input into the job at the first meeting with the builder's representative. No husband, no wife, is too busy to be at that meeting.

The initial input of information both from the family and the builder or his representative is vital to the success of the entire job. If someone can't be there and they come up with a good idea two weeks later, the idea, no matter how important, is a roadblock. That idea can easily throw the progress of the job back to day one.

Secondly, don't make any spur-of-the-moment changes. Changes add expense and time to the job. That said, if a change has to be made, it has to be made, but realize that your time frame and bank account will suffer.

Finally, when getting a remodeling job built, make sure you have a completion date in the contract. For the date to have any teeth, daily penalties and rewards should be specified.

If your builder knows that he makes more money if the job is done fast and less money if he is slow, he will do everything possible to get the job done early, and you can brag about the result.

Late spring is the best time to clean, paint or stain your home

by Glenn Haege,
America's Master Handyman

Now is time to decide whether you are going to wash or paint the outside of the house this year. If you plan on exterior painting and the weather forecasters are right, you don't have a minute to lose. You can prepare the surface this weekend, then have a fun-filled family painting party on Memorial Day.

Late spring is also the best time of the year to wash the outside of the house. Even a house that is only a year old, or that was painted last year, should be cleaned to keep the painted wood, aluminum and even vinyl siding and trim in top condition.

There are many good products available that make cleaning the exterior easy. The Alumin-Nu Corp., (800) 899-7097, makes Nice N Easy and Power lines of Aluminum and Vinyl Siding Cleaners. Krud Kutter, (800) 466-7126, Olympic, (800)441-9695, and Armor All distributed by Momentum Marketing, (248) 888-0350, all make good vinyl siding cleaners.

Timing is critical for a good paint or stain job. The ideal temperature for exterior painting is 77 degrees Fahrenheit with 50-percent humidity. Good painting conditions are 55 to 85 degrees. I've seen projections that we may have as many as 60 90-plus-degree days this summer. Ninety plus is sit-in-the-shade weather, not painting weather.

Despite the torrential rains we've had in the past month, the summer is expected to be unseasonably dry. Hot, dry weather is not good for painting, so don't wait, start now.

If night-time temperatures are projected to drop below 50, or if rain is expected within 24 hours, put off the project for a couple of days.

Removing old paint

Preparation is the key to a long-lasting paint job. This process is more than just brushing off cobwebs. Scrape away any alligatoring, bubbling or scaling of the paint. Sand scraped areas smooth with 50 Grit Sandpaper.

If you find multiple layers of deteriorating paint, the surface may have to be stripped down to the bare wood. There is no easy way to do this. Consider ice blasting, power sanding or shaving removal procedures.

Ice Blasting, by a company such as Ice Blast Midwest (out of business) is a far more delicate procedure than sand blasting.

Most professionals use power sanders. The American-International Tool Co., (800) 932-5872, makes a product called the Paint Shaver, that looks a little like a disk sander, but shaves siding down to the bare wood.

The Professional Paint Shaver costs $399. A dust collector attachment costs an additional $99, but attaches to a Shop

Vac and eliminates a great deal of the mess. The company also makes a Dust-Free Sander Vac for traditional sanding.

In its April 1999 issue, Family Handyman magazine reported that a novice do-it-yourselfer was able to strip an average of 30 square feet an hour using the Paint Shaver system.

After sanding and/or stripping, seal all bare spots with a water-based stain kill like 1-2-3 by William Zinsser or Total One by Master Chem.

Staining and painting

Previously stained wood can be re-stained with a high-quality, solid stain that looks like paint but does not cause build up. Some quality names to look for are Thompson's Wood Protector Colorfast Stain, (800) 367-6297, Cabot's Q.V.T. Solid Color Stain, (800) 877-8246, and Behr Plus 10 Solid Color Stain, (800) 854-0133.

Every major paint manufacturer makes high-quality exterior house paints. The good stuff just costs more. Look for products such as Pittsburgh Paint's Manor Hall Premium Exterior, (800) 441-9695, Benjamin Moore MoorGard, (800) 672-4686, Sherwin Williams Duration, (800) 474-3794, or Behr Premium Plus.

Expect to pay in the high $20s for good exterior paint with a 20-year warranty. Sherwin William Duration costs about $36 a gallon, but has a limited lifetime warranty.

Chalking can be a major problem. If it is, you may want to have the house powerwashed before painting. Add Emulsa Bond by the Flood Co., (800) 321-3444, to the first coat of paint to help it adhere better.

Quality paint spreads very easily. So remember, it is not how many coats but how much paint is applied. Read the label and apply the paint to the company's specifications. Most, but not all, exterior paint should be applied at a rate of 400 square feet per gallon. Sherwin Williams best exterior paint, Duration, should be applied at the rate of 250 to 300 square feet per gallon.

If the rate is 400 square feet per gallon, compute the entire square footage of the exterior, minus doors and windows, and divide by 400. To train yourself to apply the paint properly, pour out a quart of paint and use up the entire amount on a 100-square-foot section of your house.

Do the job right and you can brag about the result. Your house will look beautiful and won't have to be re-painted for a long time to come.

MAY 27, 2000

More consumers put their foot down and demand new ceramic tile

by Glenn Haege,
America's Master Handyman

Everyone I know is either buying new or remodeling. Either way, flooring choices become a major portion of the selection process, and ceramic tile is becoming an increasingly popular option for the bathroom, foyer, great room, kitchen, rec room and hallways.

In kitchens and great rooms, tile is often used in combination with different flooring materials to provide accents, define areas, or furnish an extremely tough surface for high-traffic areas.

Many tile floors feature decorative border treatments. These antiqued ceramic tiles by American Olean have decorative floor tile corners and borders made with scalloped edges and triangular insets. Because of their strength, size and attractive designs, floor tiles are often also used on countertops and walls.

The March 2000 issue of F l o o r i n g m a g a z i n e pointed out that stone-look ceramic tile is a big fashion trend:

"C l a s s i c a l stone looks are now able to emulate those found in ancient villas with a s e m i - p o l - ished look that replicates the surface of stone that has been walked on for hundreds of years," contributing editor Robert Simpson said.

The average size of tiles has also c h a n g e d . Those little 4-inch square, 6-inch square and even 8-inch-square tiles are out. The new standard floor tile is 12 by 12, 13 by 13 and 16 by 16. Even 18-by-18 squares are becoming

The wear patterns of these Florida Tile Industries give them the look of centuries old chiseled stone. The hardness of a glaze is measured on the Moh or Mineral hardness scale. This Florida Tile has an Moh of 7 which means it can not be scratched by case hardened steel.

strong residential flooring contenders. Commercial tiles get even bigger.

Combining multisized tiles into interesting patterns is also becoming more and more popular.

"The trend to large tiles started in Europe where the equipment was developed, then became popular on both the East and West Coast and has migrated to the Midwest over the past five years," says Phyllis Schoenherr, the manager of showroom sales for Beaver Tile & Stone, (248) 299-8100, a large tile distributor.

"It seems that as soon as they got the ability to make larger tiles, the designers said, 'Let's go bigger,' and overnight everything was big tiles.

"People are looking for ways to make their homes distinctive. With tile you can make your home truly special," Schoenherr adds.

Another reason for tile's popularity, according to Dennis Langwald, one of the owners of Fairway Tile and Carpet, (866) 211-5558, "is that people can do it themselves, not just to save money, but to express themselves. When you have a beautiful-looking tile floor, you have not just something to walk on, but it can be a work of art. If you took the time to lay the floor yourself, you can take a lot of pride in the achievement," he says.

"The most difficult thing about doing a tile job is laying it out. My partner, Gene Perlman, is an engineer. When we provide the tile, Gene will often go to people's homes and show them how to do the layout," Langwald says.

"Many of the folks have been dealing with us for years. When they decide on a tile project, they borrow the tools from us, and automatically go to the back room and use our tile saw to cut any tiles that need cutting. It's like they're family," he says.

There's an old wives' tale that tile chips easily. That's definitely not true. The new glazes are actually harder than granite and fused to the tile surface by being fired at 2,000 degrees Fahrenheit.

If you're in the market for tile you will find that there is an almost infinite variety of styles, finishes, textures and colors. Tile can be glazed or unglazed, have a matte, semi-matte or polished finish. They can be machine or handmade. Some look like weathered stone or old classic tiles. Some tiles showcase the earthen look of the clay used to create the tile. Others make the glaze the star and offer an incredible array of colors.

Tile is on the upper tier when it comes to cost. The installed price of vinyl sheet goods is about $5 a foot. Custom solid vinyl tile is the next step up and costs $7 to $10 a square foot installed. The installed price for ceramic tile is in the $12 to $14 range, according to Langwald.

If you are just buying the tile separately, some imported tiles cost $2 or less per square foot. The average range for American machine-made tile is $2 to $5, but can go as high as $8. Domestic hand-made tiles are in the $15 to $20 range.

"Ceramic tile is also the ultimate no-wax flooring," Langwald says. "All you need is a little vinegar and water and a damp mop for daily maintenance. The glazes never dull, never need waxing, never need buffing or polishing," he says.

For an occasional deep cleaning, Langwald recommends Armstrong Once 'n Done, which has a little bit of ammonia and mild detergent. It will cut through any accumulated grease and grime and doesn't even have to be rinsed.

Tile's easy-to-clean, ceramic surface also means that it is an excellent substitute to solid surface flooring for people with dust allergies.

If you're looking for a long-lasting, knock-down-dead beautiful flooring material that is easy to care for, you couldn't do better than ceramic tile. It is definitely something that you'll be bragging about for years to come.

For Father's Day, give the gift – any gift – that dad can brag about

by Glenn Haege,
America's Master Handyman

Stuck on what to choose for a Father's Day gift? Fear not, the Handyman is here to help you. You can buy him a card and a sport shirt or pair of shorts. He will love you for it.

Or you could buy him something so out of the loop that he will just go ga-ga. I'm talking about things that he doesn't even know he wants or needs.

To come up with this list I assembled a panel of experts:
■ Gordon Mott, managing editor of Cigar Aficionado magazine, was the highest flyer and out-of-the-box thinker.
■ My friend Jim Williams from Williams Refrigeration showed an adventurous side that I never knew existed.
■ Paul Maderosian of Contractors Clothing was surprisingly practical.
■ Hallie Chalmers of Detroit Tigers Marketing had a suggestion that was inexpensive yet could last a lifetime.
■ George Cauley of Cauley Ferrari and Bob Crane of C. Crane Co. had suggestions that are way out there.

Many a father, the Handyman included, relishes a fine cigar.

Mott suggested gift givers concentrate on ways to enhance the cigar experience, such as a good humidor. He believes J.C. Pendergast Inc., (888) HUMIDITY, makes the best ones. They are beautifully made and provide automatic, not passive, humidification. The only problem is that price tags start at $2,495.

Aged Port is a great accompaniment to a fine cigar. Mott recommends the hard-to-find 1970 and 1977 Dow, Taylor Fladgate and Fonseca vintages. Beverage Warehouse in Beverly Hills, (248) 644-2155, has the 1977 Dow at $120 a bottle.

> *Being a dad and a grandfather I can assure you that it doesn't really matter what you give, if it is with love, he will brag about it.*

Mott confided that for his personal taste he preferred an aged rum such as the Bacardi 8 Year Old, which retails for $25. Upon hearing this, my publisher at Master Handyman Press bought the last bottle available at Alban's Bottle & Basket in Birmingham, (248) 258-5555. The store has already reordered and a new supply should be coming in this week.

Williams recommended a half-day NASCAR training school called the Fantasy Flyer at the Michigan Speedway. For $495 you get a half-day of schooling off and on the track, culminating with dressing in a fire suit and driving a 140-mph NASCAR.

The school is one of many racing-oriented schools offered at tracks around the country by Track Time Inc., (330) 793-9451. Call the company for brochures and a listing of dates and tracks.

If dad loves cars, you can rent him a Corvette Pace car or a Plymouth Prowler for a day from Cauley Ferrari. Cauley says daily rental costs are $300 plus a $2,000 deposit and dad has to be 30 years old. Call Georgia at (248) 855-4430 for more information.

Chalmers, of Tigers Marketing has an unbeatable deal for Detroit Tiger fans.

For 20 bucks over the price of a ticket, she will take you and dad up to a press box, where you and he will do a fantasy play-by-play and color commentary of an inning of baseball. Tigers Marketing will record the inning, complete with crowd noises, and you get to keep the tape and game notes.

Maderosian of Contractor's Clothing, (248) 544-7380, says that the trades all know enough to get good work clothes, but do-it-yourselfers seldom do. He suggests professional-quality Carhart bib overalls.

"Everyone should have a good pair of overall hanging in the garage," Maderosian said.

Prices range from $37 for 8-ounce white drill painters' overalls to $57 for heavy-duty blue denim or brown duct overalls. Carhart overalls almost never wear out.

Crane of C. Crane Co, (800) 522-TUNE, came up with a gift for the man who has everything and is a little bit nosy: a $2,000 hand-held spotlight. This little dandy will light up the night with six-million candlepower.

With this light Dad will be able to see things that he is not supposed to see up to one-and-one-half miles away. The Nicad battery will run for 90 minutes before recharging but the neighbors will never let him use it half that long before they call the cops.

For a mere $445 Dad can record up to 115 consecutive hours of my radio show with the CC Digital Recorder from C. Crane Co.

I have yet to find a reason why anyone would want to record 115 hours of radio, but it is nice to know that there is a recorder out there for those who do.

Most of the ideas in this column are a little extreme but the purpose is to get you to think "outside the box" so you and dad can both have fun.

Being a dad and a grandfather I can assure you that it doesn't really matter what you give, if it is with love, he will brag about it.

JUNE 10, 2000

Wood, steel or fiberglass; any old door can look as good as new

by Glenn Haege,
America's Master Handyman

If the entrance doors of your house are looking old, there is a good chance that they are just suffering from one-too-many coats of paint. Stripping the door down to the bare wood and refinishing can make that door as good as new.

Completely refinishing a door can take two or three days. That's a lot of time, but when you consider that replacement can easily cost between $1,000 and $2,000 in labor and materials, it is definitely time well spent.

This week's article is going to be about refinishing the three main kinds of doors, wood, steel and fiberglass. Next week's article will cover taking the plunge and buying a brand new door.

Wood

If you have an older house, the probability is that you have wooden doors. Wood takes a little more care than fiberglass or steel, but it is more versatile and almost infinitely repairable.

If you presently have a stained and varnished wooden door and would like to paint it, you can. If you have a wood door that has four or five coats of paint and you would prefer the stained and varnished look, you can do that too.

Always remember that a door, every door, has six sides: the front and back that you see, and the top, bottom and side edges that you don't. The edges are the most vulnerable parts of the door. Moisture that gets in through the edges can tear the door apart during repeated freeze-and-thaw cycles. It is very important that any time you paint or varnish a door you do all six sides.

The best way to work on a door is to take the door off its hinges and place it on padded saw horses. Before beginning to work on the door, remove all the hardware and mask the glass with masking or painter's tape.

Painting a varnished door is easy. Sand the surface with 80-grit aluminum oxide or garnet sandpaper. You don't have to remove all the varnish, just sand until it becomes powdery. Vacuum off the dust and wipe down with a coat of liquid sandpaper.

As soon as the liquid sandpaper is dry, wipe down the surface with a tack rag. Coat all six sides of the door with an oil-base stain kill such as Kilz Exterior by Master Chem, (800) 325-3552, or Wm. Zinsser, Cover Stain. Let dry 4 hours, then apply two coats of a good latex exterior trim paint.

Older doors with multiple layers of paint should be stripped to the bare surface. If the raw wood is in excellent condition, you can remove any remaining pigment with wood bleach. Then stain and varnish the door.

Doors with dry rot should be repaired by gouging out all traces of rot, then rebuilding with wood epoxy by Abatron,

56

Inc., (800) 445-1754. Wood epoxy is actually stronger than the wood it is replacing. The door should then be sanded, washed down with a solution of 4 ounces of TSP per gallon of water and rinsed. After drying, coat all six sides with an oil-based stain kill and two coats of a good acrylic exterior water-base trim paint.

Steel

The paint on steel entrance doors gets dull and listless over the years. Dents and minor rusting develops. You can make the door look almost as good as new. Remove the rust with Oxysolv Rust Remover by the Solv-O Corp., (800) 594-9028. Then wash down the door with a solution of 2 ounces of TSP per gallon of water, and rinse.

After the door is completely dry, fill any dents, dings or pitting with spot putty available at most auto supply stores. Sand with a fine sandpaper and wipe the surface with a tack rag.

Cover all six sides with a good water-base exterior stain kill such as Masterchem Total One, (800) 325-3552, or Wm. Zinsser 1-2-3. Finish with two coats of a good acrylic trim paint.

Fiberglass

Fiberglass doors are almost indestructible, but over time they can get pitted by the elements or you can decide you don't like the color. Scrub down the door with a solution of 4 ounces of TSP per gallon of water. Rinse copiously, then let dry for at least 2 to 4 hours. To finish, apply one coat of a water-base stain kill and two coats of a good acrylic exterior trim paint.

Now the door looks beautiful, but you're not done yet. The hardware should be cleaned and brightened with a good metal cleaner such as Flitz or Euroshine. Art Sutton of Big D Lock City, (248) 398-2030, in Berkley, suggests that you clean older, slightly cantankerous locks with WD-40, then lubricate with graphite or silicone spray.

Doug Woodcock of Universal Weather Stripping, (800) 878-0277, suggests that you replace the old weather stripping. Universal has the widest selection of weather stripping in this part of the country.

Then, just for the heck of it, put on a new brass kick plate. Your door is now looking so good, the neighbors will be gawking. You just saved $1,000. Treat yourself to dinner at a good restaurant. Then brag about it.

JUNE 17, 2000

Elaborate front doors are works of art that will ring your chimes

by Glenn Haege,
America's Master Handyman

Although Mark Iannuzzi calls it the soul of the house, you probably just call it the front door. Whatever the terminology, it is the single-most stared at part of your home. Everyone who approaches the front of your house and rings the doorbell spends a couple of minutes staring intently at your front door.

Front doors can be very modest flat affairs with just a handle and a keyhole, or they can be elaborate pieces of art.

Although not equipped with vocal cords, they say a lot about you. They project an image of your home, your personality and your place in society. During seminars at January's National Association of Home Builders Show, the designers told us that even though houses were getting smaller, the grand entrance ways still had to be grand.

The folks at Pease Industries, a large manufacturer of fiberglass and steel door systems, say that a person should budget 1 percent to 2 percent of the total cost of the house for the entry system. If you have a $100,000 house that means that a $1,000 to $2,000 door is within the budget. A $350,000 house can well have a $7,000 entrance. The math just keeps going up from there.

All that money is not going into the door itself. The entrance system is often composed of a single or double doors, side panels called sidelights and a decorative panel above the door called the transom.

Entrance costs can add up fast. Each sidelight costs at least two thirds as much as the door it accompanies. Transoms can cost far more. Starting with a comparatively modest $1,000 door, you can easily have $1,300 in sidelights, a $1,000 transom, $1,500 in staining and finishing, a minimum of $2,000 in installation costs and at least $1,000 in hardware. Your comparatively modest $1,000 door has become a $7,800 entrance.

Decorative glass can be anywhere from nonexistent or a slight accent to the major focus of the door, according to Mark Iannuzzi of Grinnell Door Co., (810) 463-8667. Doors from the International Wood Products designer series available through his company are actually signed by the artist, Shelley Jurs.

Henry Tarnow of Tarnow Doors uses digital cameras and photo imaging to show his customers exactly what their Therma Tru fiberglass doors will look like installed on their home.

According to Henry Tarnow, owner of Tarnow Doors in Farmington, (800) 466-9060, it is not usually a smart idea for the do-it-yourselfer to try and save money by installing the door themselves.

"My technicians do a wonderful job installing garage doors, but I wouldn't let anyone but a finish carpenter install an entrance door. The work is too exacting and there are many things that can go wrong," Tarnow says.

"When replacing an entrance door, measurement is critical. All too often, I see homeowners who have purchased a door that was just a little too high for the existing opening," Tarnow says. "They usually wind up cutting off either the top of the door, weakening the door, or cutting into the header above the door, weakening the structure."

different materials. The three most common are steel, fiberglass and wood. Many of the leading door manufacturers like Therma Tru, (800) 843-7628, Stanley, (800) 521-2752, and Pease, (800) 88-DOORS, make steel and fiberglass doors.

This Therma Tru Fiberglass Door is stained to look like wood with company's finishing system. The Bradford frosted glass pattern is made from two panes of double strength, safety-tempered glass for energy efficiency.

This Benchmark Legend steel door has a protective wood grain PVC coating that looks like wood when stained. For more information call Benchmark at (540) 898-5700.

A basic builder's model steel door is the least expensive door made. It is usually made of a metal "skin" wrapped around a wood frame with an insulated core. These doors are often used as temporary closures during the construction stage of very expensive homes. Other steel doors can cost thousands of dollars. The double-entry doors at my house are custom made, custom painted and cost much more.

Audia Woodworking of Utica has been making hardwood doors for more than 50 years. Each door can be made to the customer's exact specifications. These finished and unfinished doors are part of the display at the company's showroom. Prices of custom doors can range from a few thousand dollars to more than $65,000 for a 40-foot-high grand entrance way.

Fiberglass doors usually have a more realistic wood grain than steel. Most of the major manufacturers have special stain coating systems that make the doors seem very woodlike.

Custom doors are a functional art form. This entrance was designed and is signed by acclaimed California artist Shelley Jurs for International Wood Products, (800) 468-3667. It is available locally from Grinnell Door Co.

Wood doors can be made with anything from a thin wood veneer to magnificent laminated hard woods. A basic fir door can cost as little as $400. Deluxe, hand crafted hardwood doors can cost thousands.

Mark Iannuzzi of Grinnell Door Co. says that many of the best hardwoods come from the United States. Often the wood is bought in the States, then shipped to Mexico for the hand craftsmanship.

It is still possible to have a top-quality hardwood door made to your order right here in Michigan. Sam (Salvatore) Audia Sr. of Audia Woodworking & Fine Furniture Inc., (810) 296-6330, in Utica, and his family have been making

Intricate glass designs like the one on this Therma Tru Fiberglass Door is a popular entrance door upgrade. Glass can be clear, tinted, frosted or a combination of all three.

doors for more than 50 years. Audia says that although his company makes doors out of any wood that his customers request, he believes the best doors made are from Honduran Mahogany.

The Audias use their own laminating process to create a door that is much stronger and more weather proof than the original wood, then they carve designs to the buyer's exact specifications. Audia admits his doors are expensive, but they are built to give beauty and protection for many generations.

JUNE 24, 2000

Home Depot grows as everybody and their insurance companies get in line

by Glenn Haege,
America's Master Handyman

The world is changing. I just put down the latest issue of National Home Center News and started wondering how long it will be before dictionaries define home improvement with a three-word entry: The Home Depot.

I've broadcast from a number of the chain's grand openings in the past few months. It seems like the company can open a store in a new city or a couple of miles from another Home Depot and immediately the parking lot is full of cars and the checkout counters are thronged with lines of shoppers.

Last year, Home Depot opened 159 new locations, bringing its total to 877 stores and almost $37 billion in sales. It also sent shock waves through the industry by beginning to carry major appliances. You pick out the appliance at Home Depot and the manufacturer delivers it to you.

The pace is not slowing down. Through August, Home Depot is scheduled to open 48 more U.S. stores.

Not wanting to leave any major revenue stream untapped, Home Depot is testing the water selling central heating and cooling through a relationship with Trane and the manufacturer's "comfort specialist" dealers. It's being tested at nine stores in Georgia and Tennessee serviced by the company's Apex (building) Supply subsidiary.

If this works out, I wonder how long it will be before Home Depot will have its own brand, a la Sears Kenmore. Could Ridgid brand furnaces and air conditioners be far away?

According to Kitchen and Bath Business magazine, 925,216 kitchens were remodeled in the western region of the United States last year. Almost half (427,808) were done by home centers. KBB estimates that 216,704 of these were done by Home Depot. Two years ago at the Kitchen and Bath Show, the scuttle butt was that within five years one half of all the Certified Kitchen Designers would work for Home Depot. That seems realistic now.

Not content to rule the building materials warehouse scene, Home Depot management is opening new stores under different formats. Villager's Hardware is set to tackle mom and pop hardware stores. Expo Design Centers are going for the high-end market with deluxe flooring, cabinetry and hardware.

The first two Expo Design Centers in Metro Detroit are due to open in Troy and West Bloomfield Township before the end of the month. The company expects to have a 200-store chain of Expos around the country by 2005.

Home Depot, which is already the nation's largest retailer of carpeting, will soon open its first stand-alone flooring specialty store in Dallas.

The company's phenomenal growth has been fueled, not only by a tremendously focused marketing team led by Arthur Blank, Home Depot's president and CEO, but by baby boomers and do-it-yourselfers. Baby boomers wanted bigger, better, more. Arthur Blank and Bernie Marcus saw the trend and gave the boomers what they wanted at a bargain price. Home Depot business boomed.

According to the National Association of Home Builders, home remodeling is expected to grow to $150 billion this year. According to a national survey by Owens Corning, nearly three quarters of all homeowners in the 23- to 35-year-old age group are actively engaged in home improvement projects.

And because more boomers are hitting 50 and would rather buy it themselves but let somebody else swing the hammer, Home Depot is expanding mightily into installed sales.

Oh, I almost forgot the Internet. Home Depot already has a big internet presence and is scheduled to have an e-commerce capability this summer. A major focus of the site will be builder sales. They hope to be able to have a contractor's internet order processed and ready for pick-up at the nearest Home Depot within two hours of his e-commerce order.

Just to be helpful, Allstate Insurance has decided that "you are in good hands with Home Depot." From now on, the insurance company will refer homeowners with property damage claims directly to the nation's largest home improvement warehouse. According to Daniel Hoppes, director of national insurance programs for Home Depot, the agreement currently only covers flooring replacement, the most common property damage claim.

Right now, the alliance is only expected to increase Home Depot sales by $40 million. But don't feel too badly. Allstate pays out between $1.8 and $2 billion annually in property damage claims. Home Depot's new relationship gives them a good chance of getting a major portion of that business.

Now you know why the checkout lines get so darned long. Everybody and their brother really is shopping there.

Women flex their muscles to kick off First Lady Build in Detroit

by Glenn Haege,
America's Master Handyman

On any given day, somewhere in the United States, the wives of a couple of governors and close to 300 other women flock to a construction site and build a Habitat for Humanity Home from scratch.

The Governor's First Lady, Michelle Engler and Detroit's First Lady, Judge Trudy DunCombe Archer, take a break during the Habitat for Humanity First Lady Build at Detroit's Creekside Community.

Since April 24, 1999, women governors and governors' wives have been spearheading a Habitat for Humanity drive called the First Lady Build. The intent is to build one house in every state of the union. The actual result will be many times that number.

Janet Huckabee, the first lady of Arkansas, launched the Build program in Little Rock last April. Last month, Michigan First Lady Michelle Engler and Detroit Mayor Dennis Archer's wife, Judge Trudy DunCombe Archer, joined with Huckabee and Cathy Keating, the first lady of Oklahoma, to launch the Michigan First Lady Build program.

It started June 12 in Detroit's Creekside Community with two homes sponsored by Masco Corp. and Detroit Edison. The homes are being built in large part by women volunteers from Masco, Detroit

Edison and other Metro Detroit companies and organizations.

Michelle Engler launched Builds in Lansing, Saginaw, Grand Rapids and Negaunee/Marquette on four consecutive days last month. By the time she is finished, she will have started 36 homes in Michigan communities.

The Midwest is a Habitat hotbed, according to Fiona Eastwood of Habitat for Humanity International. The Michigan program is the most ambitious in the nation.

First ladies may grab the headlines, but it is the massive number of women volunteers that is most impressive. At the Masco-sponsored site, about 100 women volunteers, led by Dr. Lillian Bauder, president of the Masco Charitable Trust, were out there swinging hammers, raising partitions and hanging siding.

Michigan's First Lady, Michelle Engler, and Habitat for Humanity women volunteers raise the front wall of the First Lady Build House sponsored by Masco Corp. at Detroit's Creekside Community.

The Masco commitment is so extensive that more company volunteers are simultaneously building a second home right next door to the First Lady Build project. Last year, Masco employees provided more than 100,000 volunteer hours, while the company's charitable trust made a

$1-million commitment over several years to Habitat for Humanity.

The National Association of Women in Construction has 6,500 members in 200 chapters in 47 states and three Canadian provinces. Between 1995 and 1999 the number of women in construction-related jobs increased from 762,000 to 886,000. This number represents almost 10 percent of the total construction labor force of 8,987,000, according to the Bureau of Labor Statistics.

Interestingly, most of those jobs are not involved with the traditional hammer-swinging construction trades. According to the National Association of Home Builders Director of Research Gopal Ahluwalia, the real story is the number of women who are not in the business.

Michigan First Lady, Michelle Engler, Janet Huckabee the First Lady of Arkansas, and Cathy Keating, the First Lady of Oklahoma join other womem volunteers attaching the roof overhang to the front of a Habitat for Humanity house in Detroit's Creekside Community.

According to the U.S. Labor Department, there is a huge need for at least 240,000 new workers every year in the construction business. Despite the need and the fact that women make up 46.5 percent of the country's overall labor force, they make up only single digits in the core construction trades.

Department of Labor statistics show that women make up only 1.2 percent of the carpenters, 1.3 percent of the brick and stone masons, 1.8 percent of the plumbers and pipefitters, 6.4 percent of the painters, 1.9 percent of the roofers,

2.3 percent of the electricians, 3.5 percent of the concrete finishers and 3.6 percent of the drywall installers.

Three years ago Ahluwalia did a major study to learn why there were not more women in the trades. Not surprisingly, the two biggest reasons were that women were put off by the sheer drudgery of the work, and they didn't like the harassment they got from some folks on the construction site.

Nevertheless, there is an ever-increasing window of opportunity. More and more women in the construction business are beginning to network. Valisa Naganashe, who works in commercial insurance for the Brown Rigg Companies, is president of the Detroit chapter of the women builders' group, (248) 373-5580. She reports that her group is working to improve members' bidding procedures.

In addition, both the National Association of Women in Construction national and local organizations have continuing educational scholarship and certification programs. To learn more, call the group at (800) 552-3506 and sign up before Friday for a reduced rate.

Closer to home, Oakland County Community College, (248) 232-4152, has a rough carpentry program with free tuition. According to Joe Burdzinski, program development manager, so far only five of the 117 graduates of the program have been women. Four are enrolled in the current class.

A great way to get a free taste test of the construction business would be to get involved with the current First Lady Build. To learn more, call Habitat in Michigan, (517) 882-2611. Outside Michigan call (800) HABITAT. Get involved. Do some deserving folks a lot of good. Find a new career, then brag about it.

Now hear this: Options abound to reduce excess noise in the home

by Glenn Haege,
America's Master Handyman

Most of us go home for a little peace and quiet. Unfortunately, once we get there, many don't find the quiet we are looking for. Outside noise comes from sirens and other street noises, barking dogs and the neighbors' lawn mowers and other gas-powered equipment.

The sound invasion often gets even worse when you are living in an apartment or condominium. If you are planning on the transition from a house to a condominium, you might just want to clip this article and show it to your builder.

Music either soothes or irritates. If it is coming at you from the kid next door's boom box, it's noise. Come to think of it, it is even noise when the sound is coming from your son or daughter's room.

Laundry rooms, bathrooms, entertainment rooms and home offices, even kitchen appliances, all add up to demonic decibel levels that constantly bombard our ears.

How do you get away from it all?

I recently received a letter from a reader who told me that he was having a home built in Northville and wanted to know if insulating the inside walls with R-13 insulation for the purpose of noise control was a smart idea.

R-13 insulation is excellent, but it is just one of the possibilities when you are building a new house or adding a room addition. New methods of construction like Insulated Concrete Forms (ICF) and Structural Insulated Panels (SIP) should also be considered.

Even if you confine yourself to traditional methods of construction there are many things we can do to control noise pollution. Let's start with the new construction technologies, then go to the more traditional methods of combating unwanted sound.

ICF construction utilizes polystyrene foam forms for poured concrete basement and above grade walls. This method of construction includes the Reddi-Wall system pioneered by Bob Martin, (586) 752-9161, and Benchmark or the Blue Maxx System installed locally by Thermal Wall, (810) 346-2070.

Because walls are constructed from two thicknesses of foam and a solid concrete core they have excellent insulation and sound control characteristics. Add a dimpled drainage membrane, like Consella-Dorken's Delta-MS, (248) 546-1020, to the basement wall and you have a system that is not only quiet and energy efficient, but virtually waterproof.

SIPs consist of two engineered wood panels bonded with an industrial adhesive to a continuous rigid foam core. The result is a relatively light-

66

weight panel that has the strength of an I-beam with great insulation and sound control properties. For more information on this method of construction call Insulspan of Michigan, (517) 486-4844.

Both ICFs and SIPs can be used for interior as well as exterior walls. They result in very, very, quiet houses. They also cost about 10 or 15 percent more than conventional construction. However, this premium usually pays for itself in decreased heating and cooling costs within a very short period of time.

Owens Corning, (800) GET PINK, is one of the leaders in creating sound control systems for conventional construction. The company recommends specifying 2 by 6 rather than 2 by 4 exterior stud walls so that insulation can be increased to R-19 or 21.

For interior walls they recommend the addition of sound control bats of fiberglass insulation. In addition Owens Corning has developed a complete Acoustic System for noise control which includes QuietZone Acoustic Wall Framing, Floor Mats and Caulk.

QuietZone Wall Framing is made of two sections of Trus Joist MacMillan's TimberStrand LSL engineered wood connected by acoustically resilient metal clips. This specialized framing material is designed to break the path of sound vibrations so they don't make it through the walls.

The Acoustic Floor Mat is placed between the subfloor and an overlayment to create an isolation layer between floors. It deadens the sound of heavy equipment like washing machines and foot traffic.

The company's QuietZone Acoustic Caulk is a premium, nondrying, nonhardening, acrylic-based caulk. It is used to fill gaps between wall stud plates, around electrical outlets and opening surrounding air ducts.

Sound comes through doors, windows and any opening in the walls. Hollow doors create miniature echo chambers, so changing interior doors from hollow to solid core dampens sound transmission from room to room. But just adding a solid core door doesn't do the job. The tighter the fit, the better. Doorjambs should be straight and true. The gap between the door and floor should be as small as possible. The addition of a sound gasket will also seal out sound between rooms.

Double-pane windows are not only more energy efficient, they are far quieter than single-pane windows. Some manufacturers, like Weather Shield, (800) 477-6808, make windows with double strength glass for noise control. Casement windows are more efficient than double hung or slider windows for sealing out noise, cold and heat.

Spray foam can be used to very good effect to block sound transmission through electrical sockets and isolate pipes and plumbing equipment.

There's practically no end to the things you can do to control the sound in your home. But, as any builder can tell you, quiet costs. If you are willing to pay the price, your house can be as quiet as you want it to be.

JULY 15, 2000

Make sure workers are qualified before letting them paint your house

by Glenn Haege,
America's Master Handyman

My nationally syndicated radio show and Ask Glenn column in the Detroit News Feature Section on Thursdays are like homeowner surveys. You tell me what I should write and talk about. Exterior painting problems are at the top of the charts right now.

There are two sources of painting problems: Do-It-Yourselfers' self-inflicted problems and those caused by purchasing the services of incompetent painting contractors.

Do-It-Yourself exterior painting problems are so extensive that I wrote a book on the subject, Take the Pain Out of Painting - Exteriors ($12.95, Master Handyman Press). You can find copies at many libraries, Damman's, or many of the major bookstores like Borders, Barnes & Nobel and Amazon.com, direct from the publisher or call (888) HANDY 81.

I am going to concentrate on contractor problems today and cover DIY problems in a later article.

Many homeowners figure they don't have to worry because they have hired a painting professional. Most painting professionals are well qualified. It's those other guys that give professionals a bad rap.

Painting the outside of a house is not the same as Tom Sawyer white-washing a picket fence. Being able to slap a paintbrush back and forth is not a qualification. Exterior painting takes skill, energy and perseverance.

Not all professional painters want to do the extra work involved with exterior painting. The painter also has to be brave enough to walk away if the homeowner is not willing to pay for the work to be done properly.

It is often we, the homeowners, who are at fault for bad workmanship. We often go with the low bidder then complain when the paint starts peeling after two or three years. Unfortunately, even when we are willing to pay, the painter may not want to do the work the job requires.

Here's a homeowner horror story to illustrate the point. Mr. D., a personal friend of my publisher, has a relatively large, older, wood-sided home in one of Detroit's northern suburbs. He's a quality type of guy, so he always tells the painter to buy the best paint and do all the prepainting work necessary.

The average cost of painting his house is $20,000. (Gasp!) For that kind of money you would expect a top flight professional job. Unfortunately, even though quality paint with a 20-year warranty is used, he has to repaint every four years.

This year the painter was selected because he had an excellent reputation in the community and had done craftsmanlike interior painting for Mr. D.

The contractor said that he had a lot of exterior painting experience and Mr. D. believed him. Big mistake.

It turns out that most of his exterior experience was spray painting horse barns, not homes. Horse barns and houses are entirely different structures and have vastly different painting requirements. Just about everything the painter did was wrong.

Mr. D's home had two major problems.

First, the siding did not have enough ventilation, so it never dried out. Even though large vents had been installed behind the shutters, there was still not enough air circulation. Shurline vent wedges would have to be inserted every 3 feet vertically and horizontally so that the siding could breathe.

Secondly, previous coats of paint had been applied over damp, sometimes spongy siding. The surface had to be stripped to the bare wood and permitted to dry. Spongy wood had to be replaced. The entire surface needed to be sealed with a water-based stain kill like 1-2-3 by William Zinsser or Total One by Master Chem before the final coats of paint could be applied.

When the painter was told what needed to be done, he expressed shock because he had never heard of such a thing. Unfortunately for Mr. D, that painter was either a liar, incompetent or both.

The reason for this horror story is that I wanted to demonstrate that it could happen to anybody. It is being repeated on houses all over the area at this very moment. Smaller houses owned by people with tighter budgets (you and me) are even more prone to be improperly prepped, then painted with paint that is either inferior or applied too thinly to film build properly. If you don't put sufficient paint on the surface, it cannot last.

Compounding the problem, many newer homes were built with very absorbent, T-1-11 wood siding. Much of this siding was improperly applied and requires greater preparation, total encapsulation of edges during painting, and more attention to water drainage than solid wood siding.

You have to be very nosey if you want a proper painting job. You have to get quality contractor referrals from professional paint stores or friends and neighbors. You have to actually go out and look at the jobs when checking references. Then you have to make certain that thorough surface preparation is specified in the contract. You have to make certain the proper paint is being purchased and the correct amount of paint is being applied (usually 400 square feet per gallon, per coat).

Then, and only then, can you be sure of a paint job you can brag about. As Dr. Laura would say, "Now go and do the right thing."

JULY 22, 2000

Midquality vinyl siding is a safe bet, but don't skimp on installation

by Glenn Haege,
America's Master Handyman

Vinyl siding has come a long was since it was first introduced by the Crane Plastics Co. in 1947. The first vinyl came in a limited number of colors, was easily pitted and often visibly sagged after the first few years.

Today, vinyl siding has become so popular that it represents 41 percent of all exterior cladding, according to Walter Hoyt, director of marketing for Wolverine Siding Systems.

That means 41 percent of all the new and remodeled exterior walls are covered with vinyl.

It comes in a wide variety of styles and colors and has limited lifetime warranties. To make shopping worry-free, quality sidings are even certified by the Vinyl Siding Institute (VSI).

Certified vinyl siding has been tested by independent testing laboratories to assure that it meets strict standards. Testing is done for weather performance, wind load and impact resistance, surface distortion, heat shrinkage, expansion, color, gloss, camber, length, width and thickness.

All major vinyl siding companies now have VSI-Certified siding. To be certain a particular siding has been certified, look for the VSI Certified logo on the siding literature or check out the company and siding brand on the VSI web site at www.vinylsiding.org.

All that being said, when you get right down to it, all similarly styled vinyl sidings look pretty much alike from 20 feet.

Barring a tremendously powerful wind or excessive heat, your siding should last about 20 or 30 years whether you buy the cheapest vinyl siding or the most expensive.

Despite the similarities, the good stuff costs about twice as much as the "builders' special." So how's the homeowner supposed to tell the difference between the good stuff and the not quite good enough? How can you make sure you have a top-quality siding job? Can a do-it-yourselfer install vinyl siding and get a quality-looking job?

To learn the answers, I went to Bob Piquette. Piquette is the president of Siding World, one of the largest siding suppliers in the Midwest. Siding World,(313) 891-2902, has 15 distribution centers in Michigan, Ohio and Indiana.

Piquette and the company's sales manager, Claude "J.R." Lafnear, both said that the most important ingredient to a siding job is installation quality. If the installer attaches the siding too tightly, there will not be room for expansion and contraction during seasonal changes. If he or she hangs siding crooked or does sloppy trim work, the job will be a disaster.

The second biggest factor in a quality siding job is the thickness of the vinyl being hung on the wall. Builders' special or promotional siding often has a thickness of only 34 or 35 mills. Premium vinyl sidings may be 50 mills thick or more.

The break point between premium and promotional quality, according to Lafnear, is a vinyl thickness of 40 mills. At a thickness of 40 or more, the vinyl has the strength needed not to sag or break and won't blow off the wall in a high wind. If less than 40 mills thick, the siding will not have the rigidity for long-term good looks.

New manufacturing techniques, such as the introduction of a stabilizing rod in Wolverine's Benchmark 44 siding, can greatly increase rigidity and wind resistance. The company's new Millennium smart wall has been tested to withstand 200 mph hurricane-force winds. Call (888) 838-8100 for more information.

Although about 90 percent of all homeowners choose vinyl siding in a wood-grain pattern, there are many choices in styles, colors and trims. Vinyl siding comes in multiple widths and in lap, shake and half-round shingle styles.

Color technology has improved. All the major manufacturers like Alcoa, Certainteed and Wolverine make premium siding in 15 or 20 different colors and cover color retention in their warranties, Lafnear said.

When I asked Piquette what a vinyl siding shopper should look for, he said: "Don't just shop for price. Concern yourself with what you are going to like when you pull into the driveway for the next 20 or 30 years.

"Stay away from trendy colors because they may be hopelessly out of style 10 years from now. Take advantage of half-round and cedar shake looks and polystyrene moldings. Good trim design can make your home the most attractive house on the block."

When costing out a job, expect labor to be approximately 50 percent to 70 percent of the total cost. The exact amount depends upon the amount of detail involved. The vinyl siding and trim will each take up about half the remainder.

Hanging vinyl siding is not an overwhelming task for a do-it-yourselfer who wants to save money and has a lot of patience. Wolverine has a 111-page installation manual available and VSI has a 44-page manual that can be downloaded from its web site.

The job does require that a person be very meticulous. Lafnear had the best advice:

"If you are very particular and have the time to work slow, you can do a good job. If you want to get in and out quickly, have a professional do it."

With cooking in mind, kitchen revolutionary has designs on your home

by Glenn Haege,
America's Master Handyman

Don Silvers is a dangerous man. He thinks your kitchen is laid out wrong; the counters are too narrow; there aren't enough sinks; and you do entirely too much walking around making a meal.

He also has very definite ideas about where you put your appliances; why you can't duplicate the taste of most chefs' cooking; where you put supplies; and what you stand on.

Donald E. Silvers has a kitchen design consultancy in Los Angeles. He also teaches kitchen and bath design at UCLA. He has the audacity to voice these opinions because he is both a Certified Kitchen Designer and a chef. CNN credits him with being "the only certified kitchen designer and chef in the industry today."

During his career, Silvers designed more than 1,000 kitchens - he not only knows how to talk the talk, he actually walks the walk.

Every year my office receives magnificent, lavishly illustrated books on kitchens and kitchen design. The majority show beautiful kitchens for beautiful people. You get the idea that these rooms are for folks more interested in the kitchen as an art form than a place to cook a meal.

In his book, Kitchen Design With Cooking in Mind, Silvers shows how to create a kitchen that cooks beautifully and looks good. His thesis is that if your kitchen is strategically laid out and designed to cut meal preparation time and effort in half, you'll want to cook more.

When Silvers designs a kitchen some of his questions to clients are:
■ What is the maximum number of people you will prepare a meal for?
■ What type of food do you like to prepare for a formal meal?
■ What are your favorite informal meals?

His final kitchen plan will make meal preparation a joyful experience. He does this by throwing out the Kitchen Triangle and concentrating on workflow. The Kitchen Triangle is a concept introduced in a study by the University of Illinois in the 1950s. It based design on three major kitchen appliances: the stove, refrigerator and sink; then squished everything else around them.

There are three problems with this concept: Many important appliances and cooking gear that should be in daily use are stored out of view in difficult-to-reach places. Adding one or two cooks means you have to work on top of one another and get in each other's way. When you try to prepare an elaborate meal you usually wind up trying to use a sink for food prep that is already filled with dirty pots and pans.

Techniques Silvers uses to combat these problems are "furring out" the cabinets six inches from the wall; adding a cleaning sink; and laying out the kitchen using a sub system approach.

"Furring out" is the technical term for placing standard 24-inch-deep base cabinets 6 inches from the wall. This provides 30-inch-deep kitchen counters rather than the standard 24-inch depth. The additional 6 inches permits you to store all your major appliances on the counter top, while still providing a 2-foot-deep work area. Silvers says this little trick doubles the available work area in most kitchens and simplifies food preparation by having most small appliances already set up and ready to use.

When a second sink is added, one sink is designated for food preparation, the other for cleaning. The cleaning sink and dishwasher are located away from the food preparation area.

Using a sub system approach to kitchen design means laying out the kitchen for specific tasks in such a way that they complement, not interfere with one another. Cold and dry storage is convenient to food preparation and cooking. Clean up is easy, out of the way and does not interfere with food prep.

Sound impossible? Not when you understand the fundamentals. They are all laid out in less than 100 pages in Silvers' book. Kitchen Design With Cooking in Mind is available for $24.95 from Amazon.com. or direct from the author at (800) 900-4761, or on his web site at www.donsilvers.com.

The book includes in-depth explanations on how to improve kitchen design, the pros and cons of different style cabinets, counter tops, sinks, all major appliances, flooring and lighting. At the end of the book is a copy of the questionnaire Silvers gives his clients, which will help you find out about yourself and your kitchen needs.

Silvers has many interesting insights. Among them:

■ The reason most of us can't duplicate chef's recipes is that commercial cook top burners put out twice the BTU's as residential burners.

■ Vinyl flooring is the least expensive, most comfortable to stand on and easiest to care for.

■ Movable islands make putting away supplies, food preparation and serving much easier.

We have many good local kitchen designers, but if you read the book and want to move to California so Silvers can design your kitchen, you can save the trip. He consults by phone and does 40 or 50 out-of-state designs every year. If this sounds interesting, Silvers returns from vacation in mid-August.

AUGUST 5, 2000

Stop mosquitoes from bugging you with several simple solutions

by Glenn Haege,
America's Master Handyman

Quick: How many different kinds of mosquitoes are there? (Between 2,000 and 3,000.) How many different kinds of mosquitoes are there in the United States? (Estimates vary between 170 and 200.)

Why am I bugging you with mosquito trivia? Because (slap, slap) they are bugging me. This past week's rains and hot muggy temperatures have made this prime mosquito breeding time.

We do not have a major mosquito problem in Michigan, but the folks in New York, Connecticut, Massachusetts and New Jersey are doing extensive testing, and three of the four states have started spraying programs.

New York has cancelled outdoor concerts because of the potential threat of mosquitoes spreading West Nile virus. The Boston Globe reported the start of the Massachusetts spraying program on July 27 and warned that the disease could spread statewide.

West Nile virus grows in birds and is transmitted from bird to bird. The disease is transmitted to humans and horses via mosquitoes that become infected when they bite birds. According to the Massachusetts Department of Public Health, the disease, in rare instances, can be fatal.

I can drive to New York in less than a day. Driving there is no problem. What could come back with me could be. Hundreds, maybe thousands, of cars, trucks and aircraft come in from the East Coast every day. Mosquitoes can hitchhike.

The East Coast scare may just be an early warning signal. Worldwide, mosquitoes are such a big problem that a week ago the Wall Street Journal carried an editorial calling for bringing back DDT to combat malaria epidemics in Third World countries. DDT is banned in the United States because of environmental concerns.

I am not an expert on DDT. I can't do a thing about instituting a statewide anti-mosquito program. Even if I had the power, I wouldn't know what to spray. That is for the experts.

According to the Harvard School of Public Health, there are a good many things we can do as homeowners to interrupt the mosquitoes' life cycle. Mosquitoes lay their eggs in stagnant water and the larva and pupa stages cannot exist outside of water.

So, get rid of standing water and you get rid of mosquitoes. We can't do anything about swamps, but we can clean roof gutters and drain or frequently change the water in buckets, trash cans, bird baths and horse troughs. Discarded tires are a common mosquito breeding ground and need to be disposed of properly.

Drilling holes in the bottom of recycling containers, turning over plastic wading pools and wheelbarrows when not in use, and keeping pools and spas properly chlorinated all help.

Overgrown grass and shrubs retain moisture and make excellent launching pads from which mosquitoes lie in wait until their prey (you) comes along. To cut down on mosquitoes, keep the grass short and cut back the bushes.

Once the mosquito is fully grown, only the female is interested in your blood, and then only when she needs extra nourishment for egg production. The rest of the time she and her spouse are vegetarians.

If you don't want to attract her attention, the Harvard School of Public Health recommends that you wear long-sleeved clothing and slacks and avoid being outside between dusk and dawn when mosquitoes are most active.

When you go out, wear a mosquito repellent that contains DEET (diethyl-meta-toluamide) such as Deep Woods Off and Cutters.

Before an outdoor party, apply a mosquito repellent such as Bonide Mosquito Beater, (800) 536-8231. If it is a very special occasion like a wedding, consider having a pest control company spray the area. Paul LeBuhn of Maple Lane Pest Control, (800) 870-7096, says the average cost for a residential spray job is $250. He warns that a heavy rain or a high wind can destroy the effectiveness of spraying.

Some people are hypersensitive to mosquito bites. If you are, you may want to investigate the Mosquito Killing System by Environmental Products and Research. It's available in the United States from U-SPRAY Inc., (770) 985-9388; Mosquito Solutions, (281) 556-6699; or Forever Green, (203) 331-0097. Check out the science or buy direct from the web site at www.mosquitosolution.com.

This electronic gadget was developed with help from NASA. It lures the unsuspecting mosquito to its death with an intermittent gassing of carbon dioxide, mimicking the exhalation of a red-blooded animal. Once the mosquito flies into the canister looking for din din, an electric current zaps it.

Male mosquitoes and other non-blood-sucking insects are not attracted to the carbon dioxide and don't get zapped. The entire mosquito-killing system costs $575. That makes the price about equal to 350 cans of Cutters. If you decide to buy the Mosquito Killing System, let me know how it works.

AUGUST 12, 2000

Several steps will keep you from having to bail out the basement

by Glenn Haege,
America's Master Handyman

Does it ever seem to you that, no matter how fast you run, all you are doing is going around in circles?

Exactly five years ago today, the headline of my Homestyle column was "What to do if leaky cellar is draining your patience."

In last Thursday's Detroit News "Ask Glenn" column, I helped out a fellow in Toledo who had 17 inches of water in his basement. On last Saturday's radio show, I interviewed Todd Jackson of Jackson Waterproofing, (800) 404-8342, and Wayne Nichols of Hydro Flo, (800) 748-0500. Jackson is a vice-president of the National Association of Waterproofing Contractors. Nichols is a member of the group's board of directors.

Despite the recent rains and the fact that basements are being flooded in a multistate area, we are technically in the middle of a drought that has gone on at least two years.

The overlying drought may be compounding the flooding problem, according to Nichols, who is president of a basement dewatering company in Grand Rapids.

Most of the populated areas of Michigan and much of the Midwest are built on clay soil. Clay needs a certain amount of moisture to retain its strength.

Because of the prolonged drought, the clay under many of buildings is collapsing, causing cracks in unsupported foundations and basement walls.

Combine drought conditions with a building boom that continually stretches our resources, and municipalities and counties that have not seen their way clear to make the necessary upgrades in drainage and sewer lines and water treatment facilities. Then add a couple of weeks of rain to bring about flash flood conditions in many areas, and you have a prescription for disaster.

What can we as homeowners do to alleviate the problem?

First the long-term solution. As citizens, we have to let our elected representatives know that we support making the necessary upgrades in our city's, county's and state's infrastructure.

Second, when it comes time to vote for a millage to upgrade these systems, we have to put our money where our mouths are and vote to raise and spend the money. After all, when we vote for infrastructure upgrades, we are really voting to protect our own basements and safeguard our drinking water.

After we have bellied up to the bar, we have the right to let our politicians know that we will not tolerate flooded basements, water back up and polluted lakes, rivers and streams.

On a personal level, we have to do everything we can to make sure that we are part of the solution, not the problem. Many downspouts on older homes are still connected to the storm sewers. This is wrong on two counts: It plugs our own home's drainage system and over-taxes the storm lines. They just can't handle the load.

The next step is to try to put our basements on a water-free diet. Walk around the house and make sure that the downspouts are extended properly. Many direct water toward, not away from the house. Others are often pushed in the wrong direction by lawnmowers and children playing.

Climb up a ladder and make sure the gutters are clean and free flowing.

Nichols says that many of the times that his company is called in for extensive repair work, the homeowner could have saved the money if he or she had just done those two things.

If you have a sump pump draining into the back yard, the line often only goes 6 or 8 feet. Todd Jackson of Jackson Waterproofing suggests that it may be wise to extend the line another 5 or 10 feet. Too often, water from the sump pump just goes into the soil, drains under the house and is continuously re-circulated by the sump pump.

If you want to go overboard and eliminate 90 percent of all self-inflicted homeowner basement problems, make sure that proper drainage exists around the entire perimeter of your home. This means that the ground around the house should have a 1-inch drop per foot for 4 feet.

Nichols says that he would prefer an even steeper slope away from the foundation if at all possible. He would also like the slope to be topped with clay enriched topsoil so that water runs off and is not absorbed.

If the worst happens and your basement is flooded, you are stuck with the problem of whom to call. Here's a good way to separate the men from the boys among all the water proofing contractors you see in the phone book. Only waterproofers who are members of the National Association of Waterproofing Contractors subscribe to their code of ethics.

Of the NAWC membership, only those who have taken special training in soil sciences and building construction and have passed rigorous testing are Certified Waterproofing Contractors. There are only 35 certified waterproofing contractors in the entire United States and five in Michigan. Both Nichols and Jackson are certified. To find a certified contractor near you, you can contact the NAWC at (800) 245-NAWC, or check out their web site at www.waterproofers.org.

AUGUST 19, 2000

Garden gear for gals takes center stage at National Hardware Show

by Glenn Haege,
America's Master Handyman

CHICAGO

The big news at the National Hardware Show, held in conjunction with International Hardware Week, was not who was there, but who didn't come and who left early.

No-shows included some of the biggest names in the hardware business including big tool manufacturers such as Black and Decker, Skil, Bosch and Dremmel, as well as plumbing suppliers like Moen faucets and Price Pfister.

Attendance was down because Home Depot had no official presence and Wal-Mart had scheduled its own internal show for the same week.

Even so, there were still more than 3,000 exhibitors representing some 90 countries at the show. In the who-left-early group, many exhibitors from mainland China dismantled their displays and walked out of the show at 4 p.m. Monday after they discovered the Taiwanese flag flying along with all the other foreign flags representing exhibitors.

The show is much more than hardware. It also includes automotive, building supplies and tools, electrical, housewares, lawn and garden, pet products, plumbing, heating and cooling.

This week, I'll look at new products that target women, including lawn and garden items. Next week, I'll concentrate on lighting, water purification, household security and tools.

Victoria Addison designs a line of garden tools for women called Garden Gals. The tools include everything from clippers and cultivators to trowels and transplanters.

Most gardening tools are sized for men, but women actually do 65 percent of all gardening. About four years ago, Victoria Addison of Garden Pals, (800) 666-4044, was given the job of developing a line of garden tools made for women. Addison went on the Internet and asked for ideas from women gardeners on what changes they would like to see in their tools.

The result is a new line of tools called Garden Gals. The first tools included pruning shears, loppers and scissors. The tools had regular-sized blades, but were designed to reduce stress hand and wrist fatigue. In addition to being popular with women, they were so easy to use that they now carry the seal of approval of the Arthritis Foundation.

New Garden Gals tools being introduced at this year's show include mid-length and long-handled trowels, transplanters and cultivators. Each of the tools is sized smaller than a similar man's tool. The majority are made of stainless steel with soft, easy-grip handles and carry a lifetime warranty. They range in price from $4.99 to $12.99. They are carried at Wal-Mart under the Ladies Comfort private label.

The Step2 Company, (800) 347-8372, introduced two easy-on-the-back items that should be especially popular with women. The Yard Butler makes cleaning up the yard much easier. It con-

The Yard Butler by the Step2 Co. is an all-in-one lawn care companion that holds a 30-gallon paper yard waste bag, storage slots for long- and short-handled tools and a storage bin.

tains a 30-gallon paper or plastic trash bag and 4 storage slots for long-handled tools such as rakes and shovels, 3 slots for hand tools, a storage bin and an easy-grip handle. It can be easily pushed anywhere on four 7-inch poly wheels. The Yard Butler is in the $40 to $45 price range.

Lay the Step2 Tank Caddy on its side and it will lock a regular sized propane tank securely in the trunk of your car. Upright the Tank Caddy becomes a two wheeled cart that lets you move the propane take effortlessly.

Barbecue propane tanks are a necessity, but getting them from place to place can be a nightmare. The Tank Caddy by Step2 is a sturdy plastic two-wheel cart that keeps the propane tank snug while you move it. When a fill-up is required, you lift the cart into the trunk, then tip it over on its side and the tank locks upright. It is priced in the $25 to $30 price range.

Organizing the garage is going to get a lot easier, too. Knape & Vogt, (800) 253-1561, introduced a line of Storage Wizards at the show. The Tool Organizer will hold up to 3 long-handled shovels and rakes, one in front of the other, plus has hooks for three hand tools or things like clippers, whisk brooms or dust pans. The Garden Tool Organizer stores 9 items in about one foot of width.

The Tool Organizer by Knape & Vogt lets you hang tools in half the space.

Evriholder, (800) 975-0335, is introducing a fold-away wheelbarrow that will carry 110 pounds yet weighs only 71/2 pounds. The container portion is made of triple-stitched, waterproof canvas.

Most of these products should be in a hardware store or home center near you by next spring. Some even sooner.

From lasers to filters, hardware show unveils latest in safety gear

by Glenn Haege,
America's Master Handyman

CHICAGO

Your family's health and safety are your No. 1 priority. There were a few items at this year's International Hardware Show that could literally be called life-savers.

First on my list was the Magne-Flo Magnetic Excess Flow Valve. Explosions caused by gas leaks have been in the news a great deal lately. According to Neil Anderson, the president and owner of Magne-Flo, (888) 669-7356, the magnetic shut off mechanism developed by his company could have prevented those explosions.

Typically residential explosions occur when some one tampers or cuts the connection between the gas line and an appliance or the copper or brass connector becomes old and develops a pinpoint leak.

The magnetic devices Magne-Flo makes fit inside ball valves, gas connectors and adapter fittings. Once installed they act as "circuit breakers" between the gas line and each individual appliance.

In operation, the Magnetic Excess Flow Valve senses any interruption in the normal gas flow and shuts off the line.

Once the leak is fixed the valve turns the gas back on. Because the devise is magnetic, not electrical, the valve is a permanent safeguard and will continue in operation for hundreds of years.

The Magne-Flo device will increase the price of gas line connectors by $3 to $5 each. That means an entire house with gas heat and all gas appliances could be protected for about $30. That's pretty cheap insurance.

The new Faultless Spin-to-Lock deadbolt is another form of very cheap insurance. Once set, the lock is jimmy proof and the bolt even has an internal hardened steel roll bar that makes it impossible to cut.

You can set the deadbolt on the Faultless Spin-to-Lock deadbolt by just spinning the ring. Just press the extra security button on the inside and the lock will not open even with a key.

The new Faultless Spin-to-Lock deadbolt is another form of very cheap insurance. It was the star of the Taiwan Trade Center press conference. The new lock does not need a key to set the deadbolt. Just spin the outer ring and the deadbolt is set. Once set, the lock is jimmy proof and the bolt even has an internal hardened steel roll bar that makes it impossible to cut.

For maximum security inside the house, you can press a button and the lock cannot even be opened from the outside with a key. The lock should only cost about $19.95 retail.

The Taiwan Fu Hsing Industrial Co., Ltd., (877) 663-5625, manufactures the Faultless Spin-to-Lock deadbolt. It will be introduced by all Wal-Mart stores in September.

Despite the fact that America has a good water supply, purity is a growing concern. Culligan, (888) 777-7962, introduced a new under sink water filter system, the SY-2300, which can eliminate 90 percent of the methyl tertiary-butyl ether from the water supply in addition to guarding against Cryptosporidium and Giardia cysts, lead, chlorine, asbestos, mercury and many pesticides and herbicides.

According to Gary Hatch, Ph.D., Culligan's chemical engineering manager, MTBE is a fuel additive used in gasoline to reduce auto emissions. Now the Environmental Protection Agency says that it is a potential human carcinogen and has leached into the water supply in 49 of the 50 states. Culligan's new SY-2300 under-the-sink filtration system will cost about $135.

These days taking a shower can be hazardous to your health because of all the chlorine you inhale. According to Sprite Industries, more than half our daily chlorine

The Sprite 'All-in-One' filtered Showerhead is the first showerhead to filter out chlorine from hot water.

exposure comes from the daily shower. We don't just breath it in, we absorb it through the pores in our skin.

We need chlorine to disinfect our water supply, but many people drink bottled or filtered water to get away from the awful chemical taste. The problem is that hot water destroys carbon filters so it cannot be filtered unless we invest thousands of dollars in a whole house water filtration system.

Sprite Industries, (800) 327-9137, has solved the problem with a line of hot water showerheads and filters. The company's unique Chlorgon filtering media removes chlorine, trace lead, hydrogen sulfide, iron oxide, sediment, and odors. These unique showerheads

are available at Meijer locations. Prices range from $30 to $46.

Imagine being woken up in the middle of the night by the smoke detector. You stumble to the door and the hallway is full of smoke. How do you get out of the house? Statistically smoke from home fires kills more people than the fires themselves.

The new Laserlyte Safe Escape fire escape system is a sound activated laser light projector that listens for the sound of a smoke detector, then projects three laser light arrows on the floor pointing out the escape route. According to the manufacturer the laser arrows can cut through even the thickest smoke pointing the way to safety. The retail cost of a Safe Escape is $69.99. You can buy it on their web site at www.laserlyte.com.

If you are so busy that you don't know whether you are coming or going, Rayovac has a flashlight for you. They combined a compass with their outdoor flashlight line to create Compass Lites. The illuminated compass glows in the dark after you turn the flashlight off.

Stanley, has teamed up with Belkin

Components to introduce Contractor Grade surge protectors, power strips and ground fault circuit/interrupter power cords. These are not just for in the office but are extra rugged and meant for use out in the field. They will make any job site, even the one in your back yard, a whole lot safer.

Stanley's new Contractor grade surge protector comes in 6- and 8-outlet designs and has rubber outlet covers and rugged metal construction.

Follow the rules and maybe – just maybe – you'll find a good tradesman

by Glenn Haege,
America's Master Handyman

Every week I get between 15 and 50 plaintive letters and e-mails that begin:

"Please recommend someone who can paint my ..."

"My husband has had a heart attack and I am in ill health. We need a reliable handyman to ..."

"I am an 85-year-old widow. I paid a man to fix my (fill in the blank) last year, and this year it is broken again and he won't return my phone calls. Please recommend someone who will..."

"I asked five companies to give me a quote on (fill in the blank). Not one of them has returned my repeated phone calls. Please recommend a responsible person to..."

My heart goes out to these people, but I usually can't help them. I don't run a listing service. The turnover rate for craftsmen and women and even remodeling contractors is extraordinarily high. As hard as we try, my staff and I can't keep track of all the tradesmen and women who provide good dependable service to homeowners.

Nothing remains the same. My favorite painter is now a home remodeling contractor. Excellent deck builders become kitchen or basement remodelers. The reasons are simple. You make more money on a $70,000 room addition than you do on a $7,000 paint job. You don't get sun burned, mosquito bitten or have rain or snow delays when you work indoors.

Good handymen are the hardest to find. No licensing is required. If they do one job successfully, the homeowner usually has three or four more jobs lined up before they leave. The jobs also tend to get bigger. Within a few months a good handyman may become a licensed (or unlicensed) modernization contractor.

These job upgrades are the American way. On an individual basis I am glad for the people involved. Unfortunately, every time a craftsperson moves on, he leaves an almost unfillable hole in the labor pool. The demand on the remaining people just gets greater.

Labor Day is not coming a minute too soon. Most of the tradespeople and contractors I know have been working 50 or 60-hour weeks for so long they are just plain frazzled. They need a day off to get to know their families again.

When a person is overworked and stressed out, bad things happen. Jobs go bad. People get burned out and quit right in the middle of a job. You don't want these things to happen on your project.

The need to look out for what I call stress fractures makes the contractor selection process more critical than ever. If people don't show up for the initial interview or are terribly late for one or two appointments, it is a sign that they are too busy and you do not want them on your job.

Since tradespeople are so hard to find, you have to follow all the rules to get a good one.

Rule No. 1: Network. Grill your family and friends. Ask around. Be on the lookout for similar work being done in the neighborhood.

Rule No. 2: Be flexible. Kathleen, my editor at Master Handyman Press, is having the entire interior of her house painted by a young CPA who moonlights as a painter. The guy loves painting. After a full day crunching numbers he has dinner with his wife and kids, then goes out and paints for three hours. The important thing to Kathy and her husband is that the job is being done beautifully, not the painter's weird work routine. They can live with that kind of schedule. I couldn't.

Rule No. 3: Check with suppliers. Sometimes the best way to find tradespeople is where they get their supplies. For example, last week I got e-mails from two people who needed to put in french drains. One lady lived in Rochester and had been searching for two years.

French drains are specially constructed drainage fields designed to solve tricky water run-off problems. Digging a french drain takes skill and is very hard work. Most contractors don't do them.

I called Sandy at J.C. Cornellie, (586) 293-1500, a brick and gravel supplier in Roseville. He suggested the homeowners call Cornellie's Almont yard, (810) 798-8533, to get the names of people who dug french drains in the Rochester area. Problem solved.

See what I mean? Go to a roofing supply wholesaler to get recommendations on roofing contractors. Go to a siding wholesaler to get the names of good siding installers. Go to a tile wholesaler to find good tile contractors and installers.

Rule No. 4: Check references. Anybody and their uncle can say they are a tradesman or contractor. It is vital that you thoroughly check their references so you have confidence that the person or company has the time, skill and resources to get the job done.

If you do your homework you will find the handyman, carpenter, painter, craftsperson or contractor you need and be able to brag about the result.

Happy Labor Day.

SEPTEMBER 9, 2000

Let's throw a little light on those dank, dark basement windows

by Glenn Haege,
America's Master Handyman

The trouble with basements is they make you feel like you're in prison. No matter how much money you've spent redecorating, going down to the basement usually feels like going into a dungeon.

There are two reasons for this: basement stairs and basement lighting. I'll tackle the stairways another time. Today's article is on lighting, especially those awful things that are euphemistically called basement windows.

People with better karma than the majority have above-grade basements. The very fortunate few have sliding glass door walls and real windows. Their basements have real rooms with real views.

Most of us are stuck with holes in the ground barely lit and ventilated by two kinds of windows. Most prevalent are those little slits that are good for absolutely nothing except collecting mud and spider webs. I have always recommended filling standard basement windows with glass block if zoning permits. The glass block gives more light than the clear glass, and you do not get quite the feeling that you are in the cell of a maximum-security prison.

The second type of basement window holds a lot more promise. It is a full-size window, often metal-framed, that sits in a sunken window well.

Unfortunately, basement window wells are all-too-often just that, wells. Leaves and debris collect in the bottom, plugging up drainage. When a big rain hits, the water rises until pressure pushes in the window pane and water floods the basement.

Window wells should be cleaned out every couple of months. After five years or so, it is a good idea to freshen the drainage by digging out the well and putting in 3 inches of fresh gravel covered by 3 inches of sand.

Even with the best of care, all the average sunken window does is give you a little more light and a magnificent view of something that looks like a metal culvert. Not nice.

Now three relatively new concepts can make that sunken window work a lot harder for you.

The MaxLight window well liner lines the existing well with a reflective white plastic liner and a panel that actually grabs existing light from above ground and reflects it into the basement. The manufacturer says the MaxLight System increases the amount of sunlight in the basement to the same level as on the main floor.

MaxLight Systems are available direct from the manufacturer for $94 to $155, including shipping. Call (888) MAX-2039.

The MaxLight increases the light, but does not improve the view. Scenic Window Wells change the view from your sunken window to a forest glade, bubbling brook or ocean. The Welliner is a flexible polystyrene sheet upon which one of 36 different scenes has been printed with UV-protected ink. The flexible window scenes are set to retail for $129.99. Call (877) 881-8413.

Now, the best idea of all: Change your sunken window into a wall of flowers that doubles as an escape hatch if a fire, flood or other disaster hits the basement. The Bilco ScapeWel Window Well System replaces the metal culvert with a terraced wall made of high-density polyethylene panels reinforced with a structural foam core.

ScapeWel terracing can be ordered in either two or three tiers. Each tier provides planting space so the view out your window can be shrubs or flowering plants. If you want, clear polycarbonate well covers are also available for use during winter. In the event of a catastrophe, you simply open the window and climb the terracing like a short flight of stairs.

The Window Well System calls for oversize 42-, 54- or 66-inch-wide windows. Many of us would have to have some structural work done to accommodate them. To my mind this just makes sense. If you're going to work in the basement, have your kids play there, or have someone sleep there, the least you can do is ensure that you or your loved ones can escape in case of a fire.

The Bilco ScapeWel Window Well costs $450 to $650 plus installation. In Metro Detroit, the wells are available at Dillman and Upton, (248) 651-9411, or you can call Bilco at (800) 854-9724. A competitive product using metal construction is made by Monarch Manufacturing Co., (800) 343-9370.

Believe me, these windows are worth investigating. You'll improve the view and sleep better at night.

When constructing a bigger home, don't just settle for 'built to code'

by Glenn Haege,
America's Master Handyman

If automobile companies built cars using the same criteria builders use to build houses, doctors, lawyers and affluent professionals would be driving around in humongous stretch Fords and Chevrolets.

The car-buying public wouldn't put up with it. When they want to make a statement they buy Lincolns, Cadillacs, Mercedeses, Jaguars, you name it. They brag about precision motors, hand tooling, craftsmanship and mystique of their automobiles. When most of these same people buy houses, their most significant lifestyle investment, they settle for an extra 2,000 to 5,000 square feet of floor space. Most don't even get concrete tile or slate roofs, superior electronics, soundproofing and heating systems.

There are few quality homes built in our area - I'd estimate the number to be less than 5 percent of new home construction. But even here, most builders and architects content themselves with including enough granite to build a mausoleum, 10-foot basement ceilings and, if the buyer is very lucky, hydronic heat.

I expect architects and custom builders to get huffy at this point and say that buyers can have anything they want. But what does that mean? How cutting-edge would autos be if engineers and designers left it up to the buyers to specify

transmissions, engines and aerodynamics.

Quite often, high-end home buyers are dual income professional couples. They may know all about state-of-the-art in their professions, but they know next to nothing about leading-edge construction.

That's why they usually get showy exteriors and humongous floor space. The rest of the home, everything you can't see from garbage disposals to electrical is "built to code." "Built to code" means minimum acceptable. "Code plus" means that someone took the time to specify true quality.

Code plus should not just be relegated to high-end housing. It should also be available to mid-range buyers. That includes you, me, and most of the other folks reading this article.

Builders should compete on the basis of engineering, not just floor space. Real estate reporters should be knowledgeable about construction techniques and seek out architects and builders who specify and use the latest building techniques and code plus materials.

If we want quality we should support architects and builders who go the extra mile. We should get as excited about the construction quality of our houses as we are of our automobiles. We should be smart enough to know that quality construction, not just added floor space, is worth extra money. Superior materials cost more to begin with, but save money year after year.

OK, so if you're new house hunting, what should you be looking for?

Basements: Begin in the basement. Ceiling height should be 9 to 10 feet. Eventually you'll want to use the basement for living or work space. Make sure it is built for the job.

Basements should be insulated. I personally would recommend foam-insulated concrete forms like those made by Reddi Wall, (586) 752-9161. Demand waterproof, not damp-proof, basements. During the construction it is relatively easy to make a waterproof basement. After the fact, it costs many thousands of dollars.

Electrical: Upgrade the electrical. A 200-amp service should be minimum. Most basements have bad lighting. Living areas usually have the minimum, not the optimum, electrical service. Ask how many home run circuits a house has. A home run circuit is wiring that goes directly to a given area for a specific purpose. At a minimum, each bathroom should have a home run circuit and most kitchens need at least two. Your family room, home office and entertainment areas also require home run circuits so that you will have sufficient power when you need it.

Flooring: Sub floors should be plywood rather than OSB board. Plywood holds nails and screws more securely.

Bathrooms: It is a good idea to have pressure assisted-toilets in the bathrooms.

Finally, try to find a builder who will let you upgrade your new house without sending you to the poor- house. When making an upgrade, a common practice among many builders is to keep in the charge for the old material, then double the additional cost of the new flooring, cabinets, bathtub, whatever. The result is that the builder makes over 100 percent on the upgrade. A profit of 25- or 30- percent on an upgrade just makes good business sense.

When you find a builder who will build your quality house for a fair profit, you'll brag about it and him for the rest of your life.

SEPTEMBER 23, 2000

Be forewarned: Water damage can lead to danger years later

by Glenn Haege,
America's Master Handyman

The weather is just right for working on the roof. The temperature is cool enough to be comfortable, yet warm enough for materials to be easy to work with.

Keeping gutters clear and the roof watertight is one of the most important things you can do as a homeowner. Two falls ago, the weather was so nice for so long, that a number of us left gutters clogged until too late. The ice storm of January 1999 hit, and ice dams and water damage occurred all over Lower Michigan.

That water damage is returning to haunt many Michigan homeowners, according to Connie and Tom Morbach of Sanit-Air. They report that their air testing and remediation business is exploding. Much of this business is due to the ice storms' residual damage.

"Anyone who had ice damming two years ago should inspect their attic very carefully," Connie Morbach says. "Even when repairs were made, water often soaked into the attic insulation and went unnoticed. If the area never dried properly, mold spores have now had two warm summers to develop."

"By the time we are called in, penicillium and aspergillus mold have often permeated the wood and stachybotrys has attacked the drywall," Tom Morbach says. "All the old insulation, infected deck boards and even rafters may have to be replaced."

Penicillium, aspergillus and stachybotrys are molds that are often associated with respiratory and other health problems. The molds often cause allergic reaction and asthmatic-like symptoms. In the case of children and hypersensitive adults, the condition may be life-threatening.

The good news is that mold usually migrates up, not down. If the damage is confined to the attic, it may stay there. Unfortunately, water runs down hill. If the water came in through the roof and drained into the walls, damage could have spread throughout the house.

How bad can it get?

Contractors were called in to fix a little water damage around a doorframe in a house located in one of Detroit's Northwest suburbs. When they opened up the wall to remove rotted wood, the workers broke into rashes and had severe respiratory reactions. They could not breathe inside the house.

The contractor called Sanit-Air from the lawn outside the house alerting the Morbachs to the emergency. Luckily, the homeowners were out of town, so the house did not have to be vacated.

During the next few weeks, comprehensive testing was done and four or five different leaks were found. Substantial

88

portions of the entire house have to be gutted.

The problem probably started where the garage and house roofs were joined. Water leaked all the way down to the basement. Unknown to anyone, water had leaked into the cavity between the garage and kitchen walls, then wicked across the kitchen floor. More water leaked into the house down to the doorframe. By a fluke, the drain pan in the master bath shower sprung a leak. Damage extends from roof decking in the attic to the sill plate in the basement.

This is not a renovation project. Work must be done in a totally contained environment with negative air machines and huge Hepa air filters. The workmen wear Tyvek moon suits and masks. Gutted materials are double bagged and taken to a hazardous waste dump.

The sooner the damage is discovered the less of a health risk there is to residents and the lower the cost of remediation will be.

Here are some of the danger signs, according to Sanit-Air.

Attic: Look to see if the roof nails coming into the attic are rusty, then check the wood for rot or water damage. See if the insulation is wet or compressed from being wet. If an area looks suspicious, lift the insulation and check the wood or drywall underneath for damage. Penicillium looks like small white splotches. Aspergillus can be yellow. Stachybotrys mold is black and oily.

Living area: Check to see if walls or ceilings are out of alignment in the living areas. Sometimes there is so much moisture in the drywall or plaster that the paint will look slightly darker in the affected area. Mold may be visible in baths, kitchens and closets.

Basement: Look for moisture damage and wood rot in the basement. If there was ever standing water in the basement and the drywall or paneling was not pulled away from the wall, remove a section and look for mold or water damage on the back of the paneling or within the wall cavity.

Outside: Look for spongy wood, especially on the soffits.

If you find significant damage, call for testing. Two sources are Sanit-Air, (888) 778-7324, and Christopher Cote's Air Analysis, (800) 416-2323.

Just as important, make sure your house does not become an ice damage victim this winter. Make certain your roof is watertight. Keep the gutters clean and free flowing. Replace curling or damaged shingles. Make sure that the roof valleys and flashing are in good repair.

On ground level, make sure your home has proper drainage and that all downspouts direct water away from the house.

New homes will undergo dramatic changes in the next few years

by Glenn Haege,
America's Master Handyman

We all know about the house of yesterday - most of us are living in one.

A fortunate few know about the house of today - they are shopping for it.

But what about the house of tomorrow?

Last year, I pictured a house built in 1990 or 1995 and thought about how it would be different from one built in 2005 or 2010. From what the architects I listen to at the building shows say, the outward appearance of the houses will be much the same, but almost everything else will be different.

Starting at the bottom, the 1990s basement was poured concrete or block. Basement walls were 8 feet high. Plumbing was a mixture of cast iron and copper. The basement was built to damp proof, not waterproof, specifications. Basement windows were single glazed with metal frames.

The equivalent basement in 2005 or 2010 will be waterproof foam insulated concrete forms (ICF). Walls will be 10 feet high. Basement windows will be block or larger double-glazed metal, composite or vinyl framed.

In case of fire, large basement windows will open for the easy escape of basement occupants.

Plumbing will be PVC for drains and CPVC for the supply side. CPVC can't corrode, pit or scale and retains water purity. Heavy-duty plastic drains won't rust. Both are easier to use than their metal predecessors.

Most homes will have whole- house water quality systems making the water more pure than anything found in nature.

Inside the 1990's basement you usually had a forced air natural gas furnace, hot water tank, laundry tub, washer and spin-dry dryer. Homes built by the more forward-thinking builders had a laundry area that was on the first floor.

In the basement of the 2010 house, everything will be up for grabs. Heating plants will be so small that they can literally be put anywhere. Most geothermal and boiler/hydronic heating systems will still be in the basement. If you choose to have separate hot water capability, on demand units could very well be located wherever needed. Hot water will be instantaneous, no waiting.

Hot air ductwork will be a thing of the past with more efficient hot water coils in floors and walls the new standard. Cold floors and drafts will not exist unless programed into the heating system.

By 2010 joists, studs, rafters – all the load-bearing beams – may well be engineered wood, metal or some kind of a composite. The term, a "stick built house," will have faded from the vocabulary. Panelized building will have taken over. Framing will be delivered on site, constructed to exact specifications.

Wiring may be massive. The average house could well have power requirements double or triple those of residential building in the 1990s.

Rough carpentry as we think of it today may well be a thing of the past. The crew that accepts on-site delivery and is in charge of overall assembly will be highly trained professionals and paid that way. Brain will account for a lot more than brawn. Young people who are very adaptable, learn rapidly, and are hands-on, take-charge individuals could do very well in the construction trades.

Living rooms will have made way for entertainment centers. That big picture you see over most couches will have been traded in for a big, flat-screen monitor, which can be programed to segue between 50 or so of your favorite photos. If you'd rather look at the news or a favorite television show, just give a voice command.

Kitchens will be cooking/socializing centers. You have always used them that way, but by 2010 they will be built to suit your lifestyle.

Food preparation will be easier. You won't have to reach for anything on the top shelf because kitchen cabinets will pull down.

Boiling water will be just another spout on the sink.

The dishwasher will be noiseless.

The oven will be able to roast a big turkey in a half-hour. A thick steak seared on both sides should take about five minutes.

Cooktops will have highly decorative design patterns.

Counters, tables, seating, even some cabinetry will be so maneuverable that you will be able to easily adjust the kitchen floor plan to meet party arrangements.

The walls will often be concrete-filled foam forms. Ceilings will be high. Air quality will be tightly controlled, assuring a much healthier living environment than you find today.

Roofing will be fireproof and rated for the life of the structure.

If this sounds good to you, you don't have to wait. The future could be now.

You could have all this today with code-plus quality construction.

OCTOBER 7, 2000

Follow hot tips to eliminate cold rooms before winter's frigid days

by Glenn Haege,
America's Master Handyman

Last weekend was beautiful. This weekend is dreary. On a few nights, the temperature dropped into the 30s. Hopefully, we'll still have a month of fairly good weather, but cold, drafty days are part of the winter package.

Here are a few tips on keeping warm this winter.

■ When the cold is coming from an outside wall or the wall between the garage and family room, there is probably not enough insulation. Blown-in insulation is a good way to take care of either problem without tearing out drywall or paneling.

Two of many good insulation contractors are Dana Energy Savers, (800) 757-3262, of Clinton Township and Macomb Insulation Co., (810) 949-1400, of Macomb Township. Dana specializes in Cellulose, while Macomb does Fiberglass. Before deciding on an insulation contractor, it is important to go out and look at a few jobs. When insulating brick walls, the contractor has to make holes in the mortar. Depending on the quality of the applicator, those holes can be almost invisible or an obvious eyesore.

If your house has an attached garage with no drywall and no heat, consider drywalling the ceiling joists and walls. Insulate the walls before dry-walling. Insulate the attic after the ceiling is in place. The insulation will keep cold from the garage from migrating into the house. Place faced batts of insulation so that the paper side faces the garage interior.

While you're at it, check the rest of the house. The national energy code calls for R-49 insulation in attics and R-39 in cathedral ceilings. If depth of insulation is a problem, all the major companies, Certainteed, (800) 345-1145; Johns Manville, (800) 654-3103; and Owens Corning, (800) 438-7465, now have super batts of condensed, higher R-rated insulation available.

■ Cold coming from an exposed window can be blocked with shrink-to-fit interior or exterior storm window kits; magnetic interior storm windows; or removable weather sealant.

Magnetic storm windows are almost invisible and very effective in noise and draft control. Diversified Energy Control, (800) 380-0332, installs and sells do-it-yourself magnetic interior storm window kits. If you don't want to cover the windows, Liquid Nails has just released Windjammer Clear Removable Sealant. It's almost invisible and ready to use directly from the trigger-mounted spray can. Home Depot and Damman's Hardware stores just received the product.

■ Remember heat rises. If it's cold in a room with a cathedral ceiling, the temperature is probably tropical two feet over your head. Put in a ceiling fan and redirect all that nice warm air down to where you live.

■ Check to see if enough warm air is coming out of the register in cold rooms. If only a small amount of relatively cool air is coming out of these registers, while lots of warm air is coming out of registers in the warm rooms of the house, you have a lazy return air furnace problem.

The furnace doesn't care if the back bedrooms get warm. It just creates heat and dumps it the first chance it gets. Most furnaces take the air they need for combustion from the basement and release the heat in the living room and other nearby rooms.

Since little or no air is drawn into the cold air return ducts, almost no warm air goes into the coldest rooms of the house. To warm these rooms, you have to force the return registers to draw cold air out of these rooms.

Describe the problem to your heating contractor and ask him to balance the heat. He should be able to close down some of the ductwork to over-heated areas, and open ductwork to the areas where you need extra heat.

■ If that doesn't solve the problem, consider zone heating. Zone heating puts you completely in control. Your house is divided into two or three zones. Let's say, the bedrooms are Zone 1. The living room and family room, Zone 2. The kitchen and dining areas, Zone 3. Each zone is independently controlled so you can direct furnace heat or air conditioning where needed.

One contractor who specializes in retrofitting older homes with zone heating controls is Vincent's Heating of Port Huron (yes, they service the entire Metro Detroit area), (888) 985-7103. Vincent's uses an air pressure system called Comfort Zone Control TLC.

A mechanical method of zone heating is the Duro Dyne heat control system, (800) 966-6446. Installing zone heating makes you more comfortable. Turning down the heat in unused zones can usually save enough on heating bill to pay for zone heating installation in six or seven years.

■ Many homes are so air tight that we need to import fresh air so that our furnaces, fireplaces and appliances can operate efficiently and to improve our health and comfort. If you have a relatively new house, or have recently added insulation or new windows, your home could be oxygen starved. You need to bring in an unobstructed flow of outside air. Two ways to do this are with a contractor installed Skuttle Model 216 air exchanger, (800) 848-9786, of a do-it-yourself Equaliz-Air by Xavier, (734) 462-1033.

Make your house warm and cozy now and you can brag about it all winter long.

> *The national energy code calls for R-49 insulation in attics and R-39 in cathedral ceilings. If depth of insulation is a problem, all the major companies now have super batts of condensed, higher R-rated insulation available.*

93

Snow birds need to put their homes in dry-dock for the winter

by Glenn Haege,
America's Master Handyman

The ducks are practicing V-formations. The blackbirds are clustering. Hummingbirds are heading south. Monarch butterflies are long gone. Can snow birds be far behind?

Readers are already sending me questions on the best way to get summer homes ready for hibernation. For years, I recommended putting your house into winter vacation mode. That meant putting the heat down to 55- or 60-degrees Fahrenheit, turning the water heater down low, and getting a super-friendly neighbor to check the house and flush the toilets two or three times a week.

Unfortunately, vacation mode is only good for two or three weeks. If you plan to be away longer, put your home in dry-dock. Dry-dock is full hibernation, "I'll-see-'ya-sometime-in-spring" mode. My reason for recommending dry-dock is that too many houses are experiencing water damage during prolonged owner absences. A three-day over-flowing toilet, leaking water heater, dishwasher or washing machine can easily cause $50,000 or more in damage.

Putting your house in dry-dock takes a little more time, but it eliminates worrying while you're away.

What to do now

■ Take extra care during your fall walk-around. You're going south, but the house is staying here. Give it extra TLC so that your biggest investment stays safe while you're away.

■ The shingles have to be in perfect condition. Super clean the gutters and make certain that downspouts are free flowing.

■ Fill in low ground levels around your home's perimeter. The ground should slope 1-inch per foot for 5 feet away from the house.

■ Install dusk-to-dawn exterior lights to help keep bad guys at bay. It would also be nice to install a whole house surge protector before you leave.

■ Start gifting friends and family with frozen stuff from the freezer now so you won't have to work so hard before you leave.

■ If you haven't had your furnace cleaned and checked yet, make the call today. Arrange for snow removal and track down that extra good friend who is going to stop by your house weekly to check for possible damage. Don't put off asking someone until the last moment. The person has to do it willingly, or they will forget as soon as you leave.

Two weeks before you go

■ Call the police and tell them how long you are going to be away and who will be looking after your house.

■ Arrange for newspaper delivery to be cancelled and re-route postal service to your winter address.

■ Put the lights and radios that you want to stay powered on timers and plug-in outlet surge protectors.

■ Make sure that the furnace filter is clean. Have extra filters next to the furnace so your friend can change the filter if he or she thinks it's necessary.

The day you leave

This is the critical period of the dry-dock procedure. Give yourself a couple of extra hours. You do not want to be rushed or forget anything.

■ All perishable food has to be out of the house. Unplug freezers, refrigerators; prop appliance doors open.

■ All electrical equipment you don't need running should be unplugged.

■ Make certain that the appliance timers connected to lights and radios are working. Tune in a talk radio station on the plugged-in radios. Set timers to make lights and radios start and stop in different parts of the house at different times of day so that the house has that lived-in-look.

■ Turn the furnace humidifier off. That may mean turning the humidistat down to zero percent humidity.

■ Turn off the water at the water main. If no water comes into the house, no pipes can burst or fittings give way and flood the house.

■ Turn off the gas or electricity on the hot water tank. You do not even want the pilot light burning while you are away. This is a very important step. If you turn off the water and leave the water heater on, all the water could boil off and the water heater could burn the house down.

■ Flush toilets to empty their water tanks. Prop open the dishwasher door. Joe Gagnon, aka the appliance doctor, prefers that you leave a jug of water in the sink so that your friend can pour a couple of cups of water into the bottom of the dishwasher every month to keep the seal moist.

■ All plants and pets, including the gold fish, have to be out of the house and with a friendly family.

■ Turn the heat to 55- or 60-degrees Fahrenheit. This temperature is warm enough for the house yet low enough to keep the air from becoming desert dry while you are away.

Your house is now officially dry-docked. You will no longer have to worry while you watch the Weather Channel. Be sure to send your friendly neighbor oranges. Have fun.

Cobo show: The National Association of Home Builders annual Remodeling and Seniors Housing shows will be held at Cobo Center Thursday through next Saturday. Professional builders and remodelers need to be at this show both for yourself and the homeowners you serve. Call (800) 368-5242 for last-minute reservation information.

Don't fret, you still have time to clean walls and paint before holidays

by Glenn Haege,
America's Master Handyman

While the weather was nice most of us were too busy enjoying the great outdoors to worry about the inside of the house. Now that it is getting cooler, the house is closed up and suddenly we notice that the paint is scuffed and the wallpaper looks dingy. We wonder if we have time to get the place ready for the holidays.

Panic sets in. Maybe you don't like to paint, or can't stand the smell of paint. And wallpaper can be a pain to remove. No problem.

■ If the walls are dingy and scuffed, but you still like the color, there is a good chance that you can get by with deep cleaning. The best wall cleaning formula I know is still TSP (Trisodium Phosphate). But be careful what you buy. Scrubs, (out of business) on Greenfield north of 11 Mile in Southfield and all Damman Hardware Stores still carry the real thing; but many stores carry a TSP that contains no Phosphate. Naturally, this product is not nearly as good as the real thing.

To deep clean walls, start from the bottom with a mixture of 2-ounces dry measure of TSP per gallon of warm water. If the walls are extremely grimy you may have to increase the proportions to 4 ounces of TSP and add 1 cup of ammonia. This is strong stuff. Wear goggles, a long-sleeved shirt and rubber gloves. If possible make it a two-person job. One person washes, the other rinses. Use long-handled sponge mops so you don't have to climb ladders. Change the rinse water after every wall.

> *If the walls are dingy and scuffed, but you still like the color, there is a good chance that you can get by with deep cleaning. . . . If you still need to paint, don't worry about paint odor.*

You will find the change this makes in your walls and ceilings almost miraculous. Your job may be over without opening a paint can.

■ If you still need to paint, don't worry about paint odor. All the big manufacturers – ICI, Glidden, Kurfees, Sherwin Williams and Benjamin Moore – have low- or no-VOC (volatile organic chemicals) paints that are almost odor-free.

■ Removing older wallpaper can be a problem. If you succeed in getting it off, the paper will often maliciously leave a rock-hard residue behind.

When removing wallpaper, a good quality absorbent paper drop cloth is the key. The best technique is to scrape the mess off the wall and onto the drop cloth, then carefully roll the drop cloth up and throw it away.

Most wallpaper can be removed with William Zinsser's Paper Tiger and Dif Wallpaper Stripper and Paper Scraper. Rolling the Paper Tiger back and forth over the walls perforates the paper with hundreds of little holes so that the stripping solution can work its way under the paper and release the bond. There are two types of Paper Tigers on the market. The do-it-yourself version and the professional version. The professional version is well worth the extra money. It costs twice as much, but it has twice the cutting edges so you get that part of the job done in half the time.

Mix one 22-ounce container of Dif with two gallons of hot tap water and put it in a plastic garden or deck sprayer. Don't go out and buy one for this purpose, but a deck sprayer is actually the best choice because the orifice at the tip of the wand rotates and gives a better spray pattern.

Soak one entire wall with solution, then wait 15 minutes and do it all over again. After waiting an additional 15 minutes, wet a small area at the top of the wall and start removing the paper. Scrape with a 4-inch spackling knife or Zinsser's new Paper Scraper. This new removal tool has a preset blade angle that prevents accidental wall gouging. Repeat the process, working downward.

When you have removed all the paper, there will still be some residual adhesive on the wall. Spray the entire surface with the Dif solution; keep it moist for 15 minutes; then wipe off with a wet rag and rinse with clear water.

■ If the standard wallpaper removal technique does not work, Brian Santos, the Wall Wizard, gave me his secret formula for problem walls. After using the Paper Tiger on the walls, mix a bottle of Dif with one gallon of hot water, 14-cup liquid fabric softener, one cup of white vinegar, and one tablespoon of baking soda. Wet down the wallpaper three times, then cover with four-mil-thick plastic sheeting to keep the solution from drying. Let stand overnight before removing the plastic. You should be able to pull the wallpaper off in large strips starting from the bottom.

To clean off the remaining adhesive, spray the wall with Brian's solution one more time and squeegee off the residue. Wash the wall with a solution of a gallon of water and a cup of white vinegar. Rinse well.

Your walls should now be ready to paint or re-paper. Having fun? Brag about it.

If you would like more of Santos' secret formulas, ask your local bookstore to get you a copy of his book, Potions, Solutions & Recipes for the Do-It-Yourselfer.

OCTOBER 28, 2000

Older structures need a hand to meet needs of aging homeowners

by Glenn Haege,
America's Master Handyman

Last week's Remodeling Show in Detroit, held in conjunction with the Seniors Housing Show, was a big success. There were 350 exhibits, and they drew a crowd of close to 12,000 professionals. This was the biggest Remodeling Show to date.

The shows are important to homeowners because they are designed to get the building and remodeling industry up to speed on our changing needs. The exhibits were good, but the real meat of the shows was at the 60-plus seminars and press conferences. I'll write articles on some of the topics over the next few months. Today's article is designed to get you up to speed on some of the highlights.

The Remodeling and Seniors in Housing Shows are designed on two principles: Our housing needs and desires change constantly, and each of us grows one day older every day, or we're dead.

The U.S. housing stock is growing old along with us. Today, the medium-aged house is over 30. The average house was built in the 1970s. Many of the homes in the older suburbs were built in the 1950s or before.

Changing these houses to meet modern expectations is a lot of work and takes a great deal of money. Last year, according to David Seiders, chief economist of the National Association of Home Builders (NAHB), we spent $142.9 billion remodeling. This was almost as much money as we spent on new home construction. In a few years, remodeling will overtake new home construction in total spending.

As a population, we are growing older. In the next few months, the oldest baby boomers will turn 55. We baby boomers may buy one more house, but most of us have decided to age in place. Senior citizen communities are not even on our radar screen. A recent survey of people 45 years of age and older by the American Association of Retired People (AARP) found that the older we are, the more firm our conviction that we do no want to move.

From a purely physical point of view, this can cause a problem. According to Louis Tennenbaum, of Access Remodeling in Potomac, Md., a remodeling contractor who specializes in universal design work, the first scientifically designed houses were built at the end of World War II. They were engineered for the 25- to 29-year-old returning serviceman. Notice I didn't say servicewoman. The statistics were based on a prime-of-life male population in top physical condition. Housing components have been engineered to fit more or less the same model ever since.

As a generality, Tennenbaum says, "Women are half as strong as men, and 60-year-olds are half as strong as 25-to-29-year-olds.

"That means that a woman, 60, has only one quarter of the strength necessary to function efficiently in a house engineered to serve the returning serviceman of yesteryear. Even a 60-year-old man has only half the required strength and flexibility. The older couple also needs twice the light to function effectively.

The result is that seniors often become trapped in housing that does not fit their needs. The rallying cry of the Seniors Housing Movement is, "It's not you, it's the house." Cabinets and other storage is too high, too low or too hard to access. The doors and windows take too much strength to open and close. Door, faucet, shower and bath handles are too hard to move. Drawer knobs are almost impossible to grasp. Hallways, doorways and stairs are too narrow. Exterior entrances are difficult to navigate.

Bathrooms are too small to get around in. Bathtubs and showers are difficult and dangerous to enter and exit. Toilets are too low. Attractive but sturdy grab bars are needed in tub, shower and toilet areas.

Most homes have insufficient electrical service. Lighting is limited and has to be redesigned especially in kitchens, bathrooms, bedrooms and hallways. A thermostat is useless if it cannot be read. Most controls have almost impossible-to-see numbers and must be redesigned for the aging population.

If all of this sounds like there's a lot of work to be done, there is. The remodeling industry is going through the roof. Unfortunately, according to a panel of remodelers from across the country, $15,000 bath remodels, $25,0000 to $75,000 kitchen remodeling jobs and $100,000 room additions are getting most of the attention. There are few workers left to do the smaller jobs required to rehab houses for an aging population. According to the AARP study, finding a trustworthy, affordable person or company to do the work is one of the most urgent concerns of the senior citizen.

The NAHB Council on Seniors Housing is dedicated to designing more senior friendly housing and learning the best ways to adapt our current housing stock. The Seniors Housing Show is one of the ways they use to get the word out.

Getting the actual job done is the territory of Remodelers Associations and the NAHB Remodelers Council. No one at the show had any earth-shattering ideas on how to find the bodies, much less trained personnel, needed to do the work. Hopefully, the remodeling confab energized the industry to find ways to get the job done. Mom, you were right, again.

A perfect gift for the holidays:
A safe haven for your little guests

by Glenn Haege,
America's Master Handyman

The countdown is accelerating. Everyone is getting ready for the holidays. It's 2-1/3 weeks to Thanksgiving. Then comes Hanukkah, Christmas and New Year.

Most of us don't worry about making the house baby-safe. The kids are either too old or out of the house. Holiday season is different. Small fries are paraded and presented everywhere. Once these kids walk or are carried into your house, they are your responsibility. That means your house has to be child-safe for the holidays.

Any and all firearms should be stored, unloaded, in locked weapon safes or cabinets. Ammunition should be stored under lock and key in a separate location.

Everything within a toddler's reach is fair game and should be put away. All coffee and occasional tables, bookcases and desks must be cleared of potentially dangerous objects: knives, letter openers, scissors, books and bookends, crystal, pottery, ashtrays, vases and framed photos should be up, preferably out of sight.

Offices, dens, sewing rooms should be child-proofed, with the doors closed. Start getting into the habit of closing the doors now so that you close them automatically when the little ones are around.

Clear all chemicals from under the bathroom and kitchen sinks. Pantries also have to be checked and dangerous items moved up and out of the way. The laundry area, especially if you have a first-floor laundry room, has to be child-proofed. Make certain necessary evils like laundry detergents, ammonia and bleaches are out of reach. Unplug irons and take them off the ironing board.

Beer, wine and liquor are dangerous chemicals that should be stored out of reach and out of sight. Medications must be put in a secure place.

Women's purses are filled with dangerous items. They should never be left out in the open or within reach of a child.

If you really want to be safe, go through the house on your hands and knees. This is the way to see the house from a toddler's perspective. You will be surprised at all the things you didn't see before that must be put away.

Be on the lookout for sharp corners and edges, exposed electric outlets and dangling wires and cords. All sharp edges on tables, cabinets and bookcases should be covered.

If children are going to be spending the night, the outlets should be plugged and wires and cords organized so that they do not make a tempting "pull toy."

Small children can easily get tangled in window blind cords. The Easy Cleat Window Cord Keeper by Hold-It Products (248) 624-1195 of Walled Lake, is a see-through plastic cleat that is attached to the window with suction cups allowing cords to be stored out of harm's way.

Go to the hardware store and get screw-in type safety gates to block all stairways. Pressure gates seem easier to install, but even a small child can push them out of the way.

All bedrooms and bathrooms should have door locks that can be opened from the outside. The hole in the center of the knob is the emergency key entry point. Jim Damman says that if you lost the emergency key that came with the lock (and most of us have), you can special order a Kwikset emergency key, item number 1087, at any Damman. The cost is under $1.

Babies need lots of sleep. Make certain you know who is responsible for the crib. It is usually better to have the parents bring their baby's crib. If you need to get one, don't buy a crib with cutouts, corner posts or ledges that can trap clothing or vertical slats that are more than 2-3/8 inches apart and can trap hands and feet.

We all love our pets. Dogs, cats and kids look cute together. Don't trust any of the three for a minute. To a dog or cat a small child, even a baby, is a potentially dangerous invader. Their movements are erratic. They often cause pain by accident. Remember, even a good natured poke in the eye by a toddler is still a poke in the eye. If they feel threatened, dogs bite and cats scratch.

Dogs and cats like to sleep next to warm bodies. They can easily plop down on top of baby, making breathing difficult or impossible. Don't take the chance.

Make sure that bedrooms, bathrooms and hallways have nightlights. Put chimes or bells on guest room door knobs so that parents are alerted if a child starts wandering in the night.

Place towels over the top of bathroom doors at night so that a child can't get locked in the bathroom.

There are many other things to make sure that your house is child safe for the holidays and throughout the year. One of the best web sites on the subject is www.safebaby.net. This exhaustive site takes you through the house and gives safety tips on a room by room basis.

It is especially good on its coverage of child safety in the kitchen, and gives detailed tips on toys, fire safety, safe and poisonous cleaning products and plants, and lists U.S. and Canadian poison control centers.

If you take the time to child-proof your house now, you can enjoy a worry-free holiday with the little ones. Take lots of pictures.

Proper holiday lighting welcomes good guys, chases away bad guys

by Glenn Haege,
America's Master Handyman

Within a few weeks exterior Christmas lights and decorations will be springing up all over the country. The hardware stores are already filled with lights, reindeer, Santa's elves and Nativity scenes. You will probably get the bug to put up your lights before you have digested your Thanksgiving turkey.

Stringing lights is not enough. Thieves love overgrown shrubs around doors and windows. It gives them the privacy they need to break in and fill their bags with your Christmas goodies. Bring out your clippers at the same time you bring out the ladder to string the lights.

Your house isn't ready for the holidays until you've trimmed back the trees and shrubs and done the other things necessary to make your home safe and secure.

After the shrubs are trimmed, check the exterior lights. Upgrade lawn and carriage lights to weather-resistant bulbs like Philips, (732) 563-3000, Earth Light Outdoor Compact Fluorescent. It uses 75 percent less electricity than incandescent bulbs, is rated for 10,000 hours, and is protected with a shatterproof translucent cover.

While you're at it, how about installing halogen floodlights around the front, back and by the garage? Your local hardware or home center, lighting or elec-tronics store has a wide variety of lamp styles that include sensors which will turn the lights on when it gets dark or when they sense someone approaching.

Use a little bit of caution when you string the lights. Exterior electric outlets should be on a dedicated circuit. That means they have their own switch in the load center. Having a dedicated circuit means you have plenty of power to go slightly wild and run five or six strings of lights and a red-nosed reindeer.

If your builder did not call for a dedicated circuit, your exterior plugs share power with internal lights and outlets. That means that you have to be more sparing with the use of exterior lights and decorations.

String too many lights and you run the danger of overheating the wiring and blowing circuits. You can be sure that those circuits will blow during your biggest holiday party or at some other inconvenient time.

Overheated wiring can also cause an electrical fire that remains dormant until the middle of the night, then breaks into a raging fire behind the walls.

Don't be tempted to use inside electric outlets and run extension cords through open windows. That's a bad idea for three reasons.
■ It puts too much of a strain on your interior circuits.

■ It wastes a great deal of heat through partially open windows.

■ An electric wire you have sneaking through the bottom of a window is like a neon sign saying "Break in here – it's easy"

Also, make sure you use these minimum-security precautions during the holiday season. Bad guys hate light. Make them uncomfortable by leaving the outside lights on all night.

Lock exterior doors at all times. Don't leave the door unlocked and the house unguarded while you run across the street to deliver Christmas cookies or share a holiday libation.

If someone is coming in from out of town, don't change the message on your answering machine to something like: "Merry Christmas, we had to go out for a couple of hours but we'll be back by 10" This message might help your relative, but also tells a thief he has hours to do a really good job on your house.

Don't leave a key under the mat so a friend or relative can enter during the middle of the night or while you are away. A bad girl or guy will gladly use that key, rampage through your house and not even leave a thank-you note.

No matter how proud you are of your gift-wrapping prowess, don't leave boxes or parcels in plain view from the outside. The Grinch could come calling and spoil the holidays.

This is the time of year when many of us get more Fed Ex and UPS deliveries than normal. Many are left in clear sight by the door or on the front steps. Consider putting a weatherproof box on the porch so that delivery people can leave your goodies out of sight.

We are all thrilled to get expensive things on the holidays, but the boxes they came in can be dangerous. Don't advertise your bounty by throwing out boxes from newly acquired items. A computer, Play Station 2, or DVD box left on the curb on garbage collection day tells a thief: "Come and get the neat new stuff in this house"

Tear the boxes apart and dispose of them in non-see-through plastic bags.

Every neighbor shares the same concerns. Now is a good time to invite them all over for a cup of coffee and talk about Christmas plans. Make sure everyone knows who's staying, who's going away and for how long. Build a mini neighborhood watch with those you know and trust.

The more you do now to make your home well lit, safe and secure, the more you will enjoy a carefree holiday.

Good remodeling work is easy if you know the rules of the game

by Glenn Haege,
America's Master Handyman

"How do I find a good contractor?" and "How do I make sure the job is done right?" are questions I hear most often. I'm not alone.

In a recent study by the American Association of Retired People, one of the main reasons people gave for putting off necessary remodeling work was that they couldn't find a contractor they could trust.

There are ways to make sure that you are dealing with a true professional and that the work will be done, not just to code, but to accepted industry standards. In many contracting fields, the cream of the crop are not only licensed but also certified.

Licensing

The minimum threshold you should demand is that the contractor is licensed and insured for the work you need done.

A contractor with a builder's license is licensed for construction work: concrete, carpentry and roofing. Specialists such as roofers, painters and waterproofers will have licensing in just their area of expertise.

Electrical, plumbing, heating and cooling are specialties that have their own licenses, require special permits and are inspected by building inspectors expert in these specific fields.

On a big job, the general contractor gets the construction permit and his designated, appropriately licensed subcontractors pull the permits for the electrical, plumbing, heating, venting and air conditioning.

Since all licensed contractors cannot be equal, how can you make sure the contractor you choose is the cream of the crop? Read on.

Certification

I have often complained about the lack of continuing education among contractors. The National Association of Home Builders (NAHB)' Remodelors Council, a specialized unit within the organization for builders who specialize in renovation and home improvement, has addressed that problem by developing the Certified Graduate Remodeler (CGR) designation. This designation can only be used by a contractor who has taken and passed designated classes, met NAHB prescribed standards of business practice, possesses a proven track record of successfully completing projects and pledges to uphold the CGR Code of Ethics.

Not only does the contractor have to be good, but to maintain his designation he has to be re-certified every three years. If a remodeler is certified, he will always use CGR after his name on his business card.

Since the program is relatively new, some of the finest remodeling contractors in the country do not have a CGR. However, if your contractor has a CGR, you know that he is very serious about his business, has an excellent reputation among his peers and keeps abreast of the cutting edge of technology in his profession. To find a Certified Graduate Remodelor in your area, call the Remodelors Council, (800) 368-5242, ext. 8323.

The Remodelors Council is not the only organization that has expert certification procedures. Two other examples are the National Air Duct Cleaners Association, (202) 737-2926, www.nadca.com, and the National Association of Waterproofing and Structural Repair Contractors, (800) 245-6292, www.waterproofing.org.

Even the best contractor can have problems with his business. To make sure that your builder's problems never become your problems, call the Michigan Construction Protection Agency, (800) 543-6669, www.mcpanet.com, and order the Michigan Home Owners Lien Law Kit. It takes you through the construction process and gives you the forms you need to be financially secure every step of the way.

Performance guidelines

Every game has rules. The building and remodeling game is no different than any other. The problem is that most people don't know the rules of the game.

When you don't like the way a thing is done and the builder just shrugs and says, "It's built to code," that is not the end of the line. You shouldn't have to call an attorney.

The Remodelors Council and the Single Family Small Volume Builders Committee have just come out with the second edition of the Residential Construction Performance Guideline for Professional Builders & Remodelers. It outlines what is acceptable and what is not.

For instance, a new floor shouldn't sag. If it does, it has to be repaired. With the guidelines, the matter is clear, with no room for shouting. If you think your floor sags and the builder doesn't, whip out a tape measure and a level and see if the sag is more than 38-inch in 12 feet. If it is, the contractor has to fix it. If it isn't, it conforms to construction guidelines.

To make certain that your remodeling job conforms to national construction guidelines, be sure that the contract says, "All workmanship shall conform to the guidelines found in: Residential Construction Performance Guidelines for Professional Builders & Remodelers, Second Edition."

The cost of Performance Guidelines is $31.25. It's a smart investment if you're going to buy a house or have a major remodeling job done. For a copy, call the NAHB, (800) 223-2665.

A small arsenal is all you need to do battle with the holiday spills

by Glenn Haege,
America's Master Handyman

The party season has started. Thursday was Thanksgiving and the Christmas/Hanukkah/New Year's party season has begun. It's wonderful but . . . there are so many things that need to be done. You put the Christmas lights up and got finger prints all over the glass on the storm door.

Once the party has begun, what do you do when Aunt Maude spills the gravy, cousin Tom drops the Jell-O mold and your brother and sister-in-law's youngest is just so caught up with the season that he just can't contain himself . . . literally.

Here are some quick cleanup tips to get you ready for the party and some emergency tips to stop the "oopsies" from ruining the event.

Metal, glass and just about anything outdoors can still be cleaned when the temperature drops below freezing. You can clean off smudges and even dirty fingerprints with automobile windshield washing fluid. If you're going to wash all the windows outside, put on rubber gloves, pour the windshield washing fluid into a pail, sponge on, squeegee off, and wipe up drips on window sills with an old, 100-percent cotton towel.

Remember windshield washer solvent is combustible – no smoking.

If the furniture inside is getting to feel a little bit tacky and finger smudges are showing, give everything a quick coat of Doozy, (888) 851-8500. It will clean up light oils and waxes that are causing the stickies and leave a light, smudge-proof layer of protection. You can even put a protective coat on your leather or vinyl furniture. It won't show, but will give a little bit of extra luster.

Kitchen and bathroom cabinets that feel a little sticky can be cleaned with a mixture of 1 gallon of warm water and 2 ounces of Simple Green. Sponge on, wait for a minute and sponge off with clear water and another sponge. Once the cabinet exteriors and doors are clean and dry, apply a protective coat of Doozy and they will stay nice for the entire holiday season.

You can quickly mop up a vinyl floor by spraying the same 2-ounce Simple Green solution on the floor and mopping up with a bucket of rinse water. For wood, laminate or ceramic floors, spray on window washing fluid that does not contain ammonia and mop up with clear water.

When you do your party shopping, make sure you have all the ingredients needed for my Emergency Clean Up Kit. The ingredients are a couple of boxes of the cheapest facial tissue you can buy; club soda and foam-style shaving cream. Also look for spray bottles of Motsenbockers (800) 346-1633 Lift Off

No. 1 and No. 2. If pets are going to be a part of the holiday festivities, add a spray can of Spot Shot, (877) 477-6874. This small arsenal is all you need to keep your cool while cleaning up holiday spills and stains.

In fact, the club soda, shaving cream and facial tissue can solve most food and beverage spill problems all by themselves. You can whisk away even grease, food and beverage stains from an expensive tie, silk blouse, velour top, party dress, tablecloth, upholstery or carpeting. The two secret ingredients are a calm demeanor and fast action. Don't wait until the party is over. Clean up the mess right away.

When cleaning a tie, expensive party dress or blouse, start with two handfuls of facial tissue. Pour a little cold soda on one handful, then, using the other wad of tissue as backing underneath or behind the fabric, gently blot away the stain with the soda-dampened tissue. Use more tissue if needed. Always blot, never rub. Rubbing can set the stain.

If you stain a couch or deep pile carpeting, gently blot up the excess with tissue, then work in some shaving cream with your fingers. Do not spread the stain. After you have worked in the foam, scoop up the residue with wads of facial tissue. Do not rub.

If you don't get to the spot or stain until the next day, or the soda and shaving cream alone will not do the job, bring out the heavy artillery. For gravy and other grease stains or cranberry juice, coffee, red or orange Kool-Aid or red wine spray on Motsenbocker's LIFT OFF No. 2. For blood stains, Jell-O, vegetable coloring or just about any protein stain: Use Motsenbocker's LIFT OFF No. 1.

For kitten or puppy accidents, even an "oopsy" by a small child, scoop up any solid, blot with facial tissue to absorb liquid, then clean with Motsenbocker's LIFT OFF No. 1. If the spot wasn't discovered until it soaked in and dried, use Spot Shot. It is strong but very effective.

Lingering odors can be removed with a couple of sprays of Punati Chemical's Smells Be Gone, (800) 645-2882. The product does not mask odors. It destroys the bacteria that cause them.

All these ingredients work like magic. They will give you everything you need to solve the problem and keep your cool. So have fun and enjoy the party.

New generation of artificial Christmas trees gets better and cheaper

by Glenn Haege,
America's Master Handyman

The snow-tipped Ivy Berry Tree from Evergreen Home and Garden is decorated and ready to plug in when it comes out of the box. It is 40 inches high and decorated with ribbons, berries, ivy, apples and birds.

If you don't think you've got time for a Christmas tree this year, I've got you covered. I braved the Thanksgiving crowds to see what's new in artificial trees and sniff out some bargains.

I shopped three stores: Frank's, Evergreen Home and Garden and English Gardens. Frank's have stores all over. Evergreen, (586) 791-2277, has big stores in Clinton Township and Eastpointe. English Gardens, (248) 280-9500, is in Royal Oak, West Bloomfield Township, Clinton Township, Eastpointe and Dearborn.

Artificial trees are classified according to how the limbs are attached when the tree is assembled: hook, hinge and combination hook or hinge. Trees are also classified by the total number of branch tips and the diameter of the bottom layer of branches.

The limbs on a standard artificial tree are attached to the trunk by hooks.

Unless a person has vast amounts of storage space, the tree has to be disassembled at the end of every Christmas season.

To make things easier, some trees are made with limbs attached to the trunk by hinges and can just be folded up for storage. This year, English Gardens has a Northern Blue Douglas fir tree with hooks you can insert into plastic hinges, so the tree can be stored like a hinged tree if desired. This Hudson Valley beauty comes in 4 1/2- and 7 1/2-foot heights and is priced from $229 to $449. Melody Linberg, a lifelike tree expert at English Gardens, says the tree is exclusive to her stores this year.

Evergreen Home and Garden Centers has hook/hinge trees by Mountain King. Their 7 1/2-foot tree is on special for $99.

Another innovation in artificial trees is called the panel tree. All the major limbs are on six panels. To assemble, you just hook the panels to the top of the tree and boom, instant Christmas tree! Most stores have panel trees in the full range of sizes.

Frank's has a 7 1/2-foot EZ Panel Aberdeen blue spruce for $179.99. English Gardens also has a very full 7-foot fir panel tree that Linberg calls their Teddy Bear tree, at $179.98. Evergreen has a 7-foot Viking, priced at $199.

Easy assembly is not enough. Pre-lit trees were introduced a couple of years ago, for people who don't want to bother stringing lights.

Pre-lit trees come with miniature bulbs, the new, larger C-6 bulbs or Fiber Optics. Most pre-lit trees are trimmed with miniature lights. This year, Evergreen has a large selection of pre-lit trees strung with a new, traditional-looking C-6 bulb in both clear and multicolored varieties.

If you want a truly massive light display, Evergreen has a 712-foot Sylvania tree with 1,000 miniature lights priced at $199, and the Grand Mesa, a 9-foot tree with 1,500 lights for $299. English Gardens has 4 1/2- to 7 1/2-foot pre-lit trees, priced from $229 to $449.

One of the key things to look for with pre-lit trees is the warranty. Most trees have different warranties for the lights and the tree itself. English Gardens' pre-lit trees come with a three-year warranty on lights and a 10-year warranty on the tree, Linberg says.

Fiber optic trees have little points of light. They come in a smaller range of sizes, but make a spectacular presentation. Fiber Optics trees come in both the traditional and poinsettia styles.

Prices on standard fiber optic trees range from $24.99 to $119 at Evergreen. I saw 3- and 4- foot indoor fiber optic trees at Frank's priced from $59.99 to $89.99. They also had 4-foot, 5-foot and 6-foot indoor/outdoor, fiber optic trees priced from $79.99 to $179.99.

English Gardens had a full range of competitively priced fiber optic trees, but also had traditional fir-style trees with fiber optics. These trees ranged from 2 feet to 7 1/2 feet, and were priced from $39.99 to $299.99. They also carry some truly innovative designs, including a 7-foot Regency twig pencil tree, priced at $99.98; a 7 1/2-foot Charley Brown brush pine, priced at $129.88; an upside-down tree that lets you look up into the ornaments at $300; and very natural looking Alpine-style three-tree cluster groupings, priced at only $129.

The Snowmen theme tree is the most popular tree at Evergreen Home and Garden this year. It is decorated entirely with snowmen dolls, pillows and decorations.

Bob Wilk, manager at Evergreen Home and Garden, says that theme trees are very popular this year. His two biggest hits are the "Snowman Tree" a tree trimmed entirely in snowmen, and the "Top Hat Tree" crowned with a black top hat.

Evergreen also got my "nothing could be easier" award for a lavishly decorated, 40-inch, frosted needle fir tree. Priced at $120, the tree comes in a decorator pot base and is covered with a lush array of ribbons, berries, ivy, apples, even nested songbirds and 100 lights.

There's no excuse. If you have the spirit but no time to decorate, all you have to do is pull this tree out of the box to have a beautifully decorated tree for Christmas.

A do-it-yourselfer's holiday gift guide to helpful books, magazines

by Glenn Haege,
America's Master Handyman

Books and magazines head the list of gifts that handy men and women will treasure, but usually don't buy for themselves.

Here's a list to help you shop.

Magazines

You can't go wrong choosing any of these magazines for three reasons: the writers are craftsmen first and writers second; the editors have actually swung hammers, not just split infinitives; and the advertising is just as important and just as informative as the editorial copy.

Be advised that you can save money on subscriptions to some magazines by ordering online.

Fine Homebuilding, Taunton Press, $36/8 issues, (800) 888-8286, or www.finehomebuilding.com.

Every issue is filled with in-depth articles on new construction techniques, quality materials and tools, and hard-to-handle building projects.

Even a gifted professional will learn from every issue.

Today's Homeowner, Times Mirror Magazines, $17.94/10 issues, (800) 456-6369, web site: www. todayshomeowner.com.

This is a very practical guide for the average guy or gal. The editors realize that most of us want quality, but live on a budget. Advice is geared to showing handy persons how to save a buck by doing the job themselves.

Old House Journal, Hanley-Wood, $26.75/6 issues, (800) 234-3797, www.oldhousejournal.com.

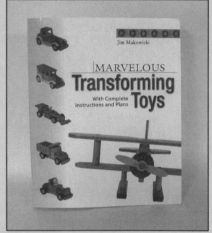

"Marvelous Transforming Toys" by Jim Makowicki contains plans and step by step directions on how to make toy boats, airplanes, cars and trucks. If grandpa is a woodworker this book will show him how to make treasures for all the little ones. It is published by Taunton Press and priced at $24.95.

Old House Journal is written for those who treasure older homes and wish to maintain them with the respect they deserve.

This magazine is my secret weapon when I get calls from folks with older homes.

This Old House magazine, Publishing Ventures, 10 issues, (800) 898-7237, www.thisoldhouse.com. A "two- fer" offer listed one subscription for you and one for a gift for $24.95.

If you like Norm Abram and the rest of the guys on PBS-TV's This Old House, you will enjoy this official show magazine. Each issue is filled with very practical advice.

Fine Woodworking, Taunton Press, $32/7 issues, (800) 888-8286, www.finewoodworking.com.

This is a must for anyone who loves the shaping of wood as an art form. Wood, woodworking tools and the objects they produce are treated with veneration but the information is very practical.

Books

The Not So Big House, A Blueprint for the Way We Really Live, by Sarah Susanka with Kira Obolensky, Taunton Press, $30, (800) 477-8727, www.taunton.com.

If you know anyone who is new-house hunting or planning on having a custom home built they need this book. An instant classic, many experts claim this book defines the future of new-home construction. Available at most book stores.

Your New House, The Alert Consumer's Guide to Buying and Building a Quality Home, 3rd edition, by Alan and Denise Fields, Windsor Peak Press, $14.95.

No philosophy but a lot about bargains and budgets. You can find it at many bookstores, or save a couple of bucks at www.bn.com, www.amazon.com or www.borders.com.

1001 All Time Best Selling Home Plans, by Home Planners LLC, $12.95.

A huge bargain, this contains every kind of floor plan you can imagine. At most bookstores.

Decorating 1-2-3, by Home Depot, $34.95.

The 1,000-pound gorilla of the Building Supply business has been putting out very practical reference books for the past several years. Very good practical advice. At most bookstores or at Home Depot.

The Art of Fine Tools, by Sandor Nagyszalanczy, and Marvelous Transforming Toys, With Complete Instructions and Plans, by Jim Makowicki. $24.95 each in soft cover. To order call (800) 477-8727, or visit www.taunton.com.

These are two of a new series of books by Taunton Press. Every craftsman loves his tools. The Art of Fine Tools is an awe-inspiring collection of photos of classic hand tools accompanied by knowledgeable commentary. The reader will want to frame the photos. Marvelous Transforming Toys contains plans and directions for building simple planes, cars and boats that are rugged works of art.

"Haege's Homestyle Articles" contains 240 of Glenn Haege's Detroit News Homestyle articles, plus special reports and a 21 page list of helpful phone numbers and web sites. A table of subjects plus a detailed subject index make it easy to track down needed information.

Haege's Homestyle Articles, The Detroit News 1995-99, by my favorite author, me.

This is a collection of 240 articles that appeared in The News' Homestyle magazine, plus special reports and 21 pages of need-to-know phone numbers and web sites. All updated and meticulously cross-indexed by subject. The book contains an in-depth article on almost every major home improvement topic. Pre-Christmas priced at $24.99, including tax and shipping. Available only from the publisher, Master Handyman Press. Call (888) 426-3981, or send check or money order to P.O. Box 1498, Royal Oak, MI 48068-1498.

Dirt filters on the latest vacuum cleaners promote healthy living

by Glenn Haege,
America's Master Handyman

A new vacuum cleaner may not make you all misty-eyed, but Barb and I gave them to our kids last year, and they loved the idea. Here's why a new vacuum cleaner for Christmas is a good idea.

Old-fashioned vacuum cleaners beat clouds of dust into the air. The air in a newly vacuumed room is often dirtier and less healthy to breathe than before vacuuming. Dirty air can cause asthma and other bronchial conditions. It is especially hard on children and older folks.

The North Carolina Department of Health and Human Services is so concerned that they are doing an environmental interventions study to see if simple preventive maintenance can halt or decrease the incidence and/or severity of asthma. The ongoing study is being reported in HFN, the news weekly of the home products industry.

In the study 96 families with asthmatic youngsters from ages 8 to 18 were given a Eureka Smart Vac with a true HEPA filter, mattress and pillow casings that create dust mite barriers and a special allergen furnace filter.

The families were told to vacuum carpeting daily and wash bed linens every other week in water that is at least 140 degrees Fahrenheit.

Initial results show that regular vacuuming with a HEPA filter-equipped vacuum cleaner makes a big difference. In one case, a 15-year old girl stopped registering as an asthmatic on peak-flow meter tests after only one month. The girl's mother, a pulmonary nurse, said her daughter was able to stop using her inhaler except before varsity volleyball practices.

Put bluntly, if you vacuum daily with a top quality filter vacuum cleaner and control dust mites, you breath easier. Eureka Ultra Smart Vacs cost around $230. You can learn more about dust mite and allergen barrier mattress and pillow encasings on the web at www.nationalallergysupply.com, or call National Allergy Supply Inc, (800) 522-1448.

The Smart Vac is just one of many good vacuum cleaners. My staff and I asked Dave Dijon, ABC Appliance Warehouse-Utica, (586) 739-1010; Benny Grossinger, United Good Housekeeper, on Coolidge in Berkley, (248) 546-0088; and Larry Sharpley, the Hoover Co., on 12 Mile in Southfield, (248) 552-6253, for their recommendations.

This year, the big buzzword is "bagless". According to HFN magazine, 40 percent of all vacuum cleaner advertising is promoting bagless products. It sounds like a very good idea, all the dirt goes into a clear plastic cup. You never have to buy another vacuum cleaner bag.

None of the pros recommended the new technology when we asked what they would buy. Sharpley at the Hoover Store explained why. "A bagless vacuum cleaner is excellent, if not buying vacuum cleaner bags is a high priority; but without a bag, you have to empty the dirt cup and clean the filter every time you vacuum," he says.

Shipley opened a bagless dirt container; the inside was covered with minute dust particles. Then he pointed to the filter that was also covered with particles. It was easy to visualize getting that fine, gritty dust all over my hands and arms while emptying the cup and cleaning the filter.

"With a bag vacuum, dirt stays in the disposable bag. When full, you just drop it into the garbage. The bag acts like a prefilter." Sharpley says.

Here are the pros' vacuum cleaner recommendations.

Dave Dion of ABC Appliance Warehouse-Utica says, "Look for a HEPA filter, a hard plastic bag container and a quiet motor." He recommended the Panasonic (800) 211-PANA) HEPA Filtered Power Wave, which starts at $159. A Performance Plus Panasonic with beltless drive can cost as high as $599. My wife Barb uses a top-of-the-line Panasonic daily and loves it.

Benny Grossinger of United Good Housekeeping's favorite vacuum cleaner is the Eureka Sanit Aire model 782, (800) 282-2886. "It is remarkably lightweight, has a micron filter and a fold-down handle that makes it very easy to store or carry up and down stairs," he says. It costs $270.

If you want a HEPA filter, Grossinger recommends the Miele White Star canister vacuum with disposable bag, (800-843-7231). "It's a great vacuum for asthmatics and people with hardwood floors," he says. A special control lets the user reduce suction when cleaning delicate surfaces. The price is $529.95.

Larry Sharpley of the Hoover Store recommends the top of the line, self-propelled Wind Tunnel with Dirt Finder. Priced at $369, it is loaded with goodies that make vacuuming easier. A self-propelled Wind Tunnel without Dirt Finder is priced at $299.95.

"Wind Tunnel vacuum cleaners have a patented air chamber that picks up more dirt than any other upright. Its disposable bag prefilters particles above 5 microns, then channels return air through a HEPA filter," he says.

Dirt-sensing devices are available on most top-of-the-line vacuum cleaners and add about $100 to the price, Sharpley says.

True HEPA filtration costs. Most HEPA filters have to be replaced every 6- to 8-months. Replacement cost ranges from $22 to $60, depending on the model. That may sound expensive, but your lungs are worth it. Put a HEPA filter vacuum cleaner under your Christmas tree this year, and you'll breath a lot easier.

DECEMBER 22, 2000

Frozen roofing can lead to water damage, but some jobs are best left for the experts

by Glenn Haege,
America's Master Handyman

A week ago, Mary and Noreen Lynch noticed wet spots on two of the ceiling tiles in the family room of their Dearborn Heights home. Melting water from their ice-covered roof was leaking into the house.

The women called Big Ike's Roofing to clear the snow off their roof. "The people were good, but I wouldn't wish this experience on anybody," says Mary Lynch. "So far, we have just had to remove two tiles, but I noticed water in the bagged insulation above the ceiling, so all that will have to be replaced before we're done."

Because of the heavy snowfall in Metro Detroit this month, almost every house has a roof covered with thick snow and roof edges lined with solid ice. Many homeowners will go through the same ordeal as the Lynches.

The phenomenon is called ice damming. Ice freezing at the gutter line of the roof builds up and stops water from the melting snow from draining away. This can eventually cause water to creep under the shingles and into the attic, causing water damage to ceilings and walls.

There are several things homeowners can do themselves to help prevent or remove ice dams, but sometimes professionals will need to be called.

If you have an ice dam problem, the one thing you shouldn't do is to climb up on the roof and try to shovel off the snow yourself. Unless you are Santa Claus, you do not belong on the roof where you are only a slip and fall away from a broken arm, leg or neck.

The only safe way to remove snow from roofs is to use a tool called a roof rake, which is basically a lightweight hoe with a wide head and a handle that extends from 12 to 20 feet.

If you have a one-story house, you can stand on the ground and rake a 3-foot swath of snow away from the drip edge. This helps prevent water backup.

Attack existing ice dams by cutting panty hose in two and filling the legs with calcium chloride flakes or pellets. Knot the open ends and place them on top of the gutters. Put a couple of these compresses on top of the gutters wherever you have icicles, and at corners and down spouts.

The calcium chloride will melt through the ice and keep the gutter free flowing. Do not substitute rock salt, however. The sodium chloride in rock salt will do serious damage to your roof.

114

Putting pantyhose compresses on the roof requires climbing a ladder. Make certain you have a helper holding the ladder steady because the bottom of the ladder may be resting on ice and could slip from under you.

Shovel a path away from the down-spouts so water can drain freely.

Unfortunately, roof rakes and calcium chloride are hard to find right now. As soon as a shipment comes in, it gets sold out.

"It's a real dilemma," says Bill Damman, vice-president of Damman Hardware. "Stocking roof rakes is a real gamble. Right now, we could sell a couple thousand if we had them. But if there is not much snow, the snow rakes just stand there, sometimes for years.

"We had about 200 roof rakes on hand at our 17 stores when the snow started. We sold out in a couple of days. We have 150 more on order, but after that there are no more in the pipeline."

If you can't find a roof rake in a store, you can jury-rig a homegrown version just like my publisher at Master Handy-man Press. He wove plastic strips in and out of the prongs of an old steel rake. Then he taped everything together with duct tape. He got the 20-foot handle length he needed by taping a Long Arm extension pole onto the rake handle.

If you don't have a steel-pronged rake, try attaching a board or piece of plastic to a garden hoe to broaden the head width. The final result won't win any beauty contests, and it weighs three times as much as an aluminum roof rake. But it works.

No matter whether you use a store-bought or homemade roof rake, use a little common sense. This is not a job for a person with a heart condition. Even if you are in top condition, you are prob-ably not used to working over your head, so pace yourself and expect sore muscles the next day.

Do not pull an avalanche of snow down on yourself or your helper. Only rake snow. Don't try to remove ice from the roof or gutters. It won't work and you could pull down the gutter.

Remember, like Detroit Edison says: Look up. A roof rake can conduct electricity. Stay away from wires.

Adam Helfman, president of Fairway Construction, believes the situation is only going to get worse. "We are in the middle of an ice dam epidemic," Helfman says. The insurance repair division of his family's Southfield-based firm is bracing for a deluge of frantic phone calls as soon as the ice begins to melt.

"If you see water coming into your home from the roof, call for help immediately. Our company maintains a 24-hour hot line, (800) 354-9310. As soon as we get a call, we rush out crews of experienced roofers and carpenters to clear the ice off the roof and repair any structural damage.

"Our emergency crews shovel off the snow, crack the ice with rubber mallets and pepper the ice with calcium chloride pellets. The average cost to the homeowner's insurance company is $650. Unfortunately, insurance won't pay for sending crews to de-ice the roof until actual water damage occurs," Helfman says.

Mark Eichol of Big Ike's Roofing in Dearborn Heights, (877) BIG IKES, believes in preventative maintenance. "If you have an ice dam problem I don't believe you should wait around for disaster," Eichol says.

His company uses a multistage process for ice dam removal. Big Ike's crews go up on the roof and shovel and rake off as much of the ice and snow as possible, then spread calcium chloride pellets on the remaining ice and leave the site for a couple of hours. When they return, they shovel off the ice that has been loosened by the calcium chloride, spread more pellets and let them work for another couple of hours before returning and shoveling away the remaining ice.

"If the ice is very thick, we take large propane heaters up on the roof and melt the ice. Unfortunately, when we do this we have to keep the crew on the roof all the time and that increases the cost of the job," Eichol says.

His firm charges $300 and up for ice dam removal. The price depends upon the depth of the ice and the pitch of the roof. Every house is not a candidate. "Two-story houses or very steep roofs are just too dangerous," he says.

Even if you get the snow and ice cleared from your house, you can't settle back in your easy chair and figure that job's done for the winter. A new snowstorm could rear up and hit at any time.

My advice is to keep your snow rake and calcium chloride pellets handy.

Ice dam problems
What you can do:
■ Minor snow removal around the roof edge: Use a roof rake.
■ Ice in roof gutters: Lay panty hose legs filled with calcium chloride on top of ice.
■ Icicles hanging from gutters: Carefully break off with broom.
■ Ice on steps from melting roof ice: Scatter calcium chloride on area. Scrape with ice chipper.

When you need to call a pro:
■ Dangerously deep snow and ice on roof.
■ You see or hear water leaking into house from roof (it may be leaking into house and draining down inside of walls, or invisibly seeping underneath attic insulation).
■ Gutters coming off soffit.
■ Roof cave in.
■ For the above three problems, be sure to call your homeowner's insurance agent for instructions. These are signs of a major water damage insurance claim and your agent may give you specific instructions. Do not settle the claim until you are certain that you know the full extent of the damage.

- Glenn Haege

Preventing frozen pipes

Another cold-weather home danger is water pipes that freeze and then burst. Preventative maintenance is best, says Jim Kronk of Universal Plumbing, (248) 542-3888, who offers these tips:

■ If you think a pipe in an enclosed area is likely to freeze, open the door and let warm air circulate around the pipe.

■ If a pipe in an enclosed area is frozen, put in a light bulb and close the door. The lit bulb will gradually thaw the pipe or fixture. If you can get at the pipe, use a hair drier or heat gun set on low.

■ Never use a propane torch or even the high setting on a heat gun. Intense heat can start a house fire.

■ If a faucet or toilet tends to freeze, let it drip by turning the handle or wedging the flapper ball up slightly.

■ You can also rent a commercial pipe thawer, which is a low-voltage transformer with a pair of cables that runs current through the pipe and melts ice from the inside out. Chet's Rent-all, (248) 853-6020, in Berkley, and Buttons Rent-It, (248) 542-5835, in Royal Oak, rent pipe thawers for $40 to $55 a day.

■ Another option is to use commercial blower heaters to circulate hot air and gradually thaw pipes. Daily rental is about $28.

- Glenn Haege

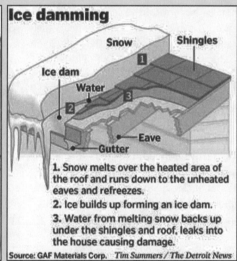

Ice damming

Snow　　Shingles

Ice dam

Water

Eave

Gutter

1. Snow melts over the heated area of the roof and runs down to the unheated eaves and refreezes.

2. Ice builds up forming an ice dam.

3. Water from melting snow backs up under the shingles and roof, leaks into the house causing damage.

Source: GAF Materials Corp.　Tim Summers / The Detroit News

Morris Richardson II / The Detroit News
A railing protects Rob Schroder as he shovels snow off the second floor porch roof of his house in Dearborn. It's too dangerous to stand on most roofs, however. A long-handled roof rake works well at removing snow on the roofs of ranch homes.

DECEMBER 22, 2000

Attic insulation is key to preventing ice dams

by Glenn Haege
Special to The Detroit News

I keep telling people that ice dams have nothing to do with the roof and everything to do with the insulation and ventilation in their home's attic.

According to Adam Helfman, president of Fairway Construction in Southfield, the ice dam phenomenon develops when it gets cold and people dial up the thermostat in their homes. Most Michigan houses have too little insulation in the attic, so warm air escapes and heats the roof. The warm roof melts the snow and water flows down the roof. The water drains into the gutters and gradually freezes over. Once the gutter is clogged, ice quickly builds up and forms a dam holding back more freezing water.

When the temperature rises, the thaw starts water rising behind the ice dam. Water backs up under the shingles, gets under the drip edge and starts flooding the attic.

"We tell people that the real answer is adding more insulation and ventilation" Mark Eichol, owner of Ike's Roofing in Dearborn Heights, says. "A cold attic does not have an ice dam problem. Proof of that is that unattached, unheated garages do not have an ice dams" Eichol says.

If you do not know whether your house has enough attic insulation, the current U.S. Department of Energy guidelines call for attic insulation of R-49. If your house has fiberglass insulation, the insulation blanket would have to be between 12 and 15 inches thick to provide that R-value.

Good ventilation is also required to keep the attic cold and the roof ice-free. Soffit vents and ridge vents or pot vents are needed to provide constant ventilation. Insulation often blocks soffit vents, so pull the insulation away from soffit vents and install rafter baffles to provide unobstructed airflow. Then push back the insulation.

If water does leak into the attic, all the insulation that gets wet has to be pulled out, but it may not have to be replaced.

"Fiberglass batt insulation that has become wet from melting ice can be pulled out, thoroughly air dried and replaced, and it will regain its insulation value," says Tim Grether, spokesman for Owens Corning. "However, loose-fill fiberglass or cellulose insulation that gets wet has to be pulled out and replaced."

If you presently have an ice dam condition, Grether recommends waiting until the ice has melted and you know your attic is dry before adding more insulation.

When it's time to reroof, Grether suggests that you tell the roofer to install Owens Corning WeatherLock or another ice shield, not just a drip edge. An ice shield creates an impermeable barrier that protects the deck boards and keeps water from getting under shingles and leaking into the house.

By installing the proper amount of insulation, ventilation and an ice shield, you have done everything you can to protect your biggest single investment from winter ice damage.

DECEMBER 23, 2000

Suggestions help you shovel your way out of snow problems

by Glenn Haege,
America's Master Handyman

We knew it was coming. We saw the TV footage of people shoveling in Buffalo. But that was Buffalo. A lot of us still got caught not holding the bag of ice melter when we needed it.

By the time most of us rushed to the hardware store or home center, the shelves were empty. We had to do without - or with whatever we had left over from last year.

The snow came down so thick, so fast, that ice melters were not much help anyway. Ice melters are not meant to be used instead of shoveling. They are merely agents used to break the bond of snow and ice so that we can shovel or run our snow blowers more effectively.

Winter has just begun, so let's go over the arsenal and be prepared next time.

Snow shovels
There are basically two different types: pushers and lifters. Pushers are the shovels with blades that look like abbreviated "Cs". Lifters are flat and wide bladed. The more modern lifting shovels have ergonomically bent handles that make lifting the snow easier on the back.

You need both. Pushing shovels are fine for light 1- or 2-inch snows but inadequate for heavy snowfalls like we just had.

You also need your summertime dirt moving shovel on hand so you can use its extra weight and sharp blade to cut through the compacted snow that the snow plow jams into your driveway.

If you have a lot of snow to move, Silver Bear Products of Calumet, Mich. makes a heavy duty push/pull snow scoop. The snow scoop is never picked up. You push it forward until its 2-by-212-foot scoop is full, then pull it away and dump it. With a snow scoop, one person can do the same work as two or three shovelers. Last time we checked, these poor folks were so inundated with calls, they were not even answering the phone.

Ice chippers have probably been around since the first cave man slipped and fell. They never wear out.

If you want to get the best out of all snow shoveling and scraping tools, coat them with a thin layer of silicone spray. The spray stops snow from sticking to the surface and makes pushing, shoveling and emptying easier.

Snow rakes are used to take snow off the roof. Some are built with handles that extend up to 20-feet. No ladder is needed.

Ice melters
All ice melters are not created equal. Some will melt ice but need relatively warm temperatures to be effective. Others create their own chemical heat and are effective even in very cold weather.

Rock salt (sodium chloride) is the least expensive. It's the stuff the cities spread all over the highway every winter. It is only effective to 20 degrees Fahrenheit. When it gets really cold, rock salt just lies there.

Magnesium chloride, potassium chloride and urea are more friendly to the environment than rock salt. They are basically fertilizers that also melt ice. These products are good to use around sensitive shrubs and are safer for pets.

Calcium chloride is the most powerful melter. It is effective down to minus 25 degrees.

Some makers blend several different melters to create a ice melter mix that is both cost effective and works regardless of the weather.

In our market, Gibraltar National, (800) 442-7258, is the biggest packager of ice melters. Their brand names for the different chemicals are Gibraltar Storm Front for calcium chloride pellets and DualFlake for Calcium Chloride flakes; Mag Chloride Pellets for magnesium chloride; and Gibraltar Ice Devil Blended Deicer for sodium chloride, calcium chloride and potassium chloride mix.

A locally available source of urea is Anti Skid by Suretrack Melt Inc., (717) 661-7179. Anti Skid also contains limestone chips for slip control. You can find it in a lot of IGA supermarkets.

Tips

■ *Remember ice melters only break the bond between ice and the under surface. Spread it like chicken feed, let it work for a half hour, then shovel away.*

■ *If you are bothered by snow and icicles on the roof, you have an insulation and ventilation problem. Fix it by blowing cellulose or fiberglass insulation into the attic. Ventilation is just as important. The soffit vents have to be clear, and you need proper pot vents or ridge vents.*

■ *To solve the short-term roof snow problem, rake 2 or 3 feet of snow away from the roof edge with a snow rake. If the gutters are frozen over, cut apart a couple of pairs of old panty hose and fill each leg with calcium chloride pellets or flakes. Knot the open ends and place them on the gutters.*

The calcium chloride will melt through the ice and keep the gutter free flowing. Put a couple of the filled panty legs on top of the gutters wherever you have icicles, around corners and down spouts. Be sure to pull the panty hose out of the gutters in the spring or people may think you are weird.

■ *Before you call it quits, shovel around the downspout to make sure the melting water has a clear path. You're done for the day, go in, get warm and have a merry Christmas.*

Planning on a spring remodeling project? Don't waste the winter

by Glenn Haege,
America's Master Handyman

It used to be that if you and your significant other were mulling over a major remodeling project in January, you could safely not start serious planning until the home and garden shows in February through April. It was OK to settle down for a long winter's nap.

No longer. During the preholiday season, I got the chance to have lunch with many of the Ask the Handyman radio show advertisers. The group is a pretty good cross-section of the movers and shakers in the home improvement industry. According to them, if you have a major remodeling project scheduled for next year, the time to start cracking is now.

Jerry Lynn, the founder of Acorn Kitchen & Bath, (248) 335-0111, said: "I thought 1999 was a banner year. Then 2000 was better. Now, we're scheduling orders well into 2001."

Despite what you read about new home construction tapering off, the remodeling business hasn't slowed. Right now, I'd bet the farm that 2001 could well be the biggest remodeling year on record. Remember, even if the economy does slow, when the economy slows people remodel more.

That means you can't waste the winter.

This is the best time of the year for interior painting, plumbing, electrical work, home office upgrades and basement remodeling. Winter is also an excellent time to have windows installed. It is an excellent time to shop for air conditioning. Even concrete and roofing can be done almost 12 months a year.

In the real estate business they call January and February the "serious season". People aren't out shopping unless they really mean business. The mind-set in the home improvement industry, too, is that you are a serious customer. That means you get better attention when you call or walk in the door and better follow-up after the initial contact is made.

Because business isn't so hectic, the salesperson has the opportunity to explain things more fully; the designer has time to put more thought into the plans; the workman is more rested and has the time to get the job done right. Back in the warehouse, the distributor may even have everything in stock. All of this means the job has a better chance of coming in on time and on budget. You, the consumer, are the big winner.

Planning is a critical part of any home modernization project. Organize, prioritize and get the entire family focused on the decision-making process. If you want to add a room, make sure that everybody huddles together and decides just exactly what that room will be used for. You'll be surprised at what good input the kids can have when you really get them involved.

If you plan to do more than one major project in a year, prioritizing is essential. Let's say you are going to put on a new roof, get new air conditioning and finish the basement. You can't do everything at once.

The roof could be the most important thing on the list. If it leaks, water can cause damage throughout the house. Not a problem. Roofing in the middle of winter is not fun but houses can be roofed year-round. If there are no leaks and you are replacing the roof because it is looking old, you have time to shop.

Now is also an excellent time to shop for air-conditioning. Do in-depth investigation and interviews on both these projects now, schedule work for first thing in the spring.

You can remodel the basement right now, but not every remodeling contractor knows how to do the project properly. Two that do are Coy Construction, (248) 363-1050, and Fairway Construction, (800) 354-9310, which is installing the new Owens-Corning basement wall system. There are a lot of other good companies, just make sure the contractor you select has a good track record.

If we are lucky, Fed Chairman Alan Greenspan may even give us lower interest rates soon. So start planning now and you won't stop bragging for years.

Projects you can do in winter
- Interior painting
- Carpeting
- Kitchen remodeling
- Bath remodeling
- Duct cleaning
- Basement remodeling
- Plumbing
- Electrical
- All floor installation and finishing
- Window replacement
- Room additions
- Waterproofing
- Deck construction
- Chimney cleaning
- Fireplace installation
- Spa installation
- Landscape planning
- Heating and air conditioning

Research now, but wait until spring
- Exterior painting
- Landscaping
- Paver installation
- Driveway construction

Chapter 1

2001 Articles reprinted from The Detroit News HOMESTYLE

Standard maintenance can help make indoor living comfortable

by Glenn Haege,
America's Master Handyman

How many of you have a runny nose, scratchy eyes, dry skin and at least someone in the family with a hacking cough or sneezing attacks?

I'll bet you also clean like crazy, but can't get rid of the dust and walking across a carpeted floor to turn on the TV can be a shocking experience.

You are not alone.

November had been pretty good, then wham, arctic cold. We've been in the deep freeze for almost a month and we have to adapt to a completely indoor environment. Most of our homes were not ready for the transition.

There are a lot of standard maintenance items you can do to make life more comfortable. These chores include carpet and duct cleaning, humidification, furnace filtration, air cleaning and daily vacuuming.

Carpet and duct cleaning are at the top of the list. Carpets should be professionally deep cleaned every six months.

If you've been using a do-it-yourself or a rental carpet cleaner, you don't really clean deep down and the machine often leaves residue on carpet fibers that attracts dirt. Only the guys with the big truck-mounted units have the power you need and even some of them don't use enough chemicals. Some of the good ones I know are Modernistic, (800) 609-1000, and Duraclean by Maryanne, (800) 372-5427. My wife swears by Chet's Cleaning, (800) 404-0017.

The big chemical and equipment companies think Modernistic is so good they hire them to train other companies on the latest cleaning techniques. Maryanne is the second biggest Duraclean cleaning franchise in the world. Chet's has a stellar reputation among people with really expensive carpeting. These companies didn't get their reputations by not doing the job right.

Most people don't clean the ducts often enough. If a house has a forced-air natural gas furnace, the ducts should be cleaned every seven years. When it gets very cold, the furnace blower motor works nonstop spreading heat, dust, dust mites and other allergens around the house.

It is also a good idea to have ducts sanitized to a sterile environment. If a family member has respiratory problems, sanitize ductwork annually.

There are a lot of good duct cleaners. Some of my favorites are A.1 Duct Cleaning, (800) 382-8256; Dalton Environmental, (800) 675-2298; Dusty Ducts, (313) 381-7801; Safety King, (800) 972-6343; Sanit-Air, (888) 778-7324; Sterling Environmental, (888) 992-1200; and Vent Corp., (248) 473-9300.

Dave Felker at Sterling just got some brand-new trucks with custom designed compressors that are very special. Safety King is the biggest in our part of the country. Sanit-Air is the only company listed that is licensed to use Ozone for the sanitizing process, all the other companies use Oxyne.

The third project is to improve humidification. If your skin feels dry and sparks fly, you don't have enough humidity. The first thing to do is check the humidity levels with a good hygrometer. Most hardware stores carry Bionaire hygrometers that only cost about $29 and allow you to check temperature and humidity levels in every room of the house.

If the humidity is down to desert levels (20 percent or lower), add humidity. Many people still have old-fashioned drum humidifiers on their furnace. If you do, treat yourself to one of the newer, flow-through kind.

(I wrote a Homestyle article on humidifiers Jan. 15 of last year that you can access by clicking here.)

When changing the furnace humidifier is not in the budget, get a warm mist portable humidifier. They are more expensive, but far more efficient than cool mist or evaporative console models.

Most people still use cheap throwaway filters that cost less than $1 and should be replaced every 90 days. Those things don't improve the quality of the air; they protect the furnace from clogging. At the minimum upgrade to a 3M Filtrete or some kind of an electrostatic filter.

Most people would do well to upgrade to a thick media filter like the Trion Air Bear, (800) 338-7466, or the Research Products Corp. Space Guard, (800) 334-6011. These filters only have to be replaced about once a year and do an excellent job for most people.

Should someone in the house have severe allergies, upgrade to an electronic air cleaner such as the Trion SE 1400 or the Honeywell F50, (800) 345-6770. They filter particulates down to .01 microns, but have to be cleaned every 90 to 120 days.

A differently designed electronic air cleaner by Dynamic, (800) 916-7873, has a disposable filter that is changed every three or four months so that you do not have to clean the entire unit.

The last thing you need to do to improve air quality in your home is also the least expensive. Vacuum daily, not just once every week or two. Not everyone can buy a new HEPA filter vacuum cleaner like I wrote about two weeks ago, but you can upgrade to an antiallergen disposable vacuum bag. These bags stop the cleaner from recirculating dust and help you breathe a lot easier.

Now, take a deep breath and get to work. You've got a lot of work to do to make the house as comfortable as it should be.

JANUARY 13, 2001

You can bring back the beauty of worn-out varnished tables

by Glenn Haege,
America's Master Handyman

Many of us have old varnished tables that we love, but the surface is worn out from years of use and countless cleanings. Bringing these surfaces back to their former beauty is a great winter project. All it takes is a little time and TLC.

Most old varnished tables were coated with a very strong, shiny lacquer. Lacquer is beautiful but becomes soft and gummy over the years. Dirt gets into scratches, and they become very obvious.

You may be able to repair the surface by just washing it down and deep cleaning it with lacquer thinner. The thinner often softens the finish enough, so that it fills the scratches and looks like new.

If you are not satisfied, wet sand the entire surface. You'll need a gallon of water and a stack of 220 or 280 black sandpaper. Wrap the sandpaper around a rubber or wood sanding block, dip it in the water and start sanding.

The water serves as a lubricant, so never let the sanding block get dry. When wet sanding, you get slush, not dust. The surface gets very smooth.

When you have finished sanding, wash the surface with clear water. Air dry, then wash it down again with Xylene and 100-percent cotton cloths.

Since Xylene is very flammable, if working in the kitchen, turn off the pilot light if you have a gas stove. Naturally, smoking is forbidden. Xylene-soaked rags should be stored outside until garbage day.

After cleaning, the surface will look dull with a great many small scratches. The scratches may be invisible after a couple of coats of Helmsman by Minwax. To find out if they will disappear, dip a clean cotton cloth into fresh water and wipe it over a small area. If you like the look, you are home free. If the scratches are still obvious, more work is needed.

Let's use the best scenario first. If you liked the look, apply two coats of Helmsman by Minwax, (800) 462-0194. Helmsman is a mixture of urethane and spar varnish. It's available at any Damman Hardware, Pontiac Paint or Dillman & Upton in Rochester, (248) 651-9411.

Here's the procedure. Brush on one coat and let it dry overnight. Next day, powder sand the finish with fine sandpaper. Do not use water. Powder sanding means you just have to roughen up the surface until a dustlike powder is visible.

The purpose of powder sanding is to prepare the surface so that the second coat bonds securely. Wipe the dust off with a damp cotton rag, then finish cleaning with a tack rag to get any stray particles. A tack rag is a special wax-impregnated cheesecloth available at paint and hardware stores.

Apply a second coat of Helmsman. When this coat dries, you're done. The surface will feel dry to the touch in just a few hours, but must cure at least 72 hours (3 days) before use.

If you didn't like what you saw after wet sanding the surface, you must sand down to the bare wood with a finishing sander. Start with 80-grit garnet sandpaper. Use progressively finer sandpaper as the job nears completion.

When the old finish is removed, the surface will look white. Wash it down with paint thinner. When dry, wipe carefully with a tack rag.

Stain with a rubbing stain until you achieve the desired color. Wear refinisher's gloves and apply the stain with a lint free, 100-percent cotton rag. Over apply the stain, then take it down to the desired color with a clean cotton rag.

The stain will raise the grain of the wood, so sand lightly with very fine sandpaper after the stain dries. Wash it down with paint thinner, then wipe with a tack rag and brush on a coat of Helmsman. Let dry over night, then powder sand.

Apply two more coats of Helmsman six hours apart. The surface will look as good or better than the day the table was brought home from the store. You worked hard and deserve the compliments that are sure to come your way, so brag about it.

Revarnishing rules

The quality of the tools you use and the area in which you work will go a long way in determining the success of the project.

■ Don't let the room temperature go below 60 degrees Fahrenheit. Furnace hot air registers in the room should be blocked, so that they are not blowing dust around. Keep people out of the work area.

■ Only soft china bristle or badger hair brushes that have never been used for paint can be used. You can get them at any quality paint store. Some places to look are Harrison Paint in Sterling Heights, (586) 268-0808; all four Shelby Paint Stores, (586) 739-0240; Walker Crawford in Royal Oak, (248) 546-466; or Pontiac Paint in Pontiac, (248) 332-4643.

■ When it comes time to apply the finish, do not work from the can. Stir well, then pour the finish through a disposable paint strainer into a clean glass container.

JANUARY 20, 2001

What do you do when the dam ice on your roof starts melting?

by Glenn Haege,
America's Master Handyman

Because of December's heavy snowfall, ice dams developed on the roofs of many area homes. Unless the dams have been removed, melting water is going to have trouble draining and might back up into your home.

Leaking roofs can be tricky; you may not even know it is happening until major damage has been done. If you are out of town and no one is checking on your home while you are away, the floors, walls and ceilings may be ruined before anyone even knows about it.

Even if you are living in a house, the roof may be leaking and you may not even know about it. Go up into the attic. Turn on all the lights and bring a very strong flashlight. Inspect the attic thoroughly. If the nails in the roof deck are rusty or wet it means you have a moisture problem.

The water may not even be coming from the outside. So much hot air may be leaking into the attic from the house below that water condenses on the underside of the roof deck.

If the attic ceiling is OK, get on your hands and knees and check the insulation in the soffit area. Wet or damp insulation means that water is coming in from the outside. It may be leaking down into the walls or the ceilings of the house.

Try to discover the water trail. Water can drain into the ceiling or walls and travel along wood or wiring to other parts of the house. It can actually flow in a horizontal plane.

If you discover major water damage call your homeowner insurance agent immediately. You may also want to call a remediation specialist such as Fairway Construction's insurance division, (800) 354-9310; or Burton Brothers, (800) 6-BURTON, in Southfield; Complete Content Restoration, (248) 650-6080, in Troy; or Inrecon, (800) 421-4141, in Macomb. All of these firms have years of experience working with insurance companies and solving water and fire damage problems.

If you cannot follow the path of the water, call Monroe Infrared Technologies, (800) 221-0163, and get them to do an infrared scan of the house while the area is still wet. Before drying, the water will show as an easily identifiable line that you can follow from initial entry point to final destination. The infrared scan will also be immensely valuable dealing with insurance adjusters because it shows the full extent of the water damage and leaves no room for guesswork.

Do everything possible to dry out the attic. Rake up and discard wet loose fiberglass or cellulose insulation. Wet attic fiberglass batt insulation can be dried and re-used, according to Owens Corning. Everything else must be thrown away.

Dry heat is needed. Turn up the furnace thermostat to 78 degrees Fahrenheit. Turn off the humidistat. Bring fans up to the attic. Connect the fans to outdoor extension cords and keep them running continuously.

If water has gotten into electric receptacles, turn off the power to the outlets and drain the fixtures.

Every wet area inside the house must be opened up and dried thoroughly, according to Connie Morbach of Sanit-Air, (888) 778-7324.

"If you have water damage in a wall or ceiling, the first thing to do is drain the area. Then remove any wet insulation. If there is just a small amount of water damage to plaster or wood you may be able to just let it dry. If the damage covers a wide area, or the affected surface is drywall, it must be cut out and replaced," she says.

"Time is critical. If you can open up the wall or ceiling, remove wet insulation and start drying the area with fans within 48 hours there is little health risk.

If an area has been wet for three days or more, never attempt to dry it with fans. After 72 hours only commercial dehumidifiers should be used safely. Blowing fans will spread contamination throughout the house.

"The reason for the time limit is that after 72 hours the bacteria count in drywall that has been soaked with clean roof water is as high as that of drywall soaked a day in sewer water. If the molds are allowed to develop, the family could have major health problems and the entire area may have to be torn out and sanitized," Morbach says.

Even water draining down the outside of a house can cause major problems, according to Don Collins of Budget Electric, (800) 400-8941. "Melting water is getting into older fabric-covered cables and draining into wall-mounted breaker boxes. If you see water coming out of the breaker box, call a licensed electrician immediately. It is only a matter of time before the box blows and there is a major possibility of fire damage or personal injury.

"There is nothing the homeowner can do to stop water from coming down and flooding breaker boxes. In the spring, they can call a company like mine and install a roof cable deicing system or insulate the attic properly and eliminate the problem. Right now all a homeowner can do is hope for the best and take immediate action if a problem develops," Collins says.

Remember what the Handyman says: "Water always wins. That's why we have a Grand Canyon."

JANUARY 27, 2001

It was the same stuff, but more of it, at annual housewares show

by Glenn Haege,
America's Master Handyman

CHICAGO

I have to confess that this year's International Housewares Show at McCormick Place in Chicago looked a whole lot like last year's Housewares Show. To see it with an entirely different set of eyes, I brought my WXYT-AM radio show producer, Dave Riger, with me and told him to tell me what products caught his eye.

Dave is a bright, live-at-home, 20-something. He knows a great deal about bowling and nothing about cooking, ironing or housewares. His picks are at the end of this article. I am going to tell you about new kitchen-oriented products today and the rest of the show next Saturday.

Just about all the major trends that we pointed out last year – like heavy-duty nonstick frying pans, professional cooking and baking ware (read extra heavy and expensive) and the retro-look – were there this year, but carried by more manufacturers.
Cookware

Viking, (662) 455-1200, the high-end appliance maker, came out with a professional line of quality pots and pans. This gave me a little bit of a chuckle because according to most of the remodeling reports I get, the people who spend the most on kitchen remodeling and high-end appliances cook the least. Now, these folks will be able to have matching high-end unused kitchen knives, sauce pans and stainless steel cookware to go with their unused, but very expensive stoves, ovens and cook tops. Viking cookware will be in the $100 to $150 per piece category.

Chef Emeril Lagasse has introduced a cookware line called Emerilware by All-Clad, (877) 659-2051. The pots and pans will also be in the $100 to $150 per piece category.

Virtually every manufacturer who makes quality nonstick frying pans (like Berndes, (888) COOK-983, Emerilware and T-Fal, (800) 395-8325) will now offer extra thick, lifetime, nonstick surfaces on which you can use metal utensils. In the real world, lifetime usually translates to a 5-year warranty.

T-Fal came up with a cute gimmick. They are now packing a Pressure Cooker Tips for Dummies booklet with their Sensor 2 stainless steel and aluminum pressure cookers. Prices will range from $80 to $130.

There is no need to worry about pouring out the peas or pasta when you use the EasyStrain cookware line by Delfre Enterprises Inc. The pans feature locking covers and built-in, large and small strainers in the pans.

Delfre Enterprises Inc., (201) 750-3245, and Chefpal Inc. have teamed up to produce the EasyStrain Cookware line of stainless steel pans with locking covers and built-in, large and small strainers. You can drain the peas or pasta without taking the cover off the pan. This cookware is just tippy-toeing into the market at some True Value hardware stores. An eight-piece set (4 pans, 4 covers) costs $250 and is available direct from the manufacturers at www.easystrain.com.

Zebra is just one of several animal china patterns by Signature Housewares. The china pattern comes in diner, lunch and salad plates, cups, saucers and mugs.

China has gone to the dogs with a wide selection of cat and dog food and water bowls, treat canisters and place mats.

China and glassware

Animal motifs were big in china. Not just pictures of animals, sometimes a close-up version of the hide. The Zebra, Pony and Cheetah pelt and Peacock feather designs by Signature Housewares, (805) 484-6666, are a prime example.

Signature is also introducing a complete line of dinnerware for your dog or cat. Fido or Fifi will love the matching ceramic water and food bowls, place mats and cookie jarlike dog and cat treat canisters. Look for them in pet catalogues and upscale pet stores.

If you are a fan of glassware that goes "thunk" instead of "ding" when you tap it, you will be glad to know that "bulletproof" top-end acrylic serving pieces and drinkware are making their way into the market. The stuff is supposed to be just about unbreakable. Manufacturers include Carlisle Home Products, (800) 339-4278, and U.S. Acrylic, (800) 232-2600. Prices will depend upon the store but should range about 40 or 50 percent more than standard acrylics.

Color is king for many of these products. Soft blues, yellows, purples and greens are in for glassware. Dramatic blacks, greens, yellows, oranges, blues and reds are very prominent in china.

The Rabbit Corkscrew by Metrokane lifts the cork from the bottle, then releases the cork with just two hand movements.

Other cool stuff

The must-have gadget of the show was the Rabbit professional corkscrew by Metrokane, (800) 724-4321. For a mere

$79.95, you can acquire a corkscrew that looks vaguely like a rabbit head complete with ears. Put it on top of a bottle of wine and squeeze. The Rabbit will pull and release the cork with just two movements of your hand.

If you are a failure in the kitchen, perhaps you are not dressed for success. Chef Revival USA, (800) 352-2433, has a complete range of high fashion chef clothing that will make you look the part. Jackets range from $36 to $70. Slacks range from $24 to $48. They even have children's sizes. Some clothing is carried by William Sonoma or you can call them direct for a catalogue.

Kim de la Villefromoy poses with two stylish chef ensembles. The full Chef Revival USA line includes chef hats, jackets, slacks and aprons. Clothing comes in both adult and youth sizes.

Dave's picks

My radio show producer at WXYT-AM, Dave Riger, liked these products:

■ Mr. Coffee by Sunbeam, (800) 882-5842, is introducing a Thermal Carafe coffee maker. It makes the coffee, then will keep it hot for five hours, and it won't break when you drop it. Prices range from $50 to $80.

■ The Ultimate Iron from Rowenta, (781) 396-0600. It takes the calcium out of the water, is very lightweight and a digital display tells you how much steam to use. Prices range from $130 to $160. It will be at Marshall Fields (Hudson's), and Damman's is considering it.

■ The Bissell Go Vac is lightweight, bagless and cordless. No bags to empty and powerful enough to clean a bachelor's condo. The price should be about $40, and it will be available at Target and Wal-Mart.

■ The Danby Countertop Dishwasher, (800) 263-2629, holds four place settings, has three cycles, connects to the kitchen tap and is small enough to fit under most cupboards. Priced at $200, Dave figures that this makes a great alternative if you don't have room to hide the dirty dishes.

FEBRUARY 3, 2001

Housewares Show's products make life easier for people and pets

by Glenn Haege,
America's Master Handyman

CHICAGO

Last week, I told you about new kitchen-oriented products at this year's International Housewares Show held recently at McCormick Place in Chicago. This week, I'll give highlights of the rest of the show, which showcases new products you'll likely find in home and housewares departments later this year. Some products are already available online.

Even though there were a few hundred thousand human-related products at the show, look at what my publisher at Master Handyman Press picked as his top three picks: the Healthy Pet Drinking Water System, the Sage King Catty Corner litter box and the Dirt Devil Spot Scrubber.

Pet supplies

Healthy Pet Drinking Water System, (626) 584-9362, is a brand-new product designed for your rugged outside dog. It comprises a 1-gallon water jug and a 30-gallon capacity Z-Filter mounted to a Health Shield antimicrobial water bowl. The Z-Filter provides your pooch with great tasting, chlorine-free water. It is priced at $19.95. The inventor said that it would save a lot of money for those who give their dogs bottled water.

The Sage King Catty Corner litter box system is an ingenious triangular litter box that makes clump removal effortless. The Catty Corner costs about $30. You can locate them on the web at www.catty-corner.com.

Every dog or cat has an occasional accident. Dirt Devil developed the Spot Scrubber to handle life's little problems. The hand-held scrubber has separate cleaning solution and dirty water tanks. It costs around $50.

For the home

Not to be outdone by the pet supply people, Elkay Water Products, (800) 432-3621, had a self-filtering water jug. Water is gravity fed through a PureSmart water filter into a porcelain water jug. The filter removes chlorine and

The Healthy Pet Drinking Water System assures good tasting, clean water by combining an anti chlorine filter cap on the 1-gallon reservoir and an antimicrobial water bowl.

If Fido has an accident, the Dirt Devil Spot Scrubber makes cleaning carpets or upholstery fast and easy. The hand held scrubber has separate cleaning solution and dirty water tanks.

Put Scrubby Toes Ice Breaker Mats on steps in the fall, and icy steps are banished forever. Ice breaks into nonslippery pieces when you step on it.

improves the smell and taste of tap water. The unit is in the $60 range.

After all the ice we've had this winter, my top product pick is the Ice Breaker Mat from Monrow Designs, (978) 372-2028. The ice breaker nonslip mat is glued or nailed onto outside steps. Just standing on the mat shatters ice into small, nonslippery pieces. Ice Breaker Mats cost about $8 and are available through catalogues such as Taylor Gifts, item No. 13827, (800) 829-1133; Improvements, item No. 199302, (800) 642-2112; and Practica, item No. G65428S, (800) 825-9817.

The Housewares Show always has some great organizers and space savers. Two of the best were the Walkway Saver Two-Place Bicycle Stand and the Smart Grip organizer.

The Walkway Saver by Jerry Kamysiak, Quick Crafter Co., of Posen, Mich., (888) 881-1880, stores two bicycles in the place of one. It costs $40 and should be at bike stores by fall. Meanwhile, you could buy direct from Kamysiak.

The unique spring system on the Smart Grip Wall Organizer Rack lets you hang any size handle just by slipping into the nonslip rubber grips.

Smart Grip Wall Organizer Rack by Idea Works, (800) 622-0089, holds everything with a handle, from tennis rackets to rakes. A unique spring system allows any size handle to slip in easily and be held instantly by sturdy nonslip rubber grips. The Smart Grip Wall Organizer Rack retails for $10. You can order online at www.ideaworksonline.com.

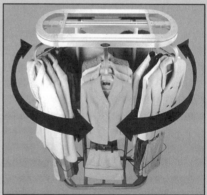

The Hongsheng Rotating Clothes Stand triples storage space. You can store up to 176 garments in an average-sized closet.

If you are so desperate for storage you are willing to spend $1,000 to triple the storage space in a closet, the Hongsheng Rotating Clothes Stand imported by Advantage WMQ of Canada, (905) 826-0882, is just the ticket. Depending on closet size, each unit can store from 40 to 176 garments. (I hope my wife doesn't read this.)

Cleaning products

If you are really serious about not letting anyone track dirt into the house or offices, ALMA's CleanStep, (800) 444-ALMA, traps dirt like flypaper. CleanStep comprises 30 24-by-30-inch layers of adhesive-coated film that remove dirt from shoes, equipment and even pet paws. Dirt is stripped from anything passing over the surface. When a layer is completely used, peel away to a clean layer. CleanStep comes in white, marble, blue, gray and sandstone and costs about $40. You can get it direct from the manufacturer at www.cleanstep.com.

Adhesive on the CleanStep 30 layer floor mat makes dirt on shoes and equipment stick to the surface. When dirty, you just peel away the top film and expose a clean adhesive layer.

Antimicrobial cloths and surfaces have been coming on strong. Foss Manufacturing, (800) 746-4019, has developed Fosshield Cleaning Wipes. The company calls it the next generation antimicrobial wipe because the feltlike cloth can be used with cold or hot water and cleaning chemicals without a drop in efficiency. The washable, reusable cloths are sold in three-packs priced from $4 to $6.

Scot Laboratories, (800) 486-7268, introduced five new products: Foame Soap, Foame, Zapit Microwave Cleaner, Furniture Treatment and Citrus Clean.

Foame Soap is an antibacterial liquid soap that turns into foam when you press the pump. The theory being that kids will have so much fun changing liquid soap to foam they may actually get their hands clean. Foame is the same product in a more grown-up container.

Zapit microwave cleaner is designed to clean hard, baked-on spills from microwave ovens. Furniture Treatment (yawn) is another citrus-based furniture cleaner/conditioner. Citrus Clean is a very concentrated water-based citrus cleaner that removes tape, tar, gum, permanent marker and glue. All five products are priced in the $2.95 to $4.95 cleaning product niche.

EcoMax is a chemical-free cleanser/scouring powder that cleans stainless steel, fiberglass, Corian and Formica. All active ingredients are fruit and vegetable based. Priced at $2, you can look for it in earth-friendly markets.

Brushtech Inc., (800) 346-0818, introduced several new specialty brushes: a window and shower door track cleaner flexible enough to get the gunk from the corners; a long, slim drain cleaner brush to clean the hair and things out of drains before they clog; and a tea pot spout cleaning kit designed to clean any configuration of tea pot spout. Prices range from $4 to $7. They will be available at discount stores and supermarkets.

If you want to know if I left anything out of this product report, there were more than 400 items in the new product display at the show. In two articles, I only had room to write about 34 of them. Don't worry, if something really important actually makes its way to the marketplace, I'll write about it here or talk about it on my radio show. Stay tuned.

FEBRUARY 10, 2001

Metro Detroit home improvement shows are brimming with ideas

by Glenn Haege,
America's Master Handyman

NOVI

Even though it was snowing last weekend, it was spring indoors at the Novi Expo Center and the beginning of the home improvement season, the 2001 Home Improvement Show.

I love home shows because you see what's new, get a feel for what's hot and talk to leading contractors, retailers and distributors. At this year's Novi show, there were eight roofing contractors, all three gutter-protection systems, 17 home remodelers, 22 kitchen and bath specialists, 40 window companies and 11 heating and cooling guys, to mention just a few of the displays. If you had a major improvement on your to-do list, you could have shopped til you dropped.

Nancy Rosen is my expert on home shows. She has handled press relations for the Novi show since it started. Rosen says, "The big change this year is that high-end is becoming mainstream."

The big stainless steel appliances, stained glass, top-of-the-line sunrooms and stamped concrete are not just for the upper crust anymore.

"People used to look, say 'wow' and walk on, but this year they are seriously shopping," says Rosen. "Average people, like you and me, are starting to express themselves with a showpiece appliance, stained glass window or stamped concrete drive or patio."

This does not mean that Sears is going to throw out Kenmore and put in all Viking appliances. It does mean stainless steel stoves, cooktops and ovens are spreading from Grosse Pointe and

Birmingham to Royal Oak, Novi and Sterling Heights.

The Gaggenau Hob Ventilator stores flat on the cooktop surface when not in use. When needed, it is raised up like a periscope and positioned over the cooking area.

One of the neatest stainless steel goodies I saw was the Gaggenau Hob Ventilator by Trevarrow Inc., (800) 482-1948. The Hob Ventilator looks like a submarine periscope that hides flush with the cooktop when not in use. When you want to use your Gaggenau barbecue grill or deep fat fryer, just pull up the ventilator and turn it directly over what you are cooking. Steam, smoke and smells are vented directly outdoors.

Hidden in the KraftMaid cabinet display by Kurtis Kitchen, (734) 522-7600, was a drawer front that pulls out into a cut-proof work table almost twice as deep as the countertop. When you

Wayne Weintraub of Kurtis Kitchen shows off the new KraftMaid pull-out tabletop. Stored, it looks like a cabinet drawer. When needed, it pulls out to provide a wide, cut-proof work area.

need extra counter space for chopping or mixing, just pull out the drawer. When done, just push the drawer back.

Every week, I get complaints from my readers and listeners about low-performance 1.6-gallon gravity-feed toilets. One high-performance model from Japan was shown by Nu-Way Supply, (800) 734-0630. These Toto G-Max toilets are so efficient the manufacturer says they equal the performance of power flush systems. These toilets are in the $500-$600 range.

The Toto Washlet Chloe adjustable toilet seat has an adjustable setting that lets the user choose men's or women's bidet setting, water temperature and pressure.

For $699, you can get the Toto Washlet Chloe adjustable seat with a built-in bidet. The electrically powered system lets you adjust the bidet spray for men or women, as well as the water pressure and temperature.

If you read my major Detroit News roofing article (Sept. 11, 1999), you know that I am a fan of the newer roofing alternatives. One of them is the cedar-shake-looking aluminum Rustic Shingle by Classic Products, and it has finally made its way to Metro Detroit. It is being installed by American Roofs Inc., (800) 287-0677. The cost is 212 to three times that of premium organic or fiberglass shingles, but it comes with a 50-year warranty. Realistically, the paint will wear off, but the aluminum should last forever.

I also enjoy checking out the Arts & Crafts area, which is one of the most attractive and affordable parts of the show. Distinguished Art Glass, (908) 637-4305, was one of the hits this year,

especially its display of decorative glass vases, bowls, plates and lampshades by Rosemarie Mazzei.

Each of Mazzei's pieces is made by placing enamels between two layers of glass. The bottom piece is hand-painted. Then the bottom and top pieces of glass are placed on a form in a kiln, and the glass is fused together. The decorative glass ranges from $75 to $175. Mazzei's work will also be on display this year at the Ann Arbor Art Fair. To learn more, check her web site, www.distinguishedartglass.com.

If you missed the Novi show, get cracking. There is a home show almost every week or two from now until the beginning of April. I've listed some of them here. Go as soon as possible. One contractor at the Novi show told me he is already 70 percent booked for the year. Make plans now. The contractors are not going to wait for you.

Breakfast club

Join me today and Sunday for Breakfast with Glenn Haege in the center court at Oakland Mall, where I'll be broadcasting my radio show from 8 a.m. to noon. Breakfast will be provided by the Coffee Beanery. Enter the mall at the main 14 Mile Road entrance.

Upcoming home show dates
■ Feb. 16-18: Macomb Home Improvement Show, Macomb Sports & Expo Center, Warren
■ Feb. 22-25: Michigan Home & Garden Show, Pontiac Silverdome
■ March 9-11: WXYT/Glenn Haege Home Show, Troy Sports Center (free admission)
■ March 22-25: GMC Builders Home & Detroit Flower Show, Cobo Center, Detroit
■ April 5-8: Spring Home & Garden Show, Novi Expo Center, Novi

FEBRUARY 17, 2001

Home show tells builders what you want

by Glenn Haege,
America's Master Handyman

ATLANTA

When you think about a building or home show, you visualize milling crowds and exhibit floors jammed with exotic displays and shining new products. The truth is that at big shows like the National Association of Home Builders' (NAHB) International Building Show, the information gathering that takes place off the exhibit floor is just as important as the exhibits.

According to the latest NAHB study, homebuyers want porches, decks, patios, landscaping and privacy. The New American Home 2001 shows how this can be accomplished on even a smaller city lot.

Did you know, for instance, that a typical home buyer wants a 2,170-square-foot house and is willing to commute to get a bigger lot and a three-car garage? This is according to a survey of actual or perspective homebuyers recently completed by the NAHB.

Finding out what buyers want, how to build it profitably and about how many buyers there will be are all-important subjects to America's professional home builders.

Every year the country's top builders and their suppliers come together to get the answers at the NAHB show.

This year, about 70,000 people from all over the world attended the 57th annual show held at the Georgia World Congress Center in Atlanta.

What they learned is not just good information for builders, it is knowledge you should have if you are grappling with questions on whether to improve or move, what's popular and what renovations will make your home more attractive at sale time.

Here are some of highlights of what we learned.

Dave Seiders, NAHB's chief economist, says that while building will be down this year, it should only drop to the levels of one or two years ago. This means that while builders may be a little less busy, there won't be any panic selling. Waiting for prices to drop will just mean you'll miss the market.

Top folks at mortgage lenders Fannie Mae and Freddie Mac assure us that there should be plenty of mortgage money in the pipeline and mortgage rates may dip below 634 percent. The Remodeling Council predicts these low interest rates will not have as great an impact on remodeling as it will have on new construction. That's because most major remodeling projects are paid for out of cash on hand, savings or investments.

140

When home owners remodel, they renovate because they love their neighborhoods and do not want to move, according to NAHB's research chief, Gopal Ahluwalia.

According to just-completed research, the average American homeowner lives in a house that is about 1,770 square feet. When we increase the size of our house, we add about 400 square feet. When we are house hunting, we look for a house that is about 2,171 square feet.

This is interesting for two reasons.

First, the median-size house sold in 2000 was 2,170 square feet, so builders are building what we want. Second, it means that Joe and Jane Average are not looking for and do not want either the 3,000- to 5,000-square-foot monsters we see popping up in the more affluent suburbs or the 1,200-square-foot boxes architects are trying to talk us into as the home of the future.

We also don't want the postage-size lots many builders love, according to NAHB research. We want a big lot with plenty of privacy. Only 5 percent of us want to live in the central city, 28 percent want to live in a close-in suburb, 36 percent want to make an outlying suburb home and 31 percent would prefer a rural address.

Think about this for a minute, with all the road rage and wasted commuting time we complain about: two-thirds of us still opt for cleaner air and wide open spaces.

What else do we want? Better Homes and Gardens (BH&G) does on-going research into what Americans want when they remodel or buy. They actually go out into the field and tour houses. Joan McCloskey, BH&G's architecture editor, was on hand to tell us her company's interpretation of what we want.

First off, we don't want a cookie cutter house. In fact, we don't want it to look like anyone else's.

We want a big, bright, beautiful kitchen and a master bedroom suite.

Third on the list is a spacious master bath. Jetted tubs are not a big thing but big, luxurious showers are.

Living rooms are unimportant, but dining rooms and a big great room are necessities. We want four bedrooms, one of which will probably be a home office. (Ahluwalia says that NABH research shows people younger than 55 want one master bedroom suite, but after 55 we want two. What does that tell you?)

Outside, we want porches, a multilevel, no-care deck or patio with a hot tub, a privacy rail/fence and beautiful landscaping. We want to be able to hang out, be snug and, above all, we want our privacy.

We also want a finished basement and lots of storage space, even a three-car garage. It would be nice if everything was energy efficient and good for the environment, but we don't really want to pay extra for these goodies.

That's a big shopping list. Next week I'll tell you about some of the new products the manufacturers have designed to fill it.

High tech products dominate national builders show in Atlanta

by Glenn Haege,
America's Master Handyman

The 1 1/2-story, 3-bedroom, 2-bath Marietta modular home was built on the National Association of Home Builders show floor. It combined state-of-the-art design, energy savings and affordability.

ATLANTA

Builders are getting serious about Smart Home and broadband technology. Twelve percent of the big builders have cable-networked communities on their drawing boards.

The recent International Builders Show in Atlanta was the place to go to get connected, literally. One whole exhibit area was devoted to ways that builders could talk to themselves, their suppliers and customers over the Internet. In addition, all the major homes built for the show were large wire (Category 5) cable and data stream wired houses.

The biggest new product at the show was as big as a house. It fact it was a house, a Marietta Modular home built on the exhibit floor by the Genesis Homes division of Champion Home Builders, (248) 276-1459.

Like two other homes built for the show - the New American Home-2001 and the Live/Work home — the Marietta used Smart Home technology. The Marietta is a state-of-the-art idea house that is available to builders and

developers now, not two or three years from now.

Final cost to the consumer should be in the $60-per-square-foot range. That gives you a 3-bedroom, 2-bath, 2,300-square foot house for about $150,000. That is a great price point for a house that has both an Environmental Protection Agency Energy Star and a Green Builder rating.

Continuing the Smart Home trend, Whirlpool, (800) 253-1301, introduced its line of interconnected, Internet-enabled appliances. Command center is a Web Tablet mounted on the refrigerator. The removable tablet can control the refrigerator, oven, dishwasher and microwave as well as make shopping lists, order groceries and leave notes for the kids.

Honeywell, (800) 345-6770, introduced the Enviracom Network that lets furnaces, air conditioners, thermostats and indoor air quality appliances talk to each other and even lets you in on the conversation while at home or work via the Home Control. Honeywell's WebPAD Internet appliance also provides portable, wireless high-speed Internet access.

Eaton Corp. introduced the Cutler-Hammer Fire-Guard. This is a new type of circuit breaker that senses wiring faults and hot spots and (hopefully) cuts off the power before an electrical fire exists. Since the majority of our houses have old, over-stressed wiring, this could be a real life saver. Check it out at www.homesafetycentral.com.

Kitchen and bath items were some of the most exciting new products at the show. Moen's, (800) BUY-MOEN, new

Pure Touch Aqua Suite series proved that you can have an elegant filtered water faucet. The faucets cost around $280 and come in 12 different finishes and two spout sizes.

If you want a high-style bath, decorative glass vessels are definitely in. Kohler is doing everything it can to make sure they become a major style feature.

Alsons, (800) 421-0001, introduced a new three-wall shower wall system with luxurious body sprays that cover you from head to toe. The new system is ADA compliant and includes a bath seat and wall-bar hand shower.

Alsons' new ADA compliant 3-wall shower wall system has body sprays that drench you from head to toe. The new system also has a bath seat and wall-bar hand shower.

A small California company, Act Inc., (800) 638-5863, introduced the hot water D'Mand System. We all hate wasting time and water waiting until the water gets hot. The D'Mand System is an electronically actuated pump system that surges hot water to your faucet at the touch of a button. Recirculating pump systems are nothing new but they are usually on timers. Electronic actuation is a smart idea.

When my group went to the show we had already been alerted to look for the Romala Stone display at the Home Depot exhibit. The new product was supposed to look like granite at about one third the price. It turns out that the new product not only looks like granite, but is real granite.

The reason for the price differential is that the vanity tops are quarried, cut and finished in China using that country's low labor rate. The tops come in only a very limited number of sizes, but give you granite priced at only $89 to $259. Home Expo stores have the same tops with fancy ogee edging, priced from $250 to $550.

Urethane pieces that look like very fancy wood millwork are nothing new, but Style Solutions (800) 446-3040, has come up with two gangbuster innovations: the miterless Corner System and the Metallon finish. The miterless corner system substitutes special corner pieces for intricate cutting. Any klutz can now measure and cut molding and cove decorations.

The Metallon series provides optional brass, nickel, copper and bronze finishes. The finishes come in either natural, so aging and weathering takes place, or lacquered, so the finish stays in like-new condition.

Hy-Lite Products, (877) 712-4013, introduced new curved wall, 2-inch-thick acrylic block units. This makes it simple to have the look of glass block for any interior wall configuration. Hy-Lite also introduced an acrylic block casement window.

Appearances

If you'd like to know more about what's new or talk to me about your home improvement project, visit me today and Sunday at the Michigan Home & Garden Show at the Pontiac Silverdome. Doors open at 10 a.m. I will be broadcasting until noon, then giving talks on the builder's stage and answering questions at the Master Handyman Press exhibit in the afternoon. Hope to see you there.

MARCH 3, 2001

Ultraviolet light is the newest weapon in battle against bad air

By Glenn Haege /
Special to The Detroit News

Many of the things we do to make our homes energy efficient – such as adding insulation, installing new windows, even caulking – save money on fuel bills but make our homes less healthy places in which to live. Sealing out drafts also seals out healthy fresh air and traps moist air, laden with household gases, inside. This moist, stagnant air is unhealthy to breathe and provides excellent breeding conditions for mold and other microorganisms.

The American Lung Association often sites U.S. Environmental Protection Agency statistics that the air we breathe in our homes may be anywhere from two to 100 times more polluted than outside air.

David Mudarri of the EPA's Indoor Environments Division believes that about 40 percent of us suffer effects ranging from dry eyes and sniffles to severe asthma attacks every week. His views and those of other experts appeared in an excellent article, "Indoor Air Pollution Can Cause a Sick Home," by Joysa Winters of the Rocky Mountain News. The complete text is available on the Indoor Air Quality News page of the International Union of Operating Engineers IAQ web site (iaq.iuoe.org/index.htm).

As consumers, there is a lot we can do to make the air in our homes cleaner.

Air infiltration devices, such as the Skuttle model 216, can bring fresh air into the house. Thick media filters and electronic air cleaners can clean the air, but they miss some of the finest particles. Cleaning and sanitizing the ductwork can cut down on dust and mold. Clean air legislation is making paints and chemicals more benign than their predecessors.

Now ultraviolet light has been added to the arsenal. The greatest source of UV is the sun. Its rays bleach furniture and fabrics and turn wooden decks gray. We use sunscreens, sunglasses and hats to protect our skin and eyes from its power.

UV waves are even more dangerous to molds and bacteria. They penetrate cell walls and change the organisms' DNA, making cell reproduction impossible.

Technology using UV has been available commercially for 40 years but has only been introduced on the residential level recently. Williams Refrigeration, (888) 268-5445, in Warren, and Sanit-Air, (888) 778-7324, in Troy, are among the pioneers and have been installing UV devices for more than two years.

To test-run the technology, I had Williams Refrigeration install UV in my heating system. My publisher at Master Handyman Press worked with Sanit-Air to test another UV system. Both of us noticed measurable improvements in air quality.

Not all UV lights are created equal. Some create ozone. Some do not. Ozone is an unstable O3 molecule. Many people consider ozone a side benefit because it zaps contaminants in the air. Connie Morbach of Sanit-Air is a licensed ozone technologist and is ultra conservative when it comes to ozone use.

"Some people are very sensitive to ozone. If there is enough ozone in the air to give a diluted bleach smell, the homeowner could experience unhealthy side effects," Morbach says.

One of the main reasons that she chose the UV system from AirPal, (877) 426-9211, was that the UV lights her company installs do not produce ozone. Roger Ferguson of Environmental Dynamics Group, (800) 916-7873, distributes the Air Pal system.

Williams Refrigeration installed the Second Wind Air Purifier, (877) 263-9463, which according to the manufacturer, produces a unique oxygen molecule called an "oxygen singlet" in addition to ultraviolet light. These molecules last only 5/100 of a second, but during this short period have a unique ability to destroy noxious gases, VOC's and Hydrocarbons.

Most UV systems cost in the $600 to $800 range. Ultraviolet lamps lose their effectiveness after a year. Replacements cost about $100.

This February, UV technology received a big boost when Honeywell introduced UV lights as part of its new Enviracaire Elite Whole-House Air Quality System. The Enviracaire Elite combines UV technology with air cleaning and humidification to promote total indoor air quality.

Honeywell uses different designs of UV lights to kill airborne bacteria in the return-air duct and to stop mold growth above the central air conditioner cooling coil. None of the UV lights in the Honeywell system produce ozone.

The entry of a large company like Honeywell into the field adds a great deal of credibility to UV technology.

If you want to improve your home's air quality, there may be a UV light at the end of the tunnel. It could help you breathe a lot easier.

A sampling of product sites

■ *AirPal:*
www.airpalspectra.com
■ *Airtech International Group Inc.:*
www.airtechgroup.com
■ *Field Controls:*
www.fieldcontrols.com
■ *Nirvana Safe Haven:*
www.nontoxic.com/air/index.html
■ *Second Wind:*
www.freshpureair.com
■ *Honeywell:*
www.honeywell.com/yourhome/uvelite/uv100a.htm

Landscaping is a remodeling job, so take it seriously

By Glenn Haege /
Special to The Detroit News

Does your planting have a plan? Does your plot have a plot? Or, to put it politely, does your landscaping look mis-begot?

Every spring, most of us look outside and say, "This is the year we make our lawn . . . garden . . . yard . . . spectacular." "We buy bushes, trees and plants that look pretty as puppies but often grow to be eyesores because they were planted too close together or too close to the house or sidewalk.

To avoid that problem, research landscaping like any other major remodeling job. Go to home shows to see landscaping displays, read magazines and tear out pictures of what you want, and talk to folks who have landscaping you like.

Landscape designs takes work to keep up. Once the landscape professional has made your yard beautiful, who will take care of it?

Also take time restraints into account and share them with the landscaping professional before plans have begun. If you have a hectic schedule or like to golf on weekends, a big garden should not be in your future unless you want to hire a full-time gardener.

Once you've done your homework, who do you call to get the work done? Gerald Salerno, an independent landscape designer who works with Superior Scape Inc., (810) 739-9630, gave a seminar on the subject at last week's Michigan Home & Garden Show.

Here are some definitions to help you pick the best landscape professional for your project.

■ Landscape architects. They are at the top of the field and know all about construction techniques, urban design and horticulture. They have a four-year degree in the subject, are quite expensive and are usually called in only on very big residential jobs.

■ Landscape designers. According to Salerno, they do much the same thing as landscape architects on the residential level. They usually have a two- or four-year degree in landscape design, but are also real plant people.

The Association of Professional Landscape Designers, (630) 579-3268, has a certification program and also has an informative web site, www.apld.com, complete with member names, addresses, phone numbers and member web sites.

■ Garden designers. They are usually people with a green thumb who love gardening and get into the business because they are good at it. You will find them at nurseries.

■ Design/build contractors. This includes big landscape companies such as Superior Scape or Stone City, (586) 731-4500. They usually have landscape designers on staff or on retainer, and have the equipment and crews to do everything from major earth moving to putting in flowerbeds.

The Associated Landscape Contractors of America, (800) 395-2522 (www.alca.org), has a certification program. Its highest degree is that of Certified Landscape Professional, but it also certifies interior and exterior technicians.

■ Arborists. If you have mature trees and are planning to reshape the ground or pave around them, trim or treat them, you need arborist. These are hands-on people who know about big trees. Arborists are certified. The National Arborist Association, (800) 733-2622 (www.natlarb.com.), can tell you how to contact professional arborist companies near you.

Remember, landscaping is a remodeling job. Before hiring anyone, get references, addresses and phone numbers. Go out to see their work and talk to the property owners. Beautiful landscapes are love affairs. Proud owners will be glad to brag about the people who made their dreams come true.

Appearances
My Spring Home Expo is this weekend. It's a chance for you to see all the things I write about all year long. This year it's at the Troy Sports Center at John R and 16 Mile (Big Beaver) 10 a.m.-6 p.m. today and 10 a.m.-4 p.m. Sunday. The show and parking are free. I'll be there broadcasting my show and answering questions both days.

Read Glenn Haege's question-and-answer column in Thursday's Detroit News. You can also call (800) 65 HANDY to ask questions during WXYT's 'Ask the Handyman' show Saturday and Sunday between 8 a.m. and noon (1270), or log on to the Master Handyman Help Site, www.masterhandyman.com.

Companies introduce more new technology at Free Home Expo

By Glenn Haege /
Special to The Detroit News

I thought I was done reporting on spring home and garden shows for the year, but several companies picked my WXYT Free Home Expo last weekend to introduce their new technologies to the retail audience. Why? Because they say my readers and listeners are the most knowledgeable home improvement folks in the country. And they're right.

Stain-proof paints

Up until now, we've had two popular types of paint: oil base and latex base. Now Muralo, a New Jersey company, has introduced water-borne resin technology. Tim Eisbrenner of Shelby Paint, (810) 739-0240, says that the new interior paint, Muralo Ultra, has no VOCs (volatile organic compounds), yet provides a finish that is as durable and flat as oil-base paint.

"Muralo Ultra is excellent for problem walls because the nonreflective dead matte finish makes surface irregularities almost invisible," Eisbrenner said.

Because resin molecules are exceptionally small and tightly packed, stains cannot sink into the surface like they can with traditional water-based paints. This makes the paint virtually stain proof.

Muralo Ultra comes in both an interior matte and an eggshell enamel. It is available only at Shelby Paint's Utica Store.

Brick that doesn't need mortar

Interlocking Novabriks are made from concrete. They are attached to furring strips with special Nova screws. No motar or footer is needed for the brick.

Brick is the most admired exterior surface in America, but it is relatively difficult to install and weathers over the years. Novabrik virtually eliminates these problems. Traditional bricks are made from clay while Novabriks are made from concrete and shaped like a checkmark with a hook at the end of the tail. The bottom of the check is the brick face. The upper portion of the brick angles back and hooks at the top.

No mortar is necessary for installation. Novabriks are screwed into furring strips attached to the wall. When bricks are placed, each new course (row) interlocks with and overlaps the bricks under it. The interlocking design makes Novabriks virtually earthquake proof, according to tests reported by the manufacturer. Overlapping creates a waterproof barrier that breathes so that water is stopped, but never trapped.

Novabrik is European technology, but is now made in Canada by Alba Products, (800) 265-2522, ext. 25. The new brick system is distributed locally by J.C. Cornellie, (586) 293-1500, a masonry company. Cornellie spokesman Ed Buchman said they added Novabrik because it's a very user-friendly, do-it-yourself product.

Concrete repairs just pour on

The Northeast and Midwest can have up to 50 freeze/thaw cycles a winter. These weather conditions cause havoc to all concrete surfaces. Water penetrates small cracks and separates the smooth outer surface from the aggregate below. This condition is called spalling. A new product, Quikrete's Concrete Resurfacer by Gibraltar, (800) 442-7258, makes repairing spalling and giving concrete a new surface easy.

The area to be repaired is first powerwashed. Once the surface dries, no additional preparation is necessary. Quikrete Concrete Resurfacer is self-leveling. It can be tinted and mixes like pancake batter. Just pour the mixed Resurfacer onto the prepared surface, squeegee into place and you're done.

Shingles that make electricity

Uni-Solar PV Shingles turn a roof top into an electric power producer. The dark blue shingle blend into the surrounding roof. They are weather proof and tested to hold fast in 60 mph winds.

Everyone I know worries about brown-outs and power failures. How would you like to make your house energy self-sufficient and maybe even sell power back to the power company?

Bekaert ECD Solar Systems LLC, of Troy, (888) 864-7652, is making solar power electrical roof systems a reality. The company makes Uni-solar PV Shingles and Architectural Metal Panels that contain photovoltaic panels. Terence Parker, Uni-Solar's manager of sales engineering, says that the solar panels – along with necessary combiner boxes, inverter and wiring – convert energy from the sun into useable electricity.

The electric power is used to run home lighting and appliances or can be stored in a battery until needed. Excess power can be sold to the electric company and channeled into its power grid.

A solar system for a 2,000-square-foot house that would supply most electric needs except during peak air condition-ing months would cost about $18,000, Parker said.

Bob Martin of Reddi-Wall Foam Insu-lated Concrete Wall Systems, (586) 752-9161, is using the solar shingles to provide electric power for an energy-efficient concrete home he is building in Genesee County. Parker said that solar power technology is most effective when used with Foam Insulated Concrete Wall and other efficient Energy Star building systems.

Times are changing and you ain't seen nothing yet. Now brag about it.

Spring into action and finish maintenance, cleaning before holidays

By Glenn Haege /
Special to The Detroit News

Can you believe that Passover and Easter are only a few weeks away? Fear not. When you team up with the Handyman to do your spring maintenance and cleaning projects, two weeks is all you need.

Start with the big jobs

Carpeting and upholstery: Small residential carpet cleaners don't have sufficient power and leave a residue, so why waste time? The big, truck-mounted carpet cleaners do the best job.

If you decide that your carpets do not have to be cleaned, do an extra good job vacuuming. Start by throwing out the old disposable vacuum bag and putting in a new one. Try the anti-allergen bags that are now available for most vacuum cleaners. They leave the air a lot cleaner.

Ducts: If you have a natural gas furnace, you should have the duct work professionally cleaned once every seven years. You need the ductwork cleaned before the central air conditioning blows dust and dust mites all over the house. Call now.

Window treatments: Drapes and other window treatments are big dust collectors. Some of them can be vacuumed. If they haven't been cleaned in a couple years, now's the time.

Walls and ceilings: Two people, two buckets and two long-handled sponge mops are what you need to wash walls and ceilings. One person cleans, the other rinses. Use 2-ounces dry measure of TSP (Trisodium Phosphate) per gallon of warm water. If you are washing down the kitchen or there are smokers in the house, add 2-ounces of ammonia. This is strong stuff so wear goggles and rubber gloves. Start at the bottom and wash up to prevent watermarks.

Wood furniture: Spring's a good time to give it a deep cleaning and oiling. First, clean wax and gunk off wood furniture by giving it a bath all over with mineral spirits. Sponge on the mineral spirits full strength, and then wipe off with facial tissue. Do not use paper toweling. Let dry overnight, then top off with a coat of Doozy, (888) 851-8500. I suggest Doozy because it contains no wax and dries to a smudge-free protective finish.

Kitchen cabinets: Cabinets can usually be deep cleaned and shined by wiping them down with Doozy. If they have the "stickies," wash them down with a 2-ounce per gallon solution of Simple Green and water. Change rinse water every couple of cabinets.

Counter tops: Deep clean, polish and seal Corian, Gibraltar, Formica or Wilsonart counter tops with Hopes Counter Top Polish, (800) 325-4026.

Mattresses: Most mattresses are sagging and full of dust and dust mites. Strip off the sheets. Then vacuum, flip, and then vacuum the other side.

Refrigerator: The condenser coils need periodic cleaning to keep the appliance running efficiently. You will find long, slim condenser brushes at appliance, appliance repair and some hardware stores.

First, unplug the refrigerator and pull it away from the wall. Get your vacuum tool and get down on your hands and knees. Brush out the under part of the refrigerator (under the door) with the coil brush, and vacuum up the mess. Do the same thing in the back. Push the refrigerator back into place and plug it back in.

Dishwasher: Joe Gagnon, the Appliance Doctor, says this is best way to clean the dishwasher: Turn on the kitchen faucet until the water gets hot. Turn on the empty dishwasher and let it cycle for about 2 minutes. Stop the dishwasher and pour in an entire bottle of Tang. Close the door and let the dishwasher complete its cycle.

Garbage disposer: Most garbage disposers are dirtier than toilets. Sanitize the disposer in a minute with Scot Laboratories Foaming Disposer Cleaner, (800) 486-7268.

Standard maintenance items

Exterior windows: To clean dirty exterior glass, mix 1 level teaspoon of liquid hand dishwashing soap and 4-ounces of vinegar to a gallon of water. Fold a 100-percent cotton towel and put it on the sill. Sponge the cleaning solution onto the window, then squeegee off. Mop up the water with the towel.

Inside windows: Mix 1 level teaspoon of liquid dishwashing soap and 4-ounces of ammonia to a gallon of water. Repeat the outside procedure. Sponge on the solution, squeegee off, and wipe up drips with the cotton towel.

Sinks, showers, toilets: Clean stainless steel with Bar Keepers Friend. Clean porcelain, tile and shower doors with The Works Tub and Tile Cleaner or Scrubbing Bubbles. Banish mold and mildew with EnviroMagic Mildew Stain Remover. It contains no chlorine and is available locally at Dammans or check it out on the web at www.ccv-product.com.

Floors: Clean vinyl flooring and tiles with 2- to 3-ounces of a good organic cleaner like Simple Green or Clear Magic to a gallon of water. Rinse with a second bucket of clear water. Wash hardwood by spraying on an nonammoniated window cleaner and damp moping. Clean ceramic tile floor with KRC 7 by Chemique (856) 235-4161.

You're done. Brag about it!

MARCH 31,2001

Take precautions to avoid high heating bills that are on the horizon

By Glenn Haege /
Special to The Detroit News

The lights have been going out in California. Consumers are screaming about more than 40 percent increases in rates. On the East Coast and in the Midwest, heating oil and natural gas customers are being trounced by scarcity and rate increases. Now the wraps are coming off Michigan's three-year price freeze, and we are bracing to see how bad we are going to get hit and what we can do about it.

Although each power company's rate increases will begin at different times, we can assume they all will be fairly consistent in the final outcome. Consumers Power had their rate for natural gas frozen at $2.84 per Mcf (thousand cubic feet) that is 28.4 cents per ccf (hundred cubic feet) of natural gas. The company has asked the Michigan Public Service Commission for permission to raise the rate up to $5.69 Mcf.

According to the utility, the average Michigan home uses 120 Mcf of natural gas a year. That makes the pre-price rise cost $340.80, against a potential of price of $682.80. The company also says on their web site that the actual price increases will be only what is needed to cover market costs (and I assume some profit).

That doesn't sound too bad, but the Alliance to Save Energy, a Washington nonprofit coalition of business, industry and governmental leaders, says that the median household natural gas bill wasn't $340.80 but $1,626 in 1999. Nationally, the average residential natural gas bills went to $2,213 in 2000. The average heating bill in 2001 will be still higher.

I believe that the Alliance numbers are closer to the real world. To prove the point, Ronda Moss, a sports reporter at WXYT-AM (1270), just moved here from Chicago. She said that the previous winter's heating bills for her two-bedroom condo averaged $75 a month. This past winter, her bill rose to $235 per month, and the heat was turned down most of the time because she was moving to Detroit and had set back the thermostat.

Chicago and Detroit enjoy much the same weather. We can expect to pay approximately the same prices, except for state taxes. We can only dodge the bullet for so long. Our three-year energy price freeze is coming to an end. Sooner or later, prices are going up big time.

When that happens, a lot of people who are already stretched thin will not be able to absorb the price increases. I asked Fred Shell, spokesman for MichCon, what people could do to cut costs. He suggested going on a budget plan that equalizes payments throughout the year. That's fine if payment is just a budgeting problem but does nothing for people who are on fixed incomes and can't afford the extra money.

What can we do?

I am very worried about lower income people, retirees and others living on a relatively low fixed income. When we think about reducing energy costs, we not only have to think about our own homes, but the homes of those we love who will bear the brunt of the rate increases.

From a practical point of view, the only way to reduce energy costs is to reduce usage. That means making homes more energy efficient. You do this on existing homes by adding insulation and ventilation and installing programable thermostats.

This doesn't take brain surgery. Murray Gula of the Michigan Construction Protection Agency has prepared a 20-page brochure on the subject that he will mail you free if you send him your address and two first class stamps. Mail them to Stop the Energy Guzzler, MCPA, P.O. Box 1037, Royal Oak, MI 48068.

The Department of Energy and the many building materials manufacturers have been telling us what to do for years. The Department of Energy has many sites that will help you. One site, the Energy Efficiency and Renewable Energy Network (EREN), has a map of all 50 states and lists the total recommended R-Values for existing homes in each state differentiated by heating source (www.eren.doe.gov/consumerinfo/ener gysavers/r-valuemap.html). I listed the complete web page designation because the EREN site is very large and you could rattle around there for hours.

The Home Energy Saver site, hes.lbl.gov/HES, developed by the Lawrence Berkley National Laboratory, has an interactive personal energy program that takes you through a series of questions on your own house, then shows you how much your present house costs and how much you would save by making your house energy efficient.

Both sites are excellent and have reams of information. The important thing now is to learn all you can about what you need, then put together an action plan. The insulation companies are already doing a land office business. If you wait until fall, they probably won't be able to get around to you until next spring.

Next week's article will go into explaining the pros and cons of the different kinds of insulation. Learn all you can before you do, but start doing NOW!

Redecorated site

My staff and I have completely redesigned my web site, www.Mas terHandyman.com. We have a report on the energy crisis and now make it easy to instantly search all my Detroit News articles and most asked for phone numbers.

Attics and outside walls need most attention when insulating

By Glenn Haege /
Special to The Detroit News

Hopefully, last week's Homestyle article convinced you that the way to insulate yourself from increased energy costs is to add insulation to your home. Attics and walls, the two places where homes lose the most energy, are the subjects of today's question-and-answer column.

Q: *How much insulation does your house need?*
A: The Department of Energy has insulation recommendations for attics, walls, floors, crawl space, concrete slabs and the interior and exterior of basement walls.

If you live anywhere other than California, Hawaii and the southern tips of Texas, Louisiana and Florida, the insulation on the floor of the attic should have a value of R-49, a cathedral ceiling needs R-38, and walls should have R-18. People with electric heat should increase attic insulation to R-60 in the coldest states.

William Jean, director of site development for the city of Windsor, says that the insulation recommendation for Ontario is R-31 for attics and R-17 for walls.

No matter which side of the border you are on, the more insulation the better.

Q: *How much insulation does your house have now?*
A: Most of us have fiberglass insulation in the attic and little or no insulation in the walls. Older U.S. houses have R-9 or less. Many Canadian homes were built before they had insulation requirements. To compute how much insulation your house has, go up to the attic with a ruler. If the insulation is 3 inches thick, the R-Value is roughly R-9. If it's 6 inches, R-19; 10 inches, R-30; and 13 inches, R-42.

Q: *What are the insulation choices?*
A: The standard insulation materials for ceilings and walls are loose or batt fiberglass insulation and loose cellulose insulation. Icynene and other foams are efficient but costly. Rock wool or slag wool insulation is available but seldom used.

Fiberglass batts are the most popular way to add insulation to attics because they are easy to use and add a pre-determined R-value. For example, Owens Corning, (800) GET- PINK, offers 61/4-inch-thick R-19 batts; 9-1/2-inch-thick R-30 batts, and special Miraflex 8-3/4-inch-thick R-25 batts. If you wanted to increase the R-value of your attic insulation by R-38, you could just lay down two R-19 batts.

Batts come faced or unfaced. Faced batts have craft paper on one side, which acts as a vapor barrier. Unfaced batts do not have the craft paper. Unfaced batts are recommended for attics. If you use faced batts in the attic, lay the batt paper side down.

Some batts also come in perforated poly wrap. This makes the batts easier to use and more expensive but does nothing to increase R-value or act as a vapor barrier.

Loose fiberglass and loose cellulose come in bags and can be poured out on the attic floor to the desired depth or poured down into wall cavities.

Both these products are usually blown into the attic by insulation contractors or sprayed into wall cavities. Cellulose for walls and cellulose for attics have different densities. Cellulose for attics has a density of 1.5 pounds per cubic foot. Cellulose sprayed into walls has a density of 3 to 4 pounds per cubic foot. The increased density prevents settling. Sprayed fiberglass and cellulose take a high level of skill on the part of the installer but give a superior job.

Q: *Which is best?*
A: I consider fiberglass and cellulose equal. Cellulose insulation is said to hold its R-value longer and do a better job of sealing out drafts than fiberglass. The Oakridge National Laboratory has recommended topping loose fiberglass insulation with 3 inches of cellulose to retain the longevity of the R-value. I asked David T. Brown, chief operating officer of Owens Corning, about this. He said that topping fiberglass was unnecessary.

Q: *Where can I find more information?*
A: Michigan is the home of two major cellulose insulation manufacturers. Nu-Wool, headquartered in Jenison – (800) 748-0128; web site, www.nuwool.com – does a good job explaining the added value of cellulose insulation. The company will actually guarantee the savings their insulation will make on energy bills.

Applegate Insulation, (800) 627-7536, is headquartered in Webberville, MI. Their web site, www.applegateinsulation.com, does a very good job reporting on the cellulose vs. fiberglass R-value controversy.

The two best American fiberglass insulation web sites are Certainteed, (800) 233-8990, www.certainteed.com; and Owens Corning, (800) 438-7465, www.owenscorning.com. Certainteed's animated attic solutions page, www.certainteed.com/solutions/attic/index.html, gives excellent explanations of roof ice damming, condensation and moisture problems and solutions.

Some local names for cellulose insulation are Dana Energy Savers (Nu-Wool), (800) 757-3262, and Sunshine (Applegate), (888) 749-8656; for fiberglass, call Macomb Insulation (Owens Corning), (586) 949-1400, or Whitson Insulation (Certainteed), (248) 362-2900.

The Residential Energy Efficiency Database, www.its-canada.com/reed, is an excellent disinterested third party site. It was created by three very energy- and environment-conscious individuals, Brian and Mary Mitchell and Martin Ryder, and has a wealth of information on every type of insulation and provides a step-by-step installation guide. (**Sorry, this fine web site did not get the support it deserved and went out of business.**)

When you add insulation, remember that the national energy code calls for added ventilation. This is called the 'cold roof' theory and I recommend it. Not everyone agrees. Next month, my web site, www.masterhandyman.com, will add information on both the solid roof and the cold roof insulation theories, as well as show the best way to insulate a storage attic, to our Energy Crisis Report.

Learn all you can before you do, but start doing now.

Quickly reshape your personal living space and save your aching back

By Glenn Haege /
Special to The Detroit News

How are you fixed for wheels? This is not about a tire recall. I want to know how in-tune you are with the rolling stock that can make life easier. No matter how hard you work to keep in shape, bending, stretching, reaching or lifting becomes more difficult and dangerous with each passing year.

In Short-cuts to Storage, (New Holland Publishers (UK) Ltd., London), British design writer, Annemarie Meintjes, recommends: "Mount it on wheels. Move it in, out and about. . . . Fix wheels to every possible earthbound design in your home and you'll be able to shape and reshape your personal space."

I agree. So do a lot of manufacturers. To get an idea of what's out there to help you save your aching back, we toured Sam's Club, Costco, Home Depot, Meijer, Office Depot and English Gardens.

Organization made easy

I've had it with cheap, ugly metal and plastic shelving. Costco has Seville Classics, (800) 323-5565, chrome plated, wheeled storage shelving for $69.99. The shelving looks so good that we are using some in the office, but it is economical enough to use in the basement or garage. Each unit is 4 feet wide by 1 1/2-feet deep and 6 feet high. Each shelf holds 300 pounds.

The same parts can also make a 2-shelf wheeled cart for moving heavy objects and a stationary 2-level shelf. Two of the four wheels lock. This shelving is great for organizing, or use the 2-shelf cart for moving heavy items out of the way.

Sam's Club has a 2-shelf, 31 1/2-inch wide and 35-inch high storage cart by the same manufacturer for $49.97.

Office Depot's 2001 catalogue, (888) 463-3768, lists a heavy-duty cabinet dolly for $59.99. The steel dolly has 4 rugged swivel casters, is rated for 1,000 pounds and fits any 2-shelf or 4-shelf 18-inch by 36-inch steel cabinet. The companion steel storage cabinets cost $139.99 for the adjustable 2-shelf and $179 for the adjustable 4-shelf cabinets. The cabinets are lockable so you have complete storage flexibility and security. These are not just catalogue items. I've seen them on display at many Office Depot locations.

Moving heavy items

Meijer has a Gleason, (800) 520-6335, 19-inch wide by 29-inch deep 4-wheel steel platform cart. It makes moving heavy objects up to 330 pounds a snap. The Gleason platform cart is built very low to the ground for maximum stability and has a folding handle for easy storage.

Lugging buckets

Spring cleaning just got easier. Armorall designed their 4-wheel Wash Caddy for washing the family car, but it can be a great help for any cleaning job that takes wash and rinse water. The price is $29.98 at Sam's Club. The Wash Caddy has two, 2-gallon pails, a seat and a pull rope, plus a sponge and a cleaning brush.

Gardening made easier

Ames True Temper tools, (800) 393-1846, is famous for their shovels but many of their new products are heavy-duty plastic designed to take the strain out of gardening. The 26-inch by 38-inch 4-wheel Planters Wagon came out a couple of years ago but most people haven't discovered it yet. It has a 13-inch by 31-inch hauling bed for bags of seed or soil, tool clips on each side store rakes, hoes or shovels, a covered tool compartment and five uncovered compartments for plants, drinks or what-ever. The back of the hauling bed pulls out so you can just tip up the wagon to unload.

Each of the four wheels rotates a full 360 degrees so the Planters Wagon is highly maneuverable. The handle folds back and becomes a bench seat. The price tag is $54.93 at Meijer.

A half-sized version called the Lawn Buddy is available at Home Depot ($29.70) and English Gardens ($32.99).

Every garden department has hose carts, but Home Depot has a 4-wheel, heavy-duty steel cart for the serious gardener. It stores 250 feet of hose and costs $79.97.

Sooner or later you have to get down on your knees and actually do something. Once completed, you have the even more serious chore of getting up again. If you read this and laugh, just wait: it only takes a few more years and a touch of arthritis to learn more than you'd ever want to know about sore joints and achy muscles.

I saw the Step 2, (800) 347-8372, Easy-Up Kneeler Seat at Home Depot for $19.97. Right side up it is a gardening stool you can sit on for pruning, etc. Upside down, it is a padded kneeler you can use when you're digging, transplant-ing and cultivating. When the job is done and it's time to (oh, my aching knees) get up, the kneeler handles give you the extra support that makes getting up easy.

If you have to get down on your knees for serious work, like staining a deck or shingling, the unique design of Fiskars, (800) 289-8288, Bucket Boss Air-Gel Knee Pads takes the weight off your knees and spreads it to the shin, eliminating knee joint strain. The inner micro-cell pad keeps the knees dry. My publisher at Master Handyman Press, used the knee pads while doing a major project and he won't stop bragging about them. They are $47.97 at Amazon.com tools Section but worth every dime if you have a major project.

Experts spill the paint on how to add a bit of color to boring concrete

By Glenn Haege /
Special to The Detroit News

Concrete can be boring. Adding color can add a little bit of interest to all those hunks and chunks of concrete we see around the house. Tinting concrete before it is poured is easy. Just add Quikrete Concrete Color Additives from Gibraltar, (800) 442-7258, to the mix.

Adding color to existing slabs is harder. Depending on the application, four different products can be used: concrete stain, epoxy paint, or latex or oil-based porch and floor paint. I often suggest staining because it is relatively inexpensive and lasts longer than old-fashioned floor paints.

Not everyone agrees. Staining concrete is not like staining wood. A great deal of preparation is required. If you don't do one thing right, the job can end in disaster. But if everything goes right, you will have a job that will add beauty to your property for years.

Large masses of horizontal concrete are found in the garage and basement floors, sidewalks and paths, and patios. Each area has different requirements.

I asked three different paint retailers for their recommendations. I quizzed retailers rather than painters because a good retailer knows not only what is possible, but also what you and I are capable of doing, and what is going to make us happy.

Tim Eisbrenner from Shelby Paint,(586) 739-0240, was very blunt. "I don't usually recommend a concrete stain to a do-it-yourselfer. The cleaning, acid bath, rinsing and neutralizing that are often required is too much work for someone trying to do a project on the weekend. Most people want to pop open the can and start staining. You can't do that with concrete. I have too much respect for my customer to set him up for failure."

Garage floors: Many homeowners want to do something to make the garage floor more attractive and protect it from stains and skid marks. Neither, Eisbrenner nor John Longstreet from Damman Hardware thinks staining garage floors is a good idea. Longstreet recommends using Epoxi Shield epoxy paint. Eisbrenner recommends using latex or alkyd (oil based) porch and floor paint.

"A latex paint will last about three years on the garage floor. A top-of-the-line Alkyd, like Benjamin Moore Alkyd Porch and Floor Enamel, can easily give 10 years of service. If either starts coming off, just repaint the affected area," Eisbrenner says.

Jamie Winfield from Pontiac Paint, (248) 332-4643, recommends Coronado Final Finish or Porter Color Seal. "Coronado is an excellent professional stain, but only comes in a limited number of colors and cannot be tinted. Porter Color Seal can be tinted in a wide rage of colors," she says.

Benjamin Moore is one of America's leading paint companies. Porter Color Seal is an excellent old-line concrete stain. Epoxi Shield is a top-notch concrete epoxy paint that I have recommended for years. Originally invented in Madison Heights, it has now been sold to Rust-Oleum, (800) 323-3584, www.rust-oleum.

Sidewalks and paths: Eisbrenner recommends H & C Concrete Stain. "Older sidewalks are so worn they don't need to be etched, just cleaned thoroughly before staining," he says.

H & C Concrete Stain is probably the best-known product of its type in the country. The company offers exhaustive, step by step directions for surface preparation, etching and staining on their web site, www.concretestain.com.

Longstreet recommends Super Deck Mason Select, (800) 825-5382, www.superdeck.com. This stain was developed a few years ago and uses the latest technology to create an extremely versatile product. A trip to their web site can give you some very exciting outdoor faux finish design ideas.

Winfield recommends Coronado Anti Skid Step Saver because the product's formulation adds traction. Coronado Paints and Stains are high quality professional products that give excellent results if you follow directions carefully.

Patios: All three experts recommend stains. Eisbrenner recommends H & C or Benjamin Moore Concrete Stain. Longstreet prefers Mason Select by Super Deck. Winfield's choice is Porter Color Seal.

Basements: Eisbrenner recommends using a Latex floor paint or Benjamin Moore Alkyd Porch & Floor Enamel. Longstreet suggests H & C Basement Stain or Epoxi Shield Basement Paint. Winfield prefers using any good latex floor paint.

"I don't believe in recommending concrete stain inside a house. Some concrete stains are Xylene-based and require an acid bath. Application can be dangerous. The smell is terrible and it permeates the entire house," she says.

Adding color to concrete can add a great deal of beauty, but you have to do it right. Learn all you can before you do. Follow directions to the letter and you will be able to brag about the result for a long, long time.

Concrete Paint & Stain Chart on next page.

APRIL 28, 2001

How to keep your cool when shopping for central air conditioning

By Glenn Haege /
Special to The Detroit News

Ah, spring! The grass is growing. The crocuses are in bloom. The birds are singing. The buds on trees are beginning to burst into new life.

Enjoy it while you can. In a few short weeks summer will be here and it well may be a scorcher.

Which brings us to the topic of today's column. Most of us can no longer get along without central air conditioning. Even those with window units count the days until they can convert to central air.

The Air-Conditioning & Refrigeration Institute says that the average air conditioner only lasts for about 13 years. Chances are that if you are not now in the market for an air conditioner, you will be within the next few years.

This week's article will give basic need-to-know information on central air conditioning. Next week, I will review some of the features on the newest models to help you make the buying decision.

A central air conditioning system consists of an indoor and an outdoor unit. In the industry, the outside is called the hot side. The inside components are the cold side.

The hot side consists of a metal box called the condenser that includes a condensing coil, a compressor and a fan.

The most important feature of the cold side is the evaporator coil, which is usually located inside the furnace. The furnace blows hot air from inside the home through the evaporator coil, cooling the air. The cooled air is then routed throughout the home, via the air ducts.

As the inside air is chilled, the refrigerant inside the evaporator coil is heated. The heated refrigerant is cycled to the hot side unit where it is cooled and compressed, then recycled indoors to cool more hot air.

The effectiveness of the central air conditioning system is rated by its SEER, or Seasonal Energy Efficiency Rating. The higher the rating, the more efficient the unit. The Department of Energy presently mandates a minimum of 10.0 SEER.

Before a contractor can make an intelligent quote on your air conditioning, he has to perform a Heat Load Study. Among other things, the Heat Load Study considers the size of your house, the amount of roof and wall insulation, number and size of windows, as well as the direction they face, the color of your home's roof shingles, your cooling requirements by time of day, and the number and type of trees giving shade and/or providing wind blocks.

You also have to tell the contractor how cool you want the house on a 95-degree Fahrenheit afternoon; where the hottest rooms in the house are located; whether it is important to have the upstairs bedrooms cool in the afternoon or if they just have to be cool in the evening.

When all this information is turned into numerical values, a simple calculation gives the contractor the information he needs to properly size your home's air conditioning.

Don't trust a contractor or salesperson who just wants to base his quote on your present unit. The average central air conditioner is 47 percent more efficient than a system that is 20 years old. On top of that, you may have re-roofed, added insulation, upgraded your windows, or at the very least, the trees have grown or died and been cleared away.

After the Heat Load Study, the contractor will probably present you with a selection of 10, 12, 13 or 14 SEER systems. At first blush, it would seem that the more efficient the system, the better – a 14 SEER system has to be better than a 12, and a 12 SEER should be better than a 10, right? But according to industry experts, more efficient is not necessarily better.

During the Clinton administration, the energy department called for an increase in the minimum SEER rating from 10 to 13 by 2006. The Bush administration just lowered the mandate down to a 12 SEER rating for central air conditioning.

Even a 12 SEER central air conditioning system may not be the best choice for most of us. The Department of Energy's own Life Cycle Cost analysis points out that 73 percent of consumers nationwide will not benefit from increasing the SEER level on air conditioning to 12. Eighty percent of the people on low or fixed incomes will not benefit from the new ratings. "Will not benefit from" is governmental legalese for "will be hurt by."

I asked Mike Shorkey of Detroit Safety Furnace, (800) 682-1538, one of the oldest and most reliable heating and cooling distributors in the Midwest, what the benefit of raising ratings from 10 to 12 SEER will be for residents of Michigan and other cool climates. Shorkey does not believe there is any consumer benefit for most of us.

The energy department says that the consumer should be able to recoup the difference in cost of a SEER 12 air conditioning system over a 10 SEER system in less than three years. According to figures the Air-Conditioning & Refrigeration Institute submitted to the government last December, the payback period will actually be between 9 and 14 years. Ouch!

As always, it pays to get all the facts before you make a buying decision.

Information can help consumers make right central air choice

By Glenn Haege /
Special to The Detroit News

Ruud Air Conditioning DivisionAnatomy of a quality Central Air Conditioning unit: 1. heavy duty steel cabinet; 2. fan; 3. wraparound outdoor coil; 4. base that lifts unit above slab for quick drainage; 5. scroll compressor; 6. protective high and low pressure controls to shut off compressor if it overheats or refrigerant level drops; 7. easy service access; 8. (not shown) matching furnace mounted air cooling coil.

Many Metro Detroiters are likely thinking about air conditioning after this week's summerlike temperatures.

Last week, I gave basic information on central air conditioning. This week, I will review some of the features on the newest models to help readers make the best buying decision.

Efficiency

Air conditioning and heat pump equipment are now given a Seasonal Energy Efficiency Rating (SEER) by the Air-Conditioning Rating Institute (ARI). The SEER rating projects the unit's operating efficiency over an entire cooling season. The lowest rated central air conditioner is a 10 SEER. By 2006, the threshold will be a SEER 12.

You get the most bang for the buck with a SEER 10 rated unit. The DOE (U.S. Department of Energy) says that you can save enough on energy costs to cover the increased price of a SEER 12 rated air conditioner in just 3 1/2 years.

The payback estimate is based on a seasonal average of 1,500 cooling hours. In Michigan and most northern tier states, we average 600 cooling hours. Our payback period is 2.5 times longer than the national average.

If you lived in the southern tip of Florida you would average 2,800 cooling hours. It would only take about half the national average time to start saving with a more efficient air conditioner.

Jim Williams of Williams Refrigeration, (888) 268-5445, says that the average Detroiter will only save $20 or $30 a year with a SEER 12 unit. Savings would increase if electric rates go up.

Refrigerant

Most air conditioners use a refrigerant called R-22. This refrigerant will not be manufactured after 2020. A new refrigerant called R-410A will take its place. Current trade names of R-410A are Puron by Bryant, Prozone by Ruud, Environ by Lennox and Genetron AZ-20 by Allied Signal Inc.

R-410A is more environmentally friendly than R-22 but many air conditioning experts, including Williams and Mike Shorkey of Detroit Safety Furnace, (800) 682-1538, do not believe the systems are perfected enough to recommend them.

On the pro side, the new refrigerant has no chlorine, which is better for the atmosphere. On the good/bad side, the operating pressure of an R-410A compressor is 50 percent higher than conventional models. This requires increased sound insulation resulting in a quieter compressor.

On the con side, an R-410A system is highly susceptible to moisture damage. According to Williams, once moisture gets into the system it is almost impossible to get out. "The recommended fix has gone from repair to replace," Williams said.

Shorkey agrees. "If you buy one of the new systems you better love your installation contractor or pray that nothing goes wrong. Only a few contractors and technicians are licensed to work with R-410A. When something goes wrong on a hot day, there will be almost no one else to call if your contractor is busy."

I should point out that Williams is a big Lennox dealer and Shorkey is a major Ruud distributor. Both sell R-22 and R-410A systems. They are costing themselves business by warning against the new system.

Trane Co., (888) 872-6335, the manufacturer of the 18.0 SEER XL 1800, the most efficient air conditioner on the market, devotes a page on their web site, (www.trane.com), explaining why they are sticking with R-22.

Scroll type compressors

Most air conditioners use noisy piston-type compressors. The Copeland Co. has developed a revolutionary scroll technology that is quieter, more efficient and longer-lived than piston compressors. Scroll compressors are now included in most air conditioning manufacturers' top-of-the-line units. The Rheem and Ruud companies put them on all residential air conditioners.

Two-speed motors

Air conditioners can have one or two speeds. Single-speed motors create a draft that pushes cold air through the ductwork at a high rate of speed. Two-speed air conditioners use a lower speed the majority of the time to create a more comfortable airflow, cut the fluctuation in room temperature and reduce humidity. Two speed motors are worth the extra money.

One final word. Most central air conditioning systems are composed of an external compressor unit and a furnace mounted coil. These two pieces can be purchased separately and some contractors oversize one or the other trying to "fine tune" the system for greater efficiency. Both Williams and Shorkey warn that the new systems are so finely engineered that you may burn out the compressor by not using the exact coil specified.

Choices

Here's a quick scan of air conditioning brands.

■ Bryant, (800) 428-4326. Efficiency ratings from 10 to 16.5 SEER, big proponent of R-410A, some 2-speed fans, piston and scroll compressors. Contractors include Flame, (888) 234-2340; Bergstroms, (734) 522-1350; Royal Oak Heating and Cooling, (248) 644-0123.

■ Carrier, (800) 227-7437. Efficiency ratings from 10 to 18 SEER, big proponent of R-410A, some 2-speed and variable speed fans, Sound Silencer technology. Contractors include: Lizut Heating and Cooling, (248) 858-7730; H. A. Sun Heating and Cooling, (248) 335-4555; and Parent Heating and Cooling, (248) 616-9980.

■ Lennox, (972) 497-5000. Efficiency ratings from 11 to 15.75 SEER, R-22 and R-410A units, direct drive fans, piston and scroll compressors. Contractors include: Williams Refrigeration, (888) 268-5445; Hinson Heating, (248) 541-7007; Aladdin, (586) 758-5900.

■ Ruud/Rheem, (800) 548-7433. Efficiency ratings from 10 to 14 Seer, R-22 and R-410A, 1 and 2 speed fans, all scroll compressors. Ruud: Detroit Safety Furnace, (800) 682-1538; Rheem: Williams Refrigeration, (888) 268-5445.

■ Trane, (888) 872-6335. Efficiency ratings from 10 to 18 SEER, R-22 refrigerant only, 1 and 2 speed fans, piston and scroll compressors. Contractors include: Air Master, (248) 399-1800; Crown, (313) 534-1200; Reckinger, (313) 562-5656; and Sears.

Laminates can floor you with their good looks, affordability

By Glenn Haege /
Special to The Detroit News

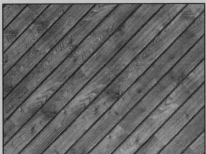

Karndean International
This ship's decking design was created with Indian Teak plank laminate, offset with a design strip between each plank. In real wood, this would be very time consuming and expensive. With laminate, it's easy.

Karndean International
It is very easy to customize laminated flooring. This Karndean International blue stained wood plank design is offset with oak-look design strips. The company makes over 40 different feature and design strips plus a wide selection of borders that look like they were made from wood, marble and tile.

"Should I or shouldn't I buy laminate flooring?" "Is laminate as good as wood?" "How long will it last?" "Will I be happy with it?"

When I get questions like this in Metro Detroit, I tell the person to go have a cup of coffee at the Mudee Waters Coffee Shop (sorry, out of business). At Mudee Waters, you see a large expanse of sort of, almost, looks like wood. You walk in and hear the distinctive, slightly hollow, clip clop of footsteps on laminate. You see where the sun has caused fading. You can also get a great cup of coffee.

The laminated surface looks good. It stands up to traffic and is easy to clean with a damp mop. Perfect.

But not for everyone. Retailers keep telling me horror stories about customers

who buy laminate, then have it yanked out because they can't live with it.

So what gives?

To find out, I went to Dick Walters, owner of Erickson Flooring and Supply Co. His company, headquartered in Ferndale, (800) 225-9663, has offices in Grand Rapids, Chicago and Indianapolis. The organization is nationally known for prefinished and unfinished hardwood, but also distributes very high quality European laminated flooring.

"Real wood, ceramic tile or stone are lifetime commitments. Once installed, they are a permanent feature and you work with them and around them when you re-decorate," Walters says.

"Laminated flooring is like a coat of paint. You use it to make a statement. If

Laminated flooring can look like anything. Dick Walters, owner of Erickson Flooring and Supply Company, is shown here holding a piece of textured laminated Karndean International laminate that looks like weathered tile. The display behind him shows laminated flooring samples that look like wood, granite, marble and ceramic tile.

you don't like the color of your walls, you put on another coat of paint. If you change your mind about the look of laminated flooring, you tear it out and put in something new."

Laminated flooring is really a big photograph you can walk on. A picture of a forest, mountain, lake or flower garden can be beautiful, but it is not a forest, mountain, lake or flower garden. Just as long as you are OK with that distinction and do not expect the picture to be what it's not, you will not be disappointed.

"All the laminated flooring in the world is made with photographs shot by Meade Paper," Walters says. "They bond the photograph to a piece of backing, and cover it with silicone carbide. The silicone carbide is called by different names and comes in different thicknesses. Expensive laminates have thicker coats of silicone carbide."

Since all the pictures and protective coating are much the same, Walters believes the biggest difference in laminated flooring is the backing. "Some backings are cheap, some are scientifically engineered wood, some are covered with a plastic undercoat to protect against moisture," he says.

The best time to use laminated flooring is when you want the look of wood, ceramic tile or stone, but for some reason do not want to use the real thing.

"A young couple moving into a new home really may want hardwood floors in the family room or stone in the foyer, but be strapped for cash. With a quality laminate, they can have the look without the price tag. When finances change, they can pull out the laminate and install the real thing. If they have kids and decide they would rather sink their savings into college funds than flooring, the laminated flooring will look beautiful for a long, long time," Walters says.

Laminated flooring is also an excellent choice if you want flooring that compliments a particular interior design, says Walters. "Say for some reason you

want blue-stained pine flooring. I would never recommend that you actually stain pine blue, but they make it in laminate. If you want it, buy it. When the fad changes, tear it out and put in something new."

Manufacturers stress how easy the new "click in," no glue floating laminate flooring is to install. Do-It-Yourselfers can find step-by-step installation guides on many web sites including Armstrong, www.armstrong.com; Bruce, www.brucelaminatefloors.com; and Witex, www.witexusa.com.

Laminated flooring is also easy to keep clean. When asked how to deep clean a laminated floor, Walters tells customers that no deep cleaning is required.

"The trick is to vacuum often and pick up any loose grit that gets tracked into the house. Once the grit is gone, damp mop and the surface is perfectly clean. If you have a party coming up and want the floor to shine, buff it," Walters says.

Mrs. Handyman tells me that the new wet Swifter pads available at most supermarkets also work like a charm.

Whether you will be happy with laminated flooring depends on what you are looking for. If you want the real thing, nothing but the real thing will make you happy. If you're looking for flooring that can look like anything you want it to be, is relatively inexpensive, simple to install and easy to care for, laminate could be an excellent choice for your next floor.

Eon decks cost more, but you save big bucks in the long run

By Glenn Haege /
Special to The Detroit News

News Flash: There may finally be a cure for "deck care dementia."

Most people buy a deck thinking they are getting a beautiful, wood-hued outdoor room. They imagine barbecue parties, early morning coffee while watching the sun come up and romantic evenings watching the stars.

What they get is a never-ending cycle of cleaning, stripping, brightening and staining. Not only is this a lot of work, deck maintenance can easily cost hundreds of dollars a year.

It's enough to drive most homeowners a little bit crazy, which is why I call it deck care dementia. In fact, this is the biggest source of questions on my summer Ask the Handyman radio shows. The need for reliable deck care information is so great I have my entire deck care book posted on my web site, www.MasterHandyman.com, so people can download it free.

Unfortunately, there is nothing you can paint, spray or nail on an existing deck that will make it maintenance-free and still look like a wooden deck.

The good news is that if you are just building a deck, there is now a product that looks like wood, that they say will never gray, fade or splinter, and should last as long as your house. It's called eon and is made by CPI Plastics of Mississauga, Ontario, Canada. The only bad thing about it, is the price.

The new eon decking material by CPI Plastics looks like wood but never grays, fades or splinters. Its easy-to-use screw-based fastening system eliminates nails.

Brad Upton of Dillman and Upton, (248) 651-9411, told me that when he tells people that eon is four times the price of cedar decking on a square foot basis, they are shocked. "But when they consider the advantages, they buy," Upton says.

To judge the product, look at the alternatives.

People expect decks to look beautiful forever. They don't. Once you build a wooden deck, you have to choose between constant maintenance or watching your investment turn gray, split, splinter and gradually disintegrate.

There are excellent cleaner/brighteners on the market like Bio-Wash Wood Wash, Superdeck Wood Brightener, Cabot Stains Problem Solver, Wolman Deck & Fence Brightener and Penofin Weatherblaster. All have the ability to return a gray deck back to its original color; but unless you stain that deck it will just turn gray again.

There are top-of-the-line stains and sealers like Penofin Ultra, Wolman Extreme, and Flood CWF-UV. They protect and beautify the wood, but the protection only lasts 18- to 24-months on a horizontal surface. After that, the old stain and seal coat has to be removed, the wood has to be cleaned and brightened and a new coat of stain has to be applied.

All these products require hours of hard, sweaty work. Even if you have the money to hire it done, finding someone decent to do the job can be as time-consuming as doing it yourself.

To get around the problem, Anchor Decking Systems, (888) 898-4990, came out with the Durable Deck. Durable Deck vinyl strips fasten directly over existing deck boards eliminating the need to stain or seal the deck forever. It also makes your deck look like it is covered with pieces of plastic.

Composite-decking materials such as TimberTech, (800) 307-7780; Smart Deck, (888) 7DECKING; and TREX, (800) 289-8739, give a more woodlike appearance. These composite materials don't rot and are much longer lasting than wood, but they all turn gray. Penofin, (800) 736-6346, www.PENOFIN.com, is the only coatings manufacturer that creates a stain exclusively for these products.

Each of these products costs as much or more than cedar, but they either don't look like wood or gray worse than the real thing.

Blair of trumpets! Enter eon.

CPI Plastic's new product is a thermoplastic material manufactured from virgin or recycled plastic. The top of an eon deck plank looks like it could be stained hardwood. It is impervious to weather, insects, rot, water and will not splinter, crack or fade. The reason it doesn't fade is because UV inhibitors are a part of its chemical composition and it is the same color throughout.

While eon looks and feels like wood, its real beauty is that the only maintenance needed is an occasional rinsing with a garden hose.

"When you consider that it costs at least $2 a square foot to have a deck professionally cleaned, striped and restained, and that expense is repeated every couple of years, eon pays for itself within five years. After that, it just keeps saving you money," Upton said.

Dillman and Upton has an eon decking display at the Rochester store and has already sold half a truckload of the product. Distributed by H.A. Davidson Lumber, (800) 543-0469, eon is currently sold at 48 lumber yards and home centers throughout Michigan. The manufacturer's web site, www.eonoutdoor.com, lists distributors and retailers throughout the US and Canada.

If you're building a new deck, there is no longer a reason to spend time cleaning, brightening, stripping and staining, unless that is what you really want to do. Like the ladies in the hair coloring commercials say, eon "may cost a little more but you're worth it."

MAY 26, 2001

Enjoy Memorial Day, lest we forget those who make it special

By Glenn Haege /
Special to The Detroit News

It's the Memorial Day Weekend. Most of us are fulfilling our patriotic duty and either have gotten out of town for a long weekend or have a barbecue in the back yard planned. A few of us will round up the kids and go see the VFW, Brownies, Indian Guides, Boy and Girl Scouts and the local swim and soccer teams march down Main Street.

Most of the kids will have no idea what the parade is supposed to commemorate. Maybe that's a good thing.

All of our younger children have been blessed with comparative peace for the length of their lives. That peace, the fact that our kids have grown up without even having to grasp the concept of war, is the real memorial to those who gave the ultimate sacrifice.

If you want an idea of the majesty of this memorial, ask the kids who are dying daily in Israel or the Gaza strip, or lost a leg to a land mine in Ethiopia, Macedonia and a hundred other of the world's trouble spots.

Lasting peace is the greatest monument a warrior could ever have.

Since no other memorial can compare to this, why don't we use Monday to celebrate all the people still living who make a major impact on our lives?

Some – like police or firemen – carry guns or charge into burning buildings, but most do not. Heroism does not have to be of epic proportions. When a hero does a job, he or she does it right, on time, and with a smile. They do this despite the fact that many of their peers are doing sloppy jobs, may not show up, and when they do get to work, act as if they are doing the world a favor. You may be surrounded by these no-account peers. If you are, don't give in.

Who, exactly, are the heroes I want to memorialize?

Try the post person who delivers your mail and sometimes checks to see if older folks on their route are OK, or the person who delivers your newspaper everyday, on time, and bags it properly if it is raining.

I'd like to propose a medal for the McDonald's drive-in person who gets my entire order right, fast, the first time. Same thing for the service tech and mechanic who get my car fixed right the first time I take the car to the dealership.

The teacher who doesn't just get the kids through the day, but inspires them with the romance of numbers, history, geography and sciences, deserves a presidential citation.

Who wouldn't want to hang a medal around the neck of the home improvement contractor who gets the job done right, on time, and within budget, or the builder who answers all of your questions and builds a quality code-plus home, not just a drywalled box that fulfills minimum standards.

How about the guy or gal who, despite cutbacks, layoffs and pressures at home, make each project the best it can be? How about the dental technician who goes the extra mile cleaning your teeth or the nurse who makes you laugh as she gives you a vaccination so expertly that it really doesn't hurt all that much.

This is not a Labor Day tribute. I want to see outstanding individual effort applauded. People who make whatever they do in life a profession because they do it in a professional way deserve to be memorialized.

I know a couple of small companies staffed by these kinds of people. They don't think they are anything special. I know they are.

In another place and another time, dispatches would say that these same people had "wiped out a machine gun nest single-handed" or, though wounded, had "overcome tremendous odds fighting to protect the rest of their platoon."

The heroes of everyday life are my kind of heroes. In 1919 and 1944, they fought and died in France. Since then, they have fought and died in Korea and Vietnam, in Desert Storm and probably in many other places the government has never told us about.

Right now, some of them are helping to hold a fragile peace in Yugoslavia. Others may be flying off the coast of China or over the mountains in Columbia. But you will also see them closer to home. They're on the line at Ford and solving computer problems on the Internet. Whatever the task life allots them, they get in, get the job done and go about their business.

If you think about it, I bet these people are your kind of heroes too. Who knows? When you looked in the mirror this morning you might even have seen one of the people I'm talking about. If you did, I salute you. You make the world a better place just by being here.

The government may never get around to sending you your medal, but when you wake up this Memorial Day, be proud.

Relax and enjoy your day. You've earned it. We'll get back to home improvement next week.

Cleaning an unfinished deck is different from cleaning a stained or sealed deck

By Glenn Haege /
Special to The Detroit News

We can't put it off any longer. It is time to get out and get the job done. This is D-Day for decks.

Over the past couple of years, there has been a great deal of misinformation published about deck cleaning. Most recently, a press release from the U.S. Department of Agriculture suggested that the best product to use to clean decks was a mixture of one part household chlorine bleach, a little laundry detergent and three parts water.

The only thing good about this combination is that it is cheap. Even if you don't mind the way chlorine mangles wood fibers, the laundry detergent acts as a surfactant, causing the ground and greenery to absorb more chlorine. This is not good unless your purpose is to kill the plant life around your deck.

A few years ago, my staff and I tested cleaners, brighteners and strippers in side-by-side competitions to see which were the most effective. Most of the work was done by my publisher and my long suffering daughter, Heather, who decided she never wanted to ask her dad for a summer job again.

In order to determine the most effective product, it is necessary to define what you want done. Cleaning an unfinished deck is different from cleaning a stained or sealed deck. Cleaning a cedar, red-wood or mahogany deck requires different products than cleaning a pressure treated pine deck. Let's define our terms.

Cleaning: The removal of dirt; it does not remove gray from wood or return it to its original look.

Brightening: It will remove the gray and returns an unfinished wood deck to approximately its original condition. Brightening agents can gray redwood, mahogany and most hardwoods.

A brightener cannot remove a stain or sealer, but it will make the finish very unattractive.

Stripping: It removes a stain or sealer from the wood. A weathered deck that has been sealed or stained must be stripped, then cleaned and brightened, before it can be restained.

Cleaning

If you want to clean the dirt off a deck and live in a state that still allows TSP (trisodium phosphate), use it. Four ounces of TSP in a gallon of water was the hands down winner in our testing. Simple Green (mixed at 1/2 gallon of product per gallon of water) and Flood Dekswood (mixed at 1 quart per gallon of water) tied for second place.

Bio-Wash Simple Wash (mixed at 1/2 gallon of product per 1/2 gallon of water) came next because it costs more than double the Flood and Simple Green products.

Laundry detergent, mixed at 2 pounds of detergent per gallon of water, was dead last. By the way, we didn't start at 2 pounds of detergent per gallon of water. We started with just a few ounces and kept steadily increasing the mix until we got something that would move the dirt.

TSP is a great cleaner, but it can turn redwood and mahogany brown. Use Simple Green, Flood Dekswood or Bio-Wash Simple Wash for these woods.

Brightening

If your deck is dirty and gray, and has not been coated, use a deck brightener. You need something like Oxalic acid to remove the top layer of dead gray cells. Some good products are Bio-Wash Wood Wash, Behr Wood Cleaner Brightener Conditioner, Cabot Stains Problem Solver, Flood Dekswood, Natural Wood Brightener, Penofin Weatherblaster, Superdeck Deckdoctor, Timberseal Rescue and Wolman Deck & Fence Brightener.

These products work well on all pressure treated decks. If you have cedar or redwood, brightening may gray the wood. The manufacturer claims Penofin Weatherblaster can be used as is. Wolman Cedar & Redwood Deck & Fence Brightener is specially made for these products. Bio-Wash recommends their brightener, followed up with a separately sold blonding agent.

There is a great deal of talk about a new miracle cleaner called Oxygen Bleach. We asked around, and no one could tell us what an oxygen bleach was. Dillman and Upton, (248) 651-9411, now carry the product, Timber Wash Professional Wood Cleaner, (800) 860-6327. We bought a bottle.

The package directions are amazingly like those for Wolman Deck and Fence Brightener, which is made with Disodium Peroxydicarbonate. Even more amazing, the Wolman product now includes a stick-on label that says it has Oxygen Bleach.

We did a head-to-head comparison of the two products on our test deck. Timber Wash may have gotten the deck a little lighter, but both products were excellent. We averaged 65 square feet per gallon of mixed solution, not the 100 square feet claimed on each product label. When you buy your product, keep in mind that amateurs always use more product than the technical experts who write the directions.

Stripping

If you have a dirty, dull and peeling deck, strip the deck first, and then brighten it before restaining or resealing. We will cover these important topics next week.

If you need to know now, my entire book, Deck Care Fast & Easy, is on my internet web site, www.MasterHandyman.com, as a database. Just click on the picture of the deck care book, and you can get everything you need.

JUNE 9, 2001

The old finish has to be removed when the deck turns dull

By Glenn Haege /
Special to The Detroit News

If you are a wood worker, you stain a piece of furniture lovingly and it lasts for 50 or 100 years. If you have a deck, you have to strip and stain that sucker every couple of years. Stripping and staining decks is hard work. If you are not pleased with the result, you probably will not be a very happy camper.

A lot of unhappy campers call my radio show. The problem is usually that they tried to get by too cheap, were hurried and tried to skip a step, or expected products to do what they were never intended to do.

If you just had a dull gray, unfinished deck, we covered the problem last week. If you have a previously finished deck that has now turned dull, gray and splotchy, the job is more labor intensive. The old finish has to be stripped and all the goop has to be cleaned off. Then the wood has to be brightened as we described last week. With a few exceptions, you then have to let the deck dry a day or two before the new finish is applied.

Most of the major deck care product manufacturers like Penofin, Bio-Wash, Behr, Duckback Superdeck, Cabot, Wolman and Flood now make an entire line of products: strippers, brighteners, clear coats and stains. Each manufacturer tweaks his products, so that they work well together. If you are going to buy Superdeck deck stain, it just makes sense to buy Superdeck strippers and brighteners. Ditto for all the other manufacturers.

Most decks are made from pressure-treated pine. Flood, Duckback Superdeck and Penofin make deck stains especially formulated for pressure-treated wood.

What should you buy for your deck?

New deck:
Clear wood sealer with UV. Seals the wood and adds a little protection.

2 years:
Sealer toner. Includes a little pigment for protection.

4 years:
Semi-transparent stain. Enough stain to make a color statement. Enhances the markings of cedar and redwood.

6-8 years:
Solid color stain. Gives the extra protection needed to help deck woods last a long time and hides a blemish or two.

Penofin also makes special stains for hard woods, cedar and redwood and a product for composites called Knotwood. Other manufacturers have other specialized stains and sealers.

I often get asked if decks should be pressure washed. The answer is yes and no:

Yes, pressure washing makes the final step in cleaning, brightening and stripping a deck easier, though it does not eliminate the need to agitate with a brush when called for.

No, pressure washing is unnecessary. All deck care products are made so that they can be used successfully with just normal pressure from a garden hose.

If you decide to use a pressure washer, the pressure should be between 500 psi (pounds per square inch) for the most fragile cedars to 1,200 psi for the toughest pine. Most pressure washers sold to the general public produce a spray of 1,500 to 2,500 psi and the pressure cannot be turned down.

Supposedly, you get around the high pressure by using a wide-angle spray attachment and keeping the sprayer at least two feet from the deck. The trouble is that most people are in a hurry and try to clean that tough spot by putting the sprayer close to the wood. The result is a roughened, gouged deck.

Another constant complaint is that deck stains don't last long enough. People want a stain or sealer to last at least five years. Most horizontal deck surfaces have to be restained every 18- to 24-months. Some manufacturers want their stain or sealer reapplied every year.

One manufacturer, Silvertown Products, (800) 574-4662, claims that their Rhinoguard stain lasts three to seven years. That sounds good, but they also want the wood sanded before applying their product and two coats are required.

The difference in the required number of coats and preparation technique can cause problems. Many manufacturers recommend two coats. Other products, like Superdeck, are best if their wood primer is used before their solid color deck stain.

Bio-Wash wants you to apply a coat of Mil Glaze Away before staining. All wood is chemically hot after stripping. Brightening tends to neutralize the wood, but may be uneven. Applying a quick coat of Mil Glaze Away before staining neutralizes the pH and assures that any stain will be absorbed more easily.

Decks were meant to be fun, but their care gets so complicated that I have written three books on the subject over the years. If you have more questions, the most recent book is posted on my web site, www.MasterHandyman.com, so you can read or download it free.

One final word of advice – when you go to the home center, hardware or paint store for deck care products, shop for quality, not price. The most expensive ingredient is the grease in your elbow. Follow label directions to the letter, then brag about it!

The '50s retro look is among hot trends in kitchen appliances

By Glenn Haege /
Special to The Detroit News

ORLANDO

I've been trying to write about the Kitchen and Bath Industry Show in Orlando for more than a week. Something more newsworthy always got in the way. This week, I'll write about new kitchen items. Next week, we'll take a bath. Here are the trends:

Refrigerators

Photo by Ewald Stief

Danby Retro Refrigerator is available in lipstick red and brushed stainless steel.

What's old is new again. If your mother's refrigerator went down to the basement instead of the dump, consider cleaning it off and bringing it upstairs. The '50s retro look is in. If you want old made new, the Elmira Stove Works of Canada, (800) 295-8498, has a very authentic-looking lower drawer freezer model in eight different colors. It's called the Northstar and retails in the $2,700 range.

Danby Products, (800) 263-2629, has retro-look refrigerators in lipstick red and brushed stainless steel. Not really authentic, but if Art Deco turns you on, you probably will not have a good night's sleep until you have one of these babies in your kitchen. Doug Greenway, a company rep, says they were not just in the pipeline, but are available nationwide right now. Retail prices are in the $800 to $1,000 range.

If you have a large family or do a lot of entertaining, Maytag, (800) 688-9900, introduced their new Wide-by-Side refrigerator/freezer at the show. The problem with most side-by-side refrigerator/freezers is that neither side has enough width for storing big pans or trays. Maytag's new 36-inch wide unit is built with doors and refrigerator and freezer compartments shaped like inverted Zs. Half the refrigerator and half the freezer are extra wide, eliminating storage problems.

Stoves

Photo by Ewald Stief

Godin Chatelaine French Enamel Stove has brass or gold trim. It has two European convection ovens. The color of baked on enamel finish can be custom ordered.

If you love to cook and don't want to ever have to worry about electricity blackouts or brownouts, or the escalating price of natural gas, Heartland Appliances, (800) 361-1517, has got the stove for you. It may not be new, but as long as you can find wood, the Heartland Wood Stove will keep you cooking. A side water tank heats the dishwater while you're preparing the meal. Prices for the wood burning stoves run from $2,900 to $3,500.

During the past several years we have been inundated with commercial-look stainless steel appliances. First from the big commercial kitchen guys, then all the wanna-bes followed suit.

Godin of France, (800) 550-4294, is trying to save us from saneless stainless. Godin stoves come in the same vibrant colors you see in French enamel cookware: black, white, sapphire blue, ruby red or emerald green. They will even custom color stoves to your order. One of the unique features of Godin is their distinctive brass or gold frame trim.

The Godin Chatelaine boasts two convection ovens, both with diagonal rotisseries. In European convection mode, pans can be placed directly on the oven floor increasing useable oven space. Prices for the Chatelaine series are in the $7,000 to $10,000 range. The line should be at the Troy Design Center within the next couple of months.

If you love to cook, but are afraid that the country may run out of gas, Godin makes models that burn wood, coal and fuel oil. They are not yet imported into the United States (thank heaven), but Godin will gladly ship them to us if the California energy crisis gets really out of hand.

Should you be the proud possessor of a wood lot (or a lot of wood) and want to play it safe, Heartland Appliances Inc., (800) 361-1517, has wood stoves priced from $2,900 to $3,500. Some even have hot water tanks so that when you've finished cooking and baking there is plenty of hot water for the dishes.

Design elements

If you're reading this article because you urgently, desperately need to remodel your kitchen and have access to a computer, log on to www.kitchens.com. Steve Krengel and Editor Charlotte Rowe have launched a new virtual showroom that will tell you everything you need to know about designing your kitchen including all the different formats, price ranges, colors, what's hot, even designers and builders who have offices within 60 miles of your house. They make everything but paying for the remodeling job very easy.

Photo by Ewald Stief

Maytag's extra wide, Wide-by-Side Refrigerator / Freezer has a "Z" shaped doors and interiors so that there is room in both the refrigerator and freezer for extra wide dishes.

Why settle for an ordinary kitchen when you can turn it into an art gallery? Ferguson Bath and Kitchen Gallery, (800) 373-8057, has introduced front panels for appliances called the Art Dishwasher and Art Fridge. The front panels are signed and numbered reproductions of art especially designed for the purpose by contemporary artists Jay Miller and Jeffrey Robert. Prices for the panels run about $1,000. Pricey? Yes, but you gotta have art.

Next week, we'll step out of the kitchen and into the throne room. You will find that much of the seating has been elevated to new heights.

Designer plumbing, accessories improve the bathroom experience

By Glenn Haege /
Special to The Detroit News

ORLANDO

Photo by Ewald Stief

Acorn Engineering's Neo-Comby, stainless steel one-piece toilet has everything you need in a small space.

Whether you want your bathroom to be spartan, sinfully luxurious or practical, bathroom manufacturers aim to please. They brought their newest products to the recent Kitchen and Bath Industry Show in Orlando. Here are the trends that caught my eye:

Toilets

Starting with the practical, Kohler made a big thing of their wide selection of comfort-height toilets. The toilet seats are the same height as a standard chair. While first introduced as an American with Disabilities (ADA) product, the higher toilets were immediately popular with anyone over 6-feet tall or over 40 years of age. Kohler had comfort-height toilets in all their high-style commode lines.

Reps from American Standard, (800) 442-1902, said that their company also features comfort-height toilets in all their major design lines so that customers would not have to sacrifice comfort for style.

If you are into minimalist or prison chic, the folks at Acorn Engineering Company, (800) 591-9050, introduced their Neo-Comby, one-piece toilet, paper holder, sink, storage cabinet and towel bar. All this is packed into a 32-by-33-inch package costing a mere $5,000. When you go to brush your teeth with this baby, you'll not only be set for life, you'll think you're doing 10 to 20 in maximum security.

Sinks and tubs

Photo by Ewald Stief

Rocky Mountain Hardware's custom hand made water trough and sand molded fixtures give Wild West flair with a designer price tag.

If you're in a Western mood, Rocky Mountain Hardware, (888) 788-2013, can rustle you up a hand-made sink that looks like a water trough for $2,000. Rugged Western-looking fixtures will set you back another $1,200 or so.

If you don't want your bathroom stainless steel or cast in bronze, how about carved out of granite? Stone Forest, (505) 986-8883, specializes in carved granite and marble lavatories. A classic marble or round granite sink costs about $600. Iron lav stands cost from $220 to $450. A granite lav pedestal is $600.

But why settle for just washing your hands? A 2,500-pound, six-foot long, blue/gray granite bathtub can be yours for $12,000. If it doesn't fall through the floor, it will impress the in-laws and make your rubber ducky very proud.

American Standard, (800) 442-1902, could easily lay claim to having the most luxurious bathtubs at the Kitchen and Bath Show. The flowing lines of their free standing, draped tub made it a work of art. The price of the tub including frame was around $3,200. An elegant freestanding tub with a cherry wood frame was $2,800.

Photo by Ewald Stief

American Stndard's free standing, draped tub gives a feeling of Victorian Elegance.

"Victorian Elegance" was a theme that kept repeating itself over and over again. The Soho Corp., (800) 969-SOHO, and Devon & Devon, (800) 351-0038, devoted their entire lines to ornate British designs. Baths, lavatories, commodes, faucets, showers and accessories all reminded you of a bygone era.

Delta Faucet Company, (800) 345-3358, capitalized on this theme with their new Victorian Collection of sink and bath faucets and accessories. The Delta Victorian Collection comes in chrome, a new Venetian Bronze, as well as the company's exclusive polished brass and pearl nickel Brilliance finishes.

Kohler, (800) 4-KOHLER, went back to 1929 for a retrospective look at Kohler products that were displayed at the Metropolitan Museum of Art in that year. Most attractive was their 32-inch wide, fireclay console table sink equipped with retro-look Memoirs faucet and lever handles.

Mirrors and more

Newhome Bath & Mirror, Inc., (877) 242-5327, introduced the Shower ClearMirror. This is an electrically heated 10-by-12-inch mirror that will actually stay fog free and allow you to shave in the shower.

Sanitary for All, (800) 363-5874, the American Division of a French plumb-

ing products company, introduced SaniPro, a line of toilet, sink and shower fixtures that permit you to flush up from basements below sanitary lines and from areas in the house that may be too far away from a sanitary stack to flush or drain properly. The device includes a special compacting pump that creates water flow while compacting discharge to a 3/4-inch diameter pipe. Using the new equipment, an entire flushing cycle requires less than 1 gallon of water.

Photo by Ewald Stief

An overflowing sink is no problem for the Step2 Company's new waterproof plastic vanity. It can be repeatedly soaked in water with no delamination.

If you have little ones who keep the water running until it overflows the sink, the Step2 Company, (866) 2-EN-DURE, introduced a line of water-proof plastic vanities. The vanities come in white and ivory and retail from $169 for a single door vanity to $199 for the deluxe double door style.

Far more often the culprit is not a child but a burst pipe or defective piece of equipment. Step2 creators demonstrated FloLogic, (877) 356-5644, a unique circuit breaker for the home's water supply. The FloLogic System eliminates flooding by turning off the water when it senses a burst pipe or an unusually long-running plumbing appliance.

Well, there it is filks, from the far out to the extreme practical. Now, if you'll excuse me, I gotta take a shower and go to the station for my day job.

Note to readers: Please do me a favor. If you send a question that you would like answered in my Thursday Detroit News article in the Features section, I need to know at least your first name and the city in which you live. Thank you.

JUNE 30, 2001

Some Michigan builders are giants

By Glenn Haege /
Special to The Detroit News

Professional Builder Magazine released its Big Builder rankings, and 15 of the country's top 400 housing giants are in Michigan.

This list is important for a number of reasons. The building business is a savage, dog-eat-dog endeavor. The list shows which companies have fought their way to the top of the heap. (You can find an in-depth report on the Professional Builders Giant Builder list at www.housingzone.com.)

When you get right down to it, every housing sale is an individual sale. Builders don't wholesale houses to distributors. You buy your house directly from the builder or his designated real estate agent. The Big Builder list tells us the builders who have made and kept more customers happy than anyone else in America.

To maintain their position, the top tier players spend millions of dollars taking the pulse of America. They try to learn just exactly what you want in a home, how long you plan to stay and where you want to be 10 or 20 years from now. The building giants try to incorporate the fulfillment of all these wants and needs into their product offerings.

In addition to selling the most homes, the top builders buy the most building materials. That makes them the bulls-eye customers for every manufacturer in the building materials industry. The Big Builders test, buy, decide which products are good, which products stand up, which products eliminate call backs, which products house shoppers will pay extra for. Touring model homes makes it very easy to make distinctions between winning and loosing products.

Knowing this if you are in the market for a new home and want to know what is the state of the art; or are thinking about making renovations to your current home and want to know what will enhance the value of your home, it just makes good sense to take a look at the Giant Builders in your neighborhood.

Pulte Corpation, headquartered in Bloomfield Hills, is the biggest builder in Michigan and is listed as No. 2 in the 2001 Professional Builder's list. Last year, Pulte was No. 1, but a merger of rivals dropped them temporarily to No. 2. Pulte's purchase of Del Webb, the nation's largest developer of Senior Communities, will make the company a solid No. 1 again this coming year.

Pulte has 14 major communities in Metro Detroit and 10 in the Grand Rapids area. The company builds primarily single-family and detached single-family condominiums, ranging from $140,000 to $600,000.

Pulte builds for real people, not movie stars. Their 21,781 new home closings last year amounted to more than $4.16 billion in revenue.

The second largest builder in Michigan, Crosswinds Communities of Novi, was No. 88 on the big builder list and had only slightly more than 4 percent of Pulte's sales. A specialist in starter homes, Crosswinds sold 1,115 single-family detached, condominium and town houses last year for a total of nearly $178 million in new residential sales revenue.

Village Green Companies of Farmington Hills was the third largest Michigan builder and was No. 97 on the Professional Builder list. Headquartered in Farmington Hills, the company has Michigan Village Green complexes from Clarkston all the way to Ann Arbor. Although engaged in leasing units across the entire United States, the company sold 1,158 new residential units, for a total of $161.8 million in revenue.

Robertson Brothers of Bloomfield Hills, with some homes selling for $3 million and Moceri of Auburn Hills, with some homes in the $1 million range, were the giants who built the most expensive homes. DeShano Construction Co. of Gladwin, with homes starting at just $99,000, was the low-priced leader.

If you're house hunting, thinking about renovating or just want to get some great ideas, track down the Michigan Giants in your neighborhood and learn all they have to offer. Then brag about it.

Michigan's top developers

■ Pulte Corp., Bloomfield Hills, (248) 644-7300, pulte.com.
■ Crosswinds Communities, Novi, (248) 615-1313, crosswindscommunities.com.
■ Village Green Co., Farmington Hills, (248) 851-9600, www.villagegreen.com.
■ MJC Const. Co., Macomb, (586) 263-1203, mjcbuilders.com
■ Lombardo Co., Washington Township, (586) 781-7900, lombardocompanies.com
■ Singh Dev. Co., West Bloomfield Township, (248) 865-1600.
■ Robertson Bros. Co., Bloomfield Hills, (248) 644-3460.
■ Edward Rose, Farmington Hills, (248) 539-2255.
■ Tri-Mount Vincenti Co., Novi, (248) 735-8000.
■ S.R. Jacobson Dev., Bingham Farms, (248) 642-4700, www.srj.com.
■ Moceri Co., Auburn Hills, (248) 340-9400, moceri.com.
■ Lockwood Construction Co., Bingham Farms, (248) 540-8015.
■ Eastbrook Homes, Inc., Kentwood, (616) 455-0200, east brookhomes.com.
■ Rohde Const. Co. Inc., Kentwood, (616) 698-0880.
■ DeShano Const. Co., Gladwin, (989) 426-2521, www.deshano.com.

Small company makes big strides in helping repair wood, concrete

By Glenn Haege /
Special to The Detroit News

One of my favorite sayings is "Water always wins; that's why there is a Grand Canyon." Water always finds a way in. It makes wood waterlogged so that it rots. It expands and contracts during hot and cold cycles so that concrete cracks and falls off.

If a deck board rots or splits badly, it is relatively simple to pull it up and replace it. All that takes is a trip to the lumberyard or home center to pick up the replacement board. They will even cut the plank to size at the yard if you ask them.

If your driveway or concrete patio starts spalling or cracking, Gibraltar Quickrete, (800) 442-7258, www.quikrete.com, has a multitude of products you can use to make the drive or patio look like new.

But it is not so simple when the rot has attacked a load-bearing column on the front porch, the banister of your deck or an irreplaceable piece of window frame. If the water demon has attacked an elaborate concrete cast statue or done a number on a terraced concrete staircase, the problem can be gut wrenching.

Restoration contractors encounter these problems on a daily basis. They are called upon to bring our historic buildings back from decay. Unfortunately, most of these contractors are located on the East Coast, so most of us cannot avail ourselves of their services.

This antique window sash had fallen to pieces but was still repairable with the Abatron wood repair system.

But with a little time and practice, most of us can use their restoration techniques around our houses to repair instead of replace. The trick is to know what to use and how to use it.

Three of the most powerful weapons in the restoration contractor's arsenal are products made by Abatron Inc. of Kenosha, Wisconsin, (800) 445-1754. I have been telling people about Abatron LiquidWood, WoodEpox and AboWeld for years. Unfortunately, the products have never been widely distributed because they are relatively expensive and do not sell in sufficient volume to be carried by most hardware stores

Antique wood window sash with severe dry rot was stabilized with Abatron LiquidWood, then rebuilt using WoodEpox.

and home centers. Luckily, they can all be ordered direct from the company, which also maintains a good help desk and has a very informative web site, www.abatron.com.

If the job calls for repairing a rotted load-bearing pillar, baluster, wooden door or window frame prior to painting, there are two different repair philosophies. You can stabilize the affected wood and bring back its former properties, or you can cut out the rotten or cracked wood and replace it with new wood or a wood epoxy.

Even wood that has severe dry rot and crumbles in your fingers can usually be saved by using a consolidant like Abatron's LiquidWood. When injected into the wood, it penetrates and is absorbed completely throughout the affected area. When cured, the treated wood is strong and can be nailed and painted.

If load-bearing wood, such as a column, has been damaged by fire, or sections have to be replaced for whatever reason, Abatron WoodEpox can be used to rebuild the area. WoodEpox is load bearing. It bonds to the remaining wood and can be nailed, sawed, molded or sculpted.

Many restoration projects call for a combination of LiquidWood and WoodEpox. Since the same manufacturer makes the products, they work well together.

Not all restorers believe in repairing rotted or insect-damaged wood with a consolidant like LiquidWood. John Stahl at Advanced Repair Technology, (607) 264-9040, recommends stripping away all bad wood and sanding the remainder so that all loose fibers are removed before rebuilding.

Advanced Repair Technology makes FlexTec, a two-part polymer that is squeezed out of a dual cartridge gun directly onto the surface that is being repaired. Once in place, it can be molded and shaped on the spot. The product is used extensively by wood window repair companies.

Concrete can also be mended. Fractures or pieces that have broken off decorative cast concrete can be repaired with Abatron AboWeld 55-1. The product is a structural, thixotropic adhesive paste. That is a technical way of saying you can trowel it anywhere, and it won't drip or sag. If the corner of a step has to be repaired, the AboWeld can just be troweled into place, then shaped and it will stay.

If the corner of a piece of concrete sculpture is broken off or a bird bath cracks, you can spread a light coat of AboWeld on opposing surfaces and bond the pieces together.

We live in a throwaway society. But if you take a little time to learn about companies like Abatron and Advanced Repair Technology, you can restore instead of replace, save a lot of money and brag about the result.

JULY 14, 2001

Homeowners have new insulation option in the Hot Roof Theory

By Glenn Haege / Special to The Detroit News

I have been preaching the attic insulation gospel according to the Cold Roof Theory for 18 years. The trouble is that it doesn't always work.

The Cold Roof Theory calls for insulation and ventilation to protect houses from heat loss and prevent ice dam roof damage. The insulation provides a thermal barrier, while a continuous stream of air, coming in through the soffit vents and exfiltrating through roof or ridge vents, keeps the roof deck cool.

Mike Kearns of Kearns Brothers Insulation, (313) 277-8000, called to tell me that a product called the Cobra Soft Edge by GAF is no longer available for homes whose soffits are too narrow for traditional venting. Obviously, the theory can't work if a key ventilation element is missing.

In addition to houses with narrow soffits, many older homes have floored storage attics. Other homes have essential equipment located in the attic. In both cases, covering attic floors with a 12- or 14-inch-deep layer of insulation is not an option.

When I asked the top people at Owens Corning Insulation what was the best way to insulate storage attics, their technical expert told me that there is no good way to do the job. If you can't insulate the attic using the cold roof insulation theory, there has to be another option.

Seal off attic.
Insulate roof deck.

A few years ago, the scientists at the Oakridge National Laboratory in Tennessee tested properly vented and totally sealed attics. They found that proper venting only reduced the roof deck temperature by 3 to 5 degrees Fahrenheit.

Further testing determined that not venting an attic might reduce the service life of organic asphalt or fiberglass shingles by a maximum of five years. The temperature differential did not seem to have any effect on homes with higher quality tile or metal roofing systems.

In practical terms, this means that if you throw out the Cold Roof Theory, you have to resign yourself to shortening the service life of your shingles or upgrading to a higher quality roofing system. Most organic shingle manufacturers also void their warranties if there is not sufficient ventilation.

Using the Hot Roof Theory, the attic is completely sealed. The soffit areas are packed with insulation, and the attic walls and ceiling (the roof deck) are coated with insulation. The best type of insulation for this type of a project is sprayed foam.

Icynene, a Canadian spray foam manufactured by Icynene Inc., (800) 758-7325, has been making major inroads in insulation projects using the Hot Roof Theory. By using Icynene, the attic roof deck and walls can be insulated and sealed from wind infiltration in one application.

The product is an expanding, totally benign, water-based foam with exceptional adhesion qualities and virtually no off-gassing. Unlike cellulose or fiberglass insulation, Icynene is not damaged by water, and the original R-value is restored as soon as the product dries.

When an attic is insulated using the Hot Roof Theory, the attic temperature adjusts to within 10 degrees of the ambient temperature of the house. Because the attic is heated or cooled by air that would normally escape from the house, it does not raise the load on the heating and cooling system.

If a new house is totally foam insulated, it has most, if not all, of the benefits of foam insulated concrete block construction. It is quieter than traditional wood frame construction. The heating and cooling equipment can be safely downsized, and a 30 to 50 percent reduction in total heating and cooling costs is often realized. The need for artificial humidification is also greatly reduced. Reducing humidity levels cuts mold spores and other microbials, creating a healthier home.

Because foam insulation seals the building envelope, mechanical ventilation is required. This is usually accomplished by adding vents and a small, continuously operating, whole-house fan. An Energy Recovery Ventilator installed by a heating and cooling contractor will also take care of the problem.

In southern Michigan, Icynene insulation is installed by Seal Tech Insulation, (734) 649-8584. The Icynene web site, www.icynene.com, lists installation contractors for every part of the country.

Closed-cell polyurethanes, such as Comfort Foam, produced by the Comfort Foam Division of Foam Enterprises of Minneapolis, (800) 888-3342, also can be used, according to Bill Amend, the division manager.

"When it comes to insulation, I think that P-value is even more important than the R-value. A closed-cell polyurethane foam stops air penetration. Fiberglass can't make that claim," Amend says. If you want to learn more about his views on insulation, see the company's web site, www.comfortfoam.coms.

Gabe Farkas, the technical director of Icynene Inc., says that while foam insulation is about three times more expensive than cellulose or fiberglass insulation, it is also about six times more effective.

Although both Icynene and Comfort Foam have earned the Energy Star rating, not all building inspectors have accepted or even know about the hot roof insulation theory. To learn more, contact the manufacturers, then check with your local building officials. If you get way ahead of the curve, you can earn bragging rights big time.

If you have a tough cleaning problem, write: Cleaning Question, Master Handyman Press, P.O. Box 268, Glenn, MI 49416, or e-mail askglenn@masterhandyman.com. Haege answers readers' questions in Thursday's Detroit News Features section and on his "Ask the Handyman" radio show 8 a.m.-noon Saturday and Sunday, (800) 65-HANDY. Listen on WXYT-AM (1270) and 204 other stations.

JULY 21, 2001

Midsummer's the perfect time to make those easy home repairs

By Glenn Haege /
Special to The Detroit News

What is the status of your "Summer To Do" list? In many areas, the kids go back to school the week before Labor Day. You need time to get away for a week or two. If you have to do summer jobs around the house, you are almost out of time.

Here's a list of midsummer projects to get you started.

Inside

■ Change the furnace filter. If you have air conditioning, this is the toughest time of the year on the furnace fan system. Cold air is much heavier than hot air, so the fan has to work harder, longer. If you just use a regular, inexpensive furnace filter and normally change it every ninety days, it should be changed once a month during the summer.

■ Have the duct work cleaned and sanitized. If it has been seven years or more since the duct work in your house was cleaned, call now and get an appointment. During the air conditioning season, cold air is pushed through the duct work at a high velocity. When ducts are dirty, the higher wind pressure spreads more dirt, dust, mold, mildew spores and dust mites through your home. Yuck.

If you have never had the ducts cleaned before, some of the better duct cleaners are A-1 Duct Cleaning, (800) 382-8256,

Dalton Environmental, (800) 675-2298, Dusty Ducts, (313) 381-7801, Safety King, (888) 382-8776, Sanit Air, (888) 778-7324, and Sterling Environmental, (888) 992-1200.

Outside

■ Walk around the house and see what needs to be done. Be sure to inspect the siding, caulking, trim paint and the mortar around brickwork and chimney.

■ Check all wood siding for water damage. Rusty nails mean that the siding is wet. Water may be getting behind the boards and not be able to get out. Find out what's happening now while it can still be fixed relatively inexpensively.

■ Check the caulking around windows, doors, trim, spigots, vents and any pipes, cables and wiring that enter the house. Press the caulk with a dime or your thumbnail. If it is resilient, it's fine. If it has become hard, it is no longer functioning and should be stripped out and replaced.

There are three basic types of caulking compounds for do-it-yourselfers: latex/acrylics, silicones and combinations.

Latex/acrylics are durable, easy to use, fast drying and can be painted. Soap and water cleanup is all you need. Once their service life is over, they are relatively easy to remove. One of the leading makers of latex/acrylic caulks is United Gilsonite Laboratories, (800) 272-3235.

Silicone caulks are more finicky. Good surface preparation is a must. You cannot paint them, but pretinted or clear caulks are available. They have excellent flexibility, superior durability and will stand up to extreme weather and temperature conditions. Once silicone caulks are on, they stay stuck practically forever. Getting them on is easy. Getting them off is next to impossible. Cleanup should be with alcohol or mineral spirits. GE, (800) 255-8886, Dow Silicone by DAP, (800) 543-3840, and OSI, (800) 624-7767, make latex/acrylics and silicones.

Almost all manufacturers now also make some form of siliconized latex/acrylic caulks, which try to combine the benefits of both.

A good caulking gun and a gentle hand are very important. Cut the tip of the caulk cylinder on a 45-degree angle and load it into the gun. Then pull the gun to apply the caulk (don't push it). Apply as narrow a bead as possible. Removing surplus caulk can be a mess.

■ Check wood trim. Trim is often short-changed when the house is painted. It is the last painting job to be done, and everyone wants to clean his or her brushes and rollers and go home. Mid-summer is the perfect time to repair the trim.

If you have to rebuild, coat with an oil-base stain kill such as Cover-Stain by Zinsser, then finish with a good coat of Acrylic house paint.

■ Check mortar lines on brick siding and chimneys. Mortar can easily be cracked and lost by winter freeze/thaw cycles. Empty mortar joints permit wind and water to enter the building envelope.

If just a little tuck-pointing needs to be done, you can do it yourself. Clear away the loose mortar with a cold chisel and brick hammer. Wear goggles. Clean out the damaged area with a whisk broom, then fill in the joints with Quikrete Mortar Repair, (800) 442-7258. It comes in a handy tube with a special spout.

If the job looks too big, call the Masonry Institute of Michigan, (734) 458-8544, for the name of a masonry contractor who works in your area.

One final tip: Always try to work on the side of the house that is away from the sun. You will be cooler, and the materials will go on better and cure stronger. When the day gets too hot (more than 85 degrees), go in and have a cool glass of lemonade. You've earned it.

What you don't know about having wood installed could floor you

By Glenn Haege /
Special to The Detroit News

When people ask me about flooring, they are usually asking about laminates or other man-made materials. When I've answered their question, I often ask a question of my own: "Have you considered wood?"

I get the following responses: "Too expensive." "I want something that's very durable." "I want something that's easy to care for." "I want something really unique."

The truth is that you can get wood flooring in a wide price range. Certainly it is more expensive than vinyl or very inexpensive carpeting, but prices are very competitive to high-end carpeting or laminates.

When it comes to durability, nothing but stone can outlast wood. Like stone and ceramic tile, a wood floor is rated as being for the life of the structure. Vinyl, carpeting and laminates are not.

A hardwood floor should usually be refinished every 20 years. Many go 30 or 40 years before refinishing. A professional usually takes 1/16th of an inch or less off the surface when he refinishes a floor. A factory-finished wood floor has enough surface wood so that it can be refinished twice. Solid wood flooring could easily be refinished four or five times.

Many of our historic buildings from the Revolutionary War period still have their original wood floors. That's durability.

Caring for wood is so simple all you really need is a decent vacuum cleaner, a bottle of vinegar and water, and a sponge mop. My wife, Barbara has

refined the process. She uses a bottle of non-ammoniated window cleaner and a damp mop or a damp Swiffer.

Unless you have a flood that leaves buckets of mud, you never need to get out a pail and scrub a wood floor. Wood is like most cats. It does not like water, but always stays looking good.

Dick Walters of Erickson Floor Supply says that some pre-finished hardwood flooring now have 25-year finish warranties.

When people tell me they don't want wood because they want something that will stand out, I suggest that they take a look at some of the wood my friend Dick Walters displays at Erickson's Flooring & Supply Company, (800) 225-9663, in Ferndale. The company also has offices in Grand Rapids, Chicago and Indianapolis.

I like sending people to places like Erickson's because they are a big distributor. They don't sell to the general public, so you can get information without the sales pitch.

To show you how special wood can be, we went over to Erickson's and asked Walters to show and tell us what's new.

"What's 'new' in wood? Four words: Finishes, imports, reclaimed and laser cut.

"Some people used to choose laminate over wood because of the durability of the silicone carbide protective coating. Now you can get that same very durable coating on some of the pre-finished woods, such as Armstrong's Robbins Premium Hardwood Flooring, (800) 733-3309."

Many people who want something unique are going into the exotic hardwoods, such as Doussie, Padouk and Sapele, Walters said. These particular African woods are milled in Greece by Shelman Swiss Hellenic, (732) 576-8988. Other exotic woods come from Brazil.

American woods like oak are beautiful when coated, but are naturally quite pale. African and South American woods are very dense and oily. Brazilian Cherry, by contrast, is naturally so dark and lustrous most people think that it has been stained or coated.

American wood is the most color stable in the world. This color stability is caused by North America's short growing season and long winters, which give the color time to set. By contrast, the Brazilian and African woods grow all year long, and since the color has never been locked in, it changes over time. Indoors, Brazilian and African hardwoods actually become darker.

This means that the color you see in the showroom or when the floor has just been laid is not the color you will have in 60 days. Five years later, you will have a different color still. So when you have an exotic hardwood floor, you adapt to the wood, the wood does not adapt to you.

Reclaimed wood is another item for the wood lover. Timbers are being reclaimed from large buildings like warehouses that are being demolished. With reclaimed wood, each piece has a beauty and a history all its own. If the wood came from a Chicago speak-easy, the chances are you'll know it and be able to name drop it to friends.

Intricate, laser-cut hardwood medallions by Oshkosh can now be added to hardwood floors. Medallions come in sizes from 36- to 60-inches. Custom designs are also available.

The last new innovation in hardwoods is laser cutting of decorative accents by companies such as Historic Floors of Oshkosh, (920) 582-9977.

"Decorative inlays are magnificent pieces of art and have always added great beauty to hardwood floors," Walters said. "Unfortunately the time consuming hand cutting of the individual woods made the work so expensive, only the very wealthy could afford it.

"Laser cutting technology has made beautiful medallions, borders and parquetry very affordable," Walters says. "Each piece is laser cut from different woods, then meticulously put into a border like a giant jig saw puzzle."

There is something about the look and feel of wood you can't get from any other surface. When Barb and I had our home built, we demanded hardwood. We weren't disappointed.

Laser-cut geometric and floral desigh borders by Oshkosh give floor a one-of-a-kind look but can be installed easily by any hardwood-flooring contractor.

New electrical switches can be a big turn on and safety feature

By Glenn Haege /
Special to The Detroit News

The design of the light switches used in most homes hasn't improved in more than 50 years. Oh sure, we've gone from two wire to three wire behind the walls, but what we use to flick the lights off or on hasn't changed much since great-grandfather's day.

And it's not because technological advances don't exist – it's because most of us, homeowners and builders alike, gravitate to the lowest cost way of doing things. That's too bad because technologies have existed for years that would make finding light switches and turning them on and off easy or even automatic.

It would also save money. When your dad used to yell, "Doesn't anyone know how to turn lights off in this house?" He was right. It is estimated that automatically turning off the lights in the bathroom, bedroom, living room, halls and garages when not needed could save up to 40 percent on lighting costs. And, of course, in a land of rolling black-outs where electric power companies cannot keep up with demand, turning off unneeded lights is also the responsible thing to do.

Turning off the light switch is not the only problem. Sometimes, turning on a switch is next to impossible. Finding a light switch in a dark room can be exasperating. Who hasn't had to go to the bathroom at a friend's house and groped around desperately trying to find a switch hidden by some fiendish electrician?

Not being able to turn on the lights also can be deadly. You cannot avoid a danger you cannot see. According to the Leviton Institute, the consumer education arm of Leviton Manufacturing, slip-and-fall injuries are now the sixth-leading cause of death among people 65 years or older. We need more, and easier-to-find, light switches as we grow older.

If you're handy, the problem could be eliminated in every room of your house for less than $150. Do the math:

■ A cheap 15-amp wall switch like the ones you have now, costs less than two dollars.

■ A deluxe mercury switch costs about $4.50.

■ Upgrading to an illuminated rocker switch costs $7.79 at Damman's and many other hardware stores. An illuminated rocker switch is easier than a flip switch to use, costs almost nothing to run and is easy to see in the dark. For my money, that is a bargain.

If you are not handy, installing plug-in light-sensitive night lights in halls and bathrooms also can eliminate a lot of slips and falls and make it easier to locate the light switch – all for less than $2 a unit. Some night lights are especially made to focus on the floor, so that you have a lighted path when you walk through the house at night.

Vos Systems has an IntelaVoice, which is a voice-activated switch. You just walk into the room, say "lights" in a firm voice and the lights turn on. Say "lights" when you leave and the lights turn off. IntelaVoice sells for $29 on the Vos web site, www.vossystems.com. Damman's sells the same switch for $22.99.

If you really want to go first class, consider upgrading to occupancy sensor wall switches. These switches automatically turn on when a person walks into a room and turn off when the room is empty. Most units use passive infrared detection technology to continuously monitor the room. When a person passes in or out of the sensor zone, the switch turns the light on and keeps it on as long as it senses activity.

Home Depot stocks Decora motion activated light controls for $13 to $25. The less expensive control monitors a 110-degree area. A $20 model monitors a 150-degree area. The $25 model is for 3-way two-fixture use. In all cases, the control turns the light on when you walk in the room. It will turn the light off after about 6 minutes. If you want the light to stay on, just press the light switch to override the program.

Another type of lighting control that makes turning lights on and off easy is a hand-held remote like the entry fob on most new cars. The hand-held remote sends a signal to a wall-mounted receiver that takes the place of the conventional light switch. Damman's sells the Inermatic Indoor/Outdoor remote control switch for $19.99.

In addition to advances in switches, smart bulbs are also making an impact. The bulbs are just in their infancy and only have limited distribution. Angelo Brothers, (800) 999-ABCO, www.angelobrothers.com, has introduced a Smart Guardian Bulb that is set to go on for 6 hours then automatically turn itself off for the next 18 hours. To change the program, all you have to do is turn the light off for 2 minutes, then turn it back on and the program resets.

No doubt about it, smart bulbs and smart switches are smart thinking. But you can't take advantage of the new technologies unless you keep your eyes open and see what's out there. Once you do, you move up to the front row of the home improvement class and impress your neighbors and in-laws big time.

It's that drip-drip-drip that can build into gallons of wasted water

By Glenn Haege /
Special to The Detroit News

Water restrictions are rampant and the water police are on the prowl. It wouldn't surprise me if public floggings were soon deemed the proper punishment for any unpatriotic homeowner who mistakes an even-numbered for an odd-numbered day.

Here in southeast Michigan, the Detroit Water and Sewerage Department serves a million-plus households. We live in the midst of the world's greatest supply of fresh water, so the shortage is not due to availability, but rather to processing.

To ease the strain on the water supply, most communities have gone to an even/odd day watering scheme. Some communities such as Commerce Township have even had to resort to a no-watering policy at times.

Obviously, something has to be done before our vegetable gardens die and our front lawns turn into dust bowls. I submit that a good first step would be to stop throwing away water that is not doing us any good. Stopping water waste is not only good citizenship, it will also save us thousands of dollars.

You can start with a little thing like not keeping the water running while you brush your teeth. Brushing teeth calls for less than an 8-ounce glass of water. When most of us keep the tap running, we're pouring gallons of water down the drain.

The next culprit is the real big one. About a year back the water bill of Kathy, my editor at Master Handyman Press, doubled. The Royal Oak Water Department called her to make an appointment with a water inspector.

When the big day came, the inspector did not use any space-age gadget to look for hidden leaks; he looked at the toilet water tanks. The inspector told Kathy that leaky toilets were the primary cause of water loss.

Just one leaky toilet can cause a water loss of 36,000 gallons of water during a three-month period. The Detroit Water and Sewerage Department provides water to 3 million people in Detroit and 125 suburban communities. A system that big could easily have 100,000 leaky toilets wasting 3.6 billion gallons of water every 90 days or 1.2 million gallons a month.

The third worst culprit is leaking faucets. Almost every house has at least one. Many homes have more than one faucet relentlessly dripping away.

The U.S. government has an interesting web site called Water Science for Schools, http://ga.water.usgs. gov/edu/mqanda.html. Click on Water Use on the home page of the site to access a water calculator that estimates the amount of water wasted by a leaky faucet.

If your home has one faucet that drips 20 drops per minute, it drips 28,800 drops per day or 694 gallons a year. That's almost 58 gallons a month. Individually, we may not notice the cost. Collectively the cost to our water system is staggering.

If Detroit's water system had 1 million homes, which each had one leaking faucet, the system would lose 1,902,245 gallons of drinking water a day. That is more than 57 million gallons a month.

Doing your share to fix needless water loss doesn't take a lot of money. Usually you do not have to call a plumber, and the fix will pay for itself in a few months.

If you are on the Internet, getting step-by-step directions on solving these problems is as simple as typing "leaky faucet" or "leaking toilet" in a good search engine. Either phrase will give you a choice of 10 or 12 sites, which will help you solve the problem.

One of my favorite sites for toilet problems is www.toiletology.com. A good site for help with leaking faucets is the Home Time TV show's site, www.hometime.com. Go to the site and just click on "projects."

Solving these problems is easy, even if you're not on the Internet. The cause of a leaking toilet is usually a flapper ball that no longer seats correctly. Just turn off the water at the toilet; write down the manufacturer's name and model number (both are usually on the inside of the water tank cover.)

Take off the flapper ball and take it and the toilet information to a plumbing supply house such as Universal Plumbing, (248) 542-3888. Give the counter people the information, and they will give you an exact replacement part.

Leaking faucets are just as simple to fix. There are four different types of faucets: compression, ball, disk-type cartridge and sleeve-type cartridge. If you don't know which you have, books such as Home Depot's Home Improvement 1-2-3 or the Better Home and Garden's New Complete Guide to Home Repair and Improvement have lots of pictures and complete step-by-step directions. You don't have to buy the books; they are at any library for free.

If you have one of the major brands of faucets, such as Delta or Moen, just go to the plumbing supply store with the name and model number and ask for the cartridge replacement kit. Fully illustrated directions are included in the package.

Once you get the right parts, neither a leaking toilet nor faucet should take more than a half-hour to fix and makes you a hero. You're a good citizen. You're saving water. You're saving money. Brag about it.

Home inspector isn't contractor, but outside opinion is invaluable

By Glenn Haege /
Special to The Detroit News

Every week, I get calls, letters and e-mails from people who need the name of a good home inspector. I also get frantic calls and wails of anguish from people who bought a home without a proper inspection.

Often I give people the name of Murray Gula, president of the Michigan Construction Protection Agency, (800) 543-6669. Unfortunately, Gula is not really in the home inspection business and can't go around solving everybody's problems.

You would think it should be easy to recommend a good home inspector. It isn't. Only 21 of the 50 states have any registration or licensing requirements. Michigan is not one of them. Literally anyone who buys business cards can do home inspections.

There are several associations of home inspectors. One of the oldest and most professional is the American Society of Home Inspectors, (800) 743-2744.

If you get a home inspector that has been accredited by ASHI, you know that person is in the home inspection business as a profession, not a part-time job. To gain accreditation, an applicant has to pass two written technical exams, have performed 250 fee-paid home inspections, and have been a candidate for membership for 6 months. All ASHI home inspectors are required to adhere to the ASHI code of ethics and standards of practice.

That sounds wonderful, but as a careful consumer, you should know what a home inspector doesn't do, as well as what he does. You have to know what a home inspection doesn't guarantee, as well as what it does.

When you get a good report on a home inspection, you are not home free. Just because a home inspector looks at a house and finds only minor faults does not mean the building won't collapse within 6 months. If disaster happens, it does not mean that the home inspector did not do his job.

Before you get riled at this, remember that some people die of heart attacks within days of passing a thorough physical exam. A house doesn't pass or fail a home inspection. All you get is a written report about the outwardly discernable physical condition of the dwelling. Do not expect a home inspection to be something it was not meant to be.

A home inspector's report should review the condition of the home's heating system, central air conditioning system (temperature permitting), interior plumbing and electrical systems, the roof, attic and visible insulation, walls, ceilings, floors, windows and doors, the foundation, basement and visible structure.

A visual inspection is only that. Just because the inspector looks at the heating system and says that it seems OK, doesn't mean that the furnace won't blow up or start leaking carbon monoxide the next day.

According to ASHI Standards of Practice, when a home inspector inspects the heating system, he looks at the installed equipment, vent systems and easily inspected flues and chimneys. In his report, he is supposed to describe the energy source and the distinguishing characteristics of the heating system.

He is not required and should not give an opinion on the condition of the heat exchanger, humidifier, dehumidifier or electronic air cleaner. It is not his place to determine the adequacy of the heating supply or its distribution throughout the house.

That may not be what you'd like, but it is exactly as it should be. A home inspector is not a heating contractor, and he should not try to sound like one. If you want a thorough, top-to-bottom inspection of the heating system, you have to hire a licensed heating contractor.

The same holds true with everything else. A home inspector is not a builder. He is not an architect, a plumber, a roofer, air conditioning contractor, electrician or insulation expert. He cannot tell you if the air or water quality in a house is good or bad or even if the house has termites.

A home inspector is (hopefully) a knowledgeable generalist who walks through a house and sees things you probably would not see. He or she is not required to have the knowledge or experience to tell you how to correct any problem he or she discovers. He or she is definitely not required or even permitted to offer to fix it for you.

This being the case, do I think a home inspection is worth the money?

You better believe it. To my mind, a good home inspector is worth his weight in gold. I wouldn't think of buying a house without having an inspection. If you have an older home, I even think you should have your existing house inspected to help you prioritize what needs to be done.

Home inspections are so important that I have added a listing on my web site of all the ASHI accredited home inspectors within a 100-mile radius of my offices in Troy, Michigan.

If you need a name, just go to my web site, www.masterhandyman.com, and click on "Home Inspectors" in the telephone listing on the right hand side of the page. If you live outside that area, go to the ASHI web site, ashi.com, and click on "Find an Inspector".

Learning all you can before you do is the key to buying wisely.

Cork, the newest flooring trend, is whisper quiet and totally natural

By Glenn Haege /
Special to The Detroit News

I never thought I'd be writing this article. Cork is nice natural flooring, but I can only remember one or two questions about cork flooring in the past 18 years on my radio show.

In the past week, we've received three information requests, via e-mail. One was a particularly poignant message from an older gentleman. His wife has a tendency to fall because she has a debilitating condition. He is considering cork flooring because it is a softer surface and will slightly cushion any falls.

This sounds like an excellent idea because cork is very versatile flooring. Unfortunately, we receive hundreds, sometimes thousands of e-mails and letter requests for information every week at Master Handyman Press.

Someone on staff tries to at least glance at every one, but we cannot actually answer more than a fraction. We did a study once and determined it would cost us about $600,000 a year to staff, house and train the people required to research and respond to all of your information requests. Naturally, that is impossible, so most of the mail just stacks up.

Skimming through the mail gives us a good feel for the information readers and listeners are looking for. Receiving three questions about cork flooring at a time when most information requests are on decks or painting, sounds alarm bells and we started researching story ideas.

The story process was sped up because we managed to lose the name and e-mail address of the older fellow who needed the information for his wife. This column is my way of making certain he gets the needed information.

Cork is an excellent floor and wall covering that has been suffering from a bad case of benign neglect.

Most flooring stores do not presently carry cork flooring, but that is going to change. In the July 30 issue of HFN (The Newsweekly of Home Products Retailing), Michael D. Devine, senior editor for Fashion listed cork as the big ecological flooring fashion leader. In other words, cork is now "in," according to one of the industry's top fashion gurus.

Expo Design Centers are leading the pack and already have excellent cork flooring displays. A lot of people are looking at cork, according to Amir Ashtiani, a flooring specialist at the Expo Design Center in Troy, (248) 689-3346, Ext. 2600.

So why should we care about cork?

First of all, it is a natural, environmentally friendly product. Zillions of tiny trapped air pockets make it very quiet and easy to walk on. Since it is soft and resilient, it is an excellent flooring choice for places such as kitchens, where you stand a lot. It would also be a good choice for people who have a tendency to slip and fall.

Cork is the outer bark of an evergreen tree known as the cork oak. The tree grows in the Mediterranean and can live from 150 to 500 years. Every nine to 14 years, the outer bark is stripped off the tree and processed. Harvesting is done without damaging the tree. About 50 percent of the world's cork supply comes from Portugal, 25 percent from Spain.

After flattening and boiling, some of the bark becomes corks used in wine bottles. Some is ground up and made into products like cork flooring and underlayment.

Companies such as Natural Cork, (800) 404-2675, make cork flooring into rolls, tiles and planks. Cork tiles are made in the standard 12- by 12-inch format that costs about $5.50 at Expo Design Center.

Cork planks are really a 3-layer sandwich with an upper layer of cork, a center section of processed wood, and a thin cork under layer. The retail price for cork planks at the Expo Design Center is $8.50 a foot. Installation cost for tiles and planks is $2.99 a square foot. Ashtiani says most orders can be filled within two weeks.

When used as flooring, cork is usually stained and receives its first coat of polyurethane at the factory. After installation, a second coat of polyurethane is applied. The manufacturers say that this final polyurethane coating is not a do-it-yourself project because the application has to give the cork a perfect watertight protective coating.

Cork tile and plank flooring can be stained in a variety of colors to match any decor. Both are long wearing, easy walking flooring and environmentally friendly.

Coating with polyurethane is a relatively recent development. Historically, cork floors were treated with wax.

Cork is considered to have the same wear characteristics as wood flooring. Like wood, cork planks can be sanded, restained and re-finished. Cork tiles, on the other hand, are treated with a very hard urethane coating at the factory. They last a long time, but cannot be refinished.

Cork flooring is easy care. Like hardwood, it should be swept or vacuumed daily. It can be damp mopped with a vinegar and water mixture applied using a spritzer bottle, but should never be doused in water. This inability to withstand water means cork floors are good for kitchens, hallways, bedrooms and family rooms. You would have to be very careful if you used cork in a bathroom or other place where spilled water was a problem.

If you can live with cork's waterless restriction, it is an excellent flooring choice. It is whisper quiet and totally natural. You'll have something that is not only environmentally correct, but it also will mark you as a fashion leader. That gives you big time bragging rights.

SEPTEMBER 1, 2001

New lawn and garden equipment was a big hit at hardware show

By Glenn Haege /
Special to The Detroit News

CHICAGO

The big hit at last month's International Hardware Show was all the new products at the lawn and garden displays in McCormick Center's South Hall. Gardening is the most popular do-it-yourself activity. The many excellent columnists and feature stories in Homestyle attest to the fact that it is highly popular with the readers.

I decided to devote a full column to some of the exciting lawn and garden items my staff and I saw at last month's show.

At one time or another, everyone who gardens wishes that he or she had a greenhouse so that plants could be started earlier in the spring or worked with later in the fall. The trouble is that greenhouses take up a lot of room and are a fairly expensive commitment. Once you have a green house, it is there for keeps.

Not any more. Gronhaus has introduced an entire line of greenhouses that are lightweight, tentlike structures that can be carried in a tote bag and set up in about 30 minutes. They are made from Solaron, a specially formulated woven polyethylene glazing the allows 79 percent light transmission while blocking UV rays.

"Three, full-sized greenhouses are available," says Eric Reinsfelder, director of marketing for Gronhaus. "They range from a six-sided, gazebo-shaped, 11-foot, 8-inch by 10-foot Sonnen Haus for $300, to the 10-fo ot by 81/4-foot Gable Haus, which costs $400." Center heights range from 7- to 8-feet, 3-inches.

The Gable Haus by Gronhaus is a 7-by -10-foot greenhouse that costs only $400 and can be carried in a tote bag. It can be set up in 30 minutes and adds four months to your growing season.

They are available from the manufacturer by calling (800) 317-7225 or on their web site, www.gronhaus.com.

According to Greg Severin, one of the inventors, the greenhouses should last three to five years and permit the gardener to start working 60 days earlier in the spring and keep gardening 60 days later in the fall. If you are a gardener, $400 seems like a real bargain for an extra four months of gardening time.

Another big help for the gardener is the Garden Center by Today's Plastics, (800) 258-TOYS. The Garden Center is a garden cart with a difference. It opens up to become a potting/harvesting center, complete with sink, running water and storage drawers.

The Garden Center by Today's Plastics makes it easy to wash dirt off fresh from the garden vegetables. The handy cart opens up to become a complete tool storage/potting/harvesting center.

The Garden Center and a companion Deluxe Barbecue Station will cost between $120 and $125, according to Eleanor Zeliner, marketing manager. They should be in better garden centers by next spring.

The best way to connect water to a Garden Center would be to use one of the drinking water safe coil hoses on display at the show. The coil hoses are 25- and 50-foot hoses by companies such as Water Coil Hose, (888) 443-3842, and B&G Equipment Co., (800) 544-8811.

The beauties of coil hoses are that they don't kink and when you are done using them, they snap back to easily stored 18- to 24-inch coils. Coil hoses range in price from $20 to $50.

Water Coil hoses are carried by most national hardware chains. B&G's hoses are available direct at www.sprayersdirect.com, and at hardware stores and home centers.

If you would like to save money watering, Rain Drip Inc., (888) 923-3747, has micro water-

Imelda Trujillo of Rain Drip Inc. says that Micro Watering Kits like the one she is holding can cut water use by 70 percent. Drippers can be set to trickle as low as 1/2-gallon per hour.

ing kits that water plants, vegetables, even hanging plants by the drop. Drippers can be set to run at one half to two-gallons per hour. Starter kits retail for $35. You can find them at Lowes and Home Depot according to Imelda Trujillo, international accounts manager.

If you aren't around to water, the Direct Root Co., (888) 84-SPIKE, has developed Jelled Water Spikes. The Jell is made from a cellulose-based product that is 95 percent water. The jell trickles down the water spike into the soil. Ground bacteria eat the cellulose releasing the water. This slow conversion

provides sufficient water for a plant to stay healthy for two to three weeks according to John Vause, the company's National Sales Manager.

Water spikes retail between $1.49 and $1.99. If they are not at your garden center, you can get them on the Internet at www.directroot.com.

The last two products are worthy of mention because they are made from recycled materials and are good for the environment.

International Mulch Company in St. Louis, introduced Rubberific Mulch, (866) 936-8524. The mulch is made from old rubber tires. It comes in redwood, cedar, weathered oak, earth tone, Caribbean blue and cypress. The colors are permanent, the mulch will not rot, blow away or attract termites like wooden and bark mulches. It is also nontoxic and retains moisture.

Rubberific Mulch is not available everywhere, but it is a great idea and I hope you will find it soon at a garden center near you.

Eco-Planters by WorldWise are planters that look like all the other clay, foam or plastic planters you see in stores. Their beauty lies in the fact that they are made from recycled plastic wrap that would ordinarily go to garbage dumps. Large Eco-Planters, smaller Notta Pots and Whiskey Barrels last practically forever, are flexible and never break. They are currently carried in about 10,000 garden and home centers nationwide. For the store nearest you, call WorldWise, (800) 967-5394.

Next week, I'll tell you about the rest of the hardware show.

Hardware show had hits from security to a cozy outdoor fireplace

By Glenn Haege /
Special to The Detroit News

This year's Hardware Show at McCormick Center in Chicago had as many or more new, innovative products than my staff and I have seen in years. One exciting development was that many of the manufacturers now sell direct from their web sites, so you can get the new products even if they do not yet have retail distribution in your area.

Protect yourself

According to FBI statistics, 80 percent of all break-ins are gained by simply kicking in the door. Sixty percent of all rapes and 38 percent of all assaults occur during home invasions. Two new ways of keeping your doors from being forced open caught my attention.

Protekdoor is the world's first shock-absorbing, elastic polymer door lock. The polymer slips over the door knob and is anchored to the door frame. Once set, the Protekdoor has a tensile strength of 6,500 pounds, according to Ellen Tippetts, Protekdoor's marketing director. Kick the door in and it will just bounce back. Protekdoor retails for $19.95 and can be purchased on the company web site, www.protekdoor.com.

Have you ever tried to brace a chair under the door knob to keep a door from being opened? It is a good theory, but the chair usually slips. The Door Cop by Evertex Corporation, (281) 496-0441, is a lightweight, fiberglass rod with a rubber foot that will not slip no matter what the flooring surface. Once you brace the Door Cop under a door handle, the door will withstand more than 1,000 pounds ofpressure. The Door Cop retails for $24.95 and can be bought on the company web site, www.doorcop.com.

Basement laminate flooring

Laying laminate flooring on ground level and basement concrete slabs is often a problem because of moisture. Consella-Dorken's new polyethylene waterproof air gap membrane eliminates the problem and makes it easy to install a laminated floor. The new membrane, called DELTA-FL, locks out wet and damp.

Consella-Dorken, (888)-4DELTA4, worked with Quality Craft Laminated Flooring to perfect the do-it-yourself installation system. You just lay the DELTA-FL sheets down in an overlapping pattern. Cover the sheets with a thin foam sheet and place no-glue, snap-in-place wood grain panels down to complete the floor.

The products are carried in Michigan by N.A. Mans, (734) 676-3000, and Cheboygan Cement Products, (800) 548-8093.

Give water pressure a boost

There is nothing worse than water that just dribbles when you want to take a shower. Davey Pump's new XP and HS Range pressure boosting pumps can give you all the water pressure you  need, no matter how big or small your house.

The XP series is for homes with 20 pounds or less of pressure coming into their house. The HS series can handle up to 70 pounds of pressure on the water line. The pumps range from $300 to $400. If your local plumbing distributor does not yet have them, you can buy direct at www.dav eyusa.com or call (866) DAV-PUMP.

Drain window wells automatically

The Flotec Intelipump checks for water in basement window wells or on flat roofs every 2-1/2 minutes. If water starts collecting, the Intelipump automatically pumps down to 3/16-inch depth of water. The pump costs $199 and is available by special order at Home Depot.

Measure with touch of a button

Leica Geosystems, (800) 367-9453, introduced a new line of economical, precision, hand-held laser measuring tools. The new DISTO line comes in four different models ranging from the Disto Lite, which costs $495 and measures distances up to 330 feet, to the Disto Pro, which costs about $800, has an accuracy of 1/16th of an inch and an expanded memory of up to 800 values. The tools are for sale on the company's web site, www.leica -geosystems.com,

or at many retail locations throughout the world, including Cougar Sales and Rental, (248) 348-8864, in Novi.

Time for romance

How long has it been since you said, "Come on baby, light my fire?" Fire Designs, (800) 661-4788, has created a sophisticated new outdoor fireplace that reeks of romance. It looks like a large, Japanese metal lantern. The Luminarium Outdoor Hearth is made from your choice of powder-coated aluminum, stainless steel or copper. Prices range from $795 to $1,395. The Outdoor Hearth burns a special jelled fuel that costs $9 a gallon and lasts four to nine hours.

Most natural gas and propane outdoor fireplaces are built to really pump out the BTUs (British Thermal Units), so they are too hot for most summer evenings. The Outdoor Hearth is made to pump out romance. Its relatively cool, 17,000 BTU-per-hour fire means that you can use it on your patio or deck all summer long. You can buy from the company's web site at www.firedesigns.net.

If you want to make your fires the old-fashioned way, FISKARS, (800) 500-4849, has axes that range from a 14-inch hand ax to big log splitters. The fiber-glass-reinforced handles are molded over the heads, so you never loose a head while chopping. The heads are coated with Teflon so they don't get stuck. Prices range from $29 to $59.

Learn more on their web site, www.fiskars.com, in the gardening section.

It was a good show and you are now in the know – so brag about it.

Easy-care floors come clean without using a lot of elbow grease

By Glenn Haege /
Special to The Detroit News

What exactly does "easy care" flooring mean? And, if most flooring is easy care, is there such a thing as a hard care floor anymore? How are you supposed to care for your floors anyway?

There are eight common types of residential flooring: hardwood, laminate, cork, vinyl sheet goods and linoleum, vinyl tiles, ceramic tile, stone and carpeting. Of the eight, only vinyl and linoleum solid surface, vinyl and ceramic tiles, and stone like getting wet. The rest are like cats and want to keep their association with water to a bare minimum.

The two secrets to maintaining easy care floors are floor mats at every entrance and consistent vacuuming. Most flooring can be permanently scratched by minute particles of sand and dirt being walked in from outdoors. Floor mats absorb the grit and keep it from being walked onto the flooring's high-gloss surface. Floor mats with 100-percent latex backing are preferred.

Even with mats, some grit gets by. Vacuuming is the best way to pick up grit before it can do damage. Vacuum cleaners are better than brooms because they lift up the dirt and take it away. Brooms push grit around and air currents whip dust into the air.

Hepa filter vacuum cleaners are better than low or no filter vacuum cleaners. Centralized whole house vacuums that vent to the outside are the best of all because there is no possibility of dust recirculating.

Stone floors are the only flooring surfaces that should not be vacuumed. Pushing the vacuum around could scratch the surface. Stone floors should be dust mopped. When mopping, start at the furthest point away from the entrance and mop towards the door. This stops you from accidentally spreading grit.

When it's time to wash the floor, a spritzer bottle full of vinegar and water or nonammoniated window cleaner and a damp mop do better than a pail of hot water and cleaning solution. This is the easy care part of most easy care flooring.

The hard, durable surfaces on most of today's floors do not absorb dirt, spills and stains. Since there is no place for dirt to penetrate, deep cleaning is unnecessary.

Spritz a little cleaning solution on the floor and mop it up with a damp mop. Vinegar and water cleaning solution is mixed one cup per gallon of water. The slight acidic nature of this solution makes it a good natural antimicrobial. Use nonammoniated window washing solution straight from the bottle. By the way, Windex makes an antimicrobial window cleaning solution.

Most of the leading hardwood, laminate and vinyl tile and sheet goods companies make cleaning solutions especially made for their products. The general cleaning solutions I recommend clean just as well. The proprietary products are tweaked for the specific flooring and will sometimes restore the shine if a no-wax floor is getting dull.

Vinyl and ceramic tile are used a great deal in kitchens and baths. The kitchen gets the greasiest and the bathroom gets the grungiest of any rooms in the house. Sometimes you have a crying need to get down on your hands and knees or at least wet mop these floors.

Vinyl, linoleum and tile kitchen flooring can be cleaned with a 30 to 1 solution of water and Simple Green or Clear Magic. That's 4 ounces per gallon of warm water.

Sunshine Makers, (800) 228-0709, also makes a Simple Green Anti-Microbial Cleaner for quick bathroom cleaning.

Stone floors are the only type of flooring that actually wants to be wet mopped. Stone Care International, (800) 839-1654, makes a complete line of stone cleaning products. If you have stone floors, your best bet is to use Marbalex or one of their other cleaning systems.

Stone Care International products are carried by many flooring and some hardware stores. Damman Hardware, for instance, carries the product line at their largest stores. To find a store near you that carries the products, you can call SCI direct or get cleaning instructions on the company web site, www.stonecare.com.

Carpeting should be vacuumed daily if at all possible. Daily cleaning extends the life of the carpeting and makes your home more sanitary. All the dust mites, hair, skin flakes, and crumbs you can't see, but actually accumulate at the bottom of the carpet are whisked away where they can do no harm.

I recommend truck-mounted professional cleaning by top-of-the-line companies like Chet's Carpet Cleaning, (800) 404-0017; Duraclean by Maryanne, (800) 372-5427; and Modernistic, (800) 609-1000. Only truck-mounted equipment has the power to make certain all cleaning solution is removed. Cleaning solution residue pulls dirt from the soles of your shoes and makes the carpet dirtier, faster.

Hey, the floors clean. Take the rest of the day off and come see me at my Fall Home Expo.

Fall Expo

My annual WXYT Fall Home Expo is today and tomorrow at the Southfield Civic Center, 10-1/2 Mile and Evergreen. This year, there are many seminars by experts, including Brian Santos, the Wall Wizard, on painting and wallpapering, and Mad Dog & Merril, the Grilling Buddies, on barbecuing. The show is free, so is parking. It opens 10 a.m. and closes at 6 tonight and 4 p.m. Sunday.

SEPTEMBER 22, 2001

Deciding on window tint depends on what you hope to accomplish

By Glenn Haege /
Special to The Detroit News

One of the exciting things about writing a weekday question-and-answer column in addition to my Saturday Homestyle articles is that so many questions flow over our desks that my reading audience tells me what they want to know.

I've had a lot of requests from doctors and dentists about how to tint their windows to reduce window glare and increase patient privacy. Homeowners want information on how to reduce furniture and flooring fading from the sun's UV rays.

The answer to all these questions is window film. Laminated window film can also save money on heating and air conditioning bills, stop annoying window glare and help protect your house from break-ins and severe weather conditions such as hurricanes. If you are concerned about any of these conditions you are a good candidate for window film purchase.

Some window films such as those made by the GILA Products Division of C P Films, (800) 528-4481, are advertised as do-it-yourself items. All you have to do according to the commercials is clean the window, spray it with a little water and apply the film. If you decide you do not like the look, no problem, just pull off the film. Nothing could be easier.

Product quality and selection can be excellent. There are just two problems: not all windows are candidates for film

Important terms

■ *UV Rejection (UV): A measurement of the blockage of ultraviolet A & B rays. The higher the better.*

■ *Emissivity (EMIS): Measures how efficiently the window system reflects heat back indoors. The lower the number, the better.*

■ *Solar Energy Reduction: The total amount of infrared heat and UV rays shielded by the film. The higher the number, the better.*

application and there are many different window film choices.

Many major manufacturers, such as 3M, (800) 480-1704; Llumar, (800) 2-LLUMAR; SolarGard by MSC Specialty Films, (800) 282-9031; and Vista window film by C P Films, (800) 345-6088, require professional application.

Compounding the decision process is that some window, window shade and drapery manufacturers void their warranties if window film has been applied. Some window film manufacturers or individual installers extend their warranty or offer optional warranties that can replace the original manufacturers' warranties.

Not all window films are made the same way. Some window films are just tinted film. Others include metallised, adhesive and protective layers. Some of 3M's Scotchshield films are composed of more than 40 different layers.

Window film may make your window look gray, green, blue or brown. Some film is almost color-less. Some are especially made to provide privacy.

Mike Roeder, Specialty Protective Coatings, (800) 772-1885, a local (Michigan) 3M-film installer, says most home owners' window problems are caused by solar heat. Stop the heat and you've solved their problems.

The majority of window films reduce fading and save energy by reflecting solar heat and ultraviolet radiation. Some, but not all, films also reflect escaping heat back into the house during the winter.

For instance, 3M Scotchtint Sun Control films provide between 45 and 59 percent solar heat reduction and 99 percent UV blockage, but give little protection against winter heat loss. Scotchtint Plus All Season films not only give up to 73 percent solar heat reduction and 99 percent UV blockage, but also have a .34 to .45 Emissivity rating and reduce winter window heat loss by up to 30 percent.

Vista Window Films reduce UV penetration by 99.9 percent and Solar Energy (heat) by 26 to 75 percent. Their Low E, Ambiance Film has an Emissivity rating of .33.

Window film can also protect. Florida is often hard hit by hurricanes. 3M designed 3M Scotchshield Ultra Protective Film to meet Florida hurricane standards and Scotchshield to protect windows from intruders.

Neither Scotchshield nor Scotchshield Ultra can stop a window from breaking, but they are 130 times stronger than normal 4-mill window film. These films are designed to keep the windows from shattering. The glass may break, but the Scotchshield film holds the broken glass together. In other words 3M Scotchshield Ultra Film gives residential windows much the same shatter resistance as automobile safety glass windows.

Even greater holding power can be achieved with 3M's Scotchshield Ultraflex system, which bonds the film, glass and window frame together.

In addition to breakage protection, Scotchshield Ultra provides 99 percent UV blockage, but only gives 46 percent solar heat reduction and no heat loss reduction.

Specialty Protective Coatings have installation offices in Florida and a special information telephone number for Florida hurricane resistant window films, (877) SPC-3M3M.

Window films have many benefits, but there are definite trade-offs. You have to decide which properties are most important, then learn which films can give you the results you need. Even when you decide the film you want, there is a great difference in installation contractors. Check references thoroughly. Go out and see homes with windows containing the exact film you want. Talk to the homeowners, and you will brag about your results.

SEPTEMBER 29, 2001

New alternatives to vinyl siding offers the beauty of natural wood

By Glenn Haege /
Special to The Detroit News

Wood siding is loved, but has problems. It is expensive, takes a lot of care, and can rot. As soon as a house is built, the siding has to be prepped, primed and painted. Every five to seven years thereafter, the process has to be repeated. The best thing that can be said for this process is that you can change your home's exterior color scheme every few years.

Traditional wood siding also has to be put up one board at a time by skilled craftsmen.

To bring down costs and increase ease of installation, manufactured engineered wood products like T-1-11 were developed. New home builders found that the new products went up easy and just had to be sprayed with a thin coat of stain or paint. Or they slapped on plywood and sprayed on a mixture that looked like stucco.

Both the stucco and T-1-11 looked fairly good and the public was sold on the idea that they were quality siding alternatives.

Unfortunately, some builders did not read or follow manufacturers' installation instructions. (Instructions? What instructions?) The engineered wood panels were not back primed. The stucco was not installed properly. Drainage was not built into the walls and another new product, house wrap, was often put on wrong. The resulting failure rate caused so many claims and class action suits that several of our largest building product manufacturers had to seek Chapter 11 bankruptcy protection.

Average homeowners like you and me were stumped. Traditional wood siding was expensive and had to be repainted regularly. Lower cost, engineered replacements seemed to be a disaster. What to do?

In the 1950's, aluminum siding became popular. It was relatively inexpensive and looked pretty good. Unfortunately, aluminum siding has a tendency to dent and sooner or later the paint wears off and repainting is necessary.

Then vinyl siding was born. It was so much easier to care for than wood or aluminum that it soon became the overwhelming favorite. The only problem is that even the best embossed vinyl siding is only 4.4 mills thick. It can be beautiful, but it's not wood.

So new alternatives were developed. Louisiana Pacific, (800) 566-2282, developed engineered wood sidings called SmartLap and SmartSide. They have an embossed cedar grain texture. The siding is manufactured using a borate-based chemical that resists termites and fungal decay. Each board is embossed, not cut, and a resin-saturated primer paint base is applied.

Another relatively new product is fiber-cement siding. The most highly advertised is James Hardie Hardiplank, (888) J-HARDIE. Other brand names are Georgia-Pacific Cemplank and Cempanel, (877) CEMPLANK; GAF Fiber Cement, (800) 223-1948; and CertainTeed Weather Boards, (800) 233-8990.

Fiber-cement is several times thicker than vinyl and deeply embossed to look just as good or better than wood. It can be made to look like rough sawn cedar, round or octagon-cut shingles, even stucco.

The panels are cut and attached more or less like wood. They don't rot, but can be more delicate than wood. Fiber-cement panels have to be stored absolutely flat. They have to be picked up and carried carefully or they may break.

When nailing, you have to apply just the right amount of pressure to bond the nail to the panel. Hit the nail too hard and you have to repair and re-nail. Hit the nail too gently and the panel can wear prematurely. If moisture penetrates a panel, it will degenerate during freeze/thaw cycles like any other cement-based product.

According to the James Hardie company, the fiber-cement panels have to be primed with an acrylic latex primer and painted with top-of-the-line paints like Fuller O'Brien Weather King II Flat, Sherwin Williams' Duration, PPG Industries Manor Hall or Olympic Overcoat, or Valspar Severe Weather 15 Year 100% Acrylic Exterior Latex Flat. Regular repainting is required.

If all this makes you think vinyl siding is getting to look better and better, you are like the majority of Americans. According to the records of Siding World, (313) 891-2902, one of the Midwest's largest siding suppliers, more than 90 percent of all siding sold is vinyl.

There are many different vinyl siding manufacturers including CertainTeed, (800) 233-8990; Georgia Pacific, (800) 284-5347; Owens Corning, (800) 528-0942; and Rollex Corp., (800) 251-3300.

The CertainTeed's Wolverine Siding Systems, (888) 838-8100, carried by Siding World, are among the most advanced designs in the country. The company has gone to great lengths to make installation easy. Their Millennium siding has a patented nail-tight flexible hem fastening system that permits installers to nail hard. It makes installation almost goof proof. Most siding has to be installed relatively loosely or problems develop. The product is so good that it has a "Won't Blow-Off" Warranty.

Wolverine's Benchmark 44 siding, is over 200 percent stiffer than ordinary vinyl siding and includes a fiberglass reinforcement rod that locks into place.

Dollar for dollar, you can't beat vinyl. But consider all the options before you use the most powerful tool in your tool box (your checkbook). Then you will be able to brag about the result.

OCTOBER 6, 2001

Protect your home from small critters looking for a winter shelter

By Glenn Haege /
Special to The Detroit News

Kathy, my editor at Master Handyman Press, called me frantically Tuesday morning a couple of weeks ago. There were scurryings and scratchings up and down her kitchen wall. The sounds were driving her and her two Boston Terriers crazy. Both Dolly and Jonsie were throwing themselves at the wall trying to get at whatever was making the noise. What could she do?

Luckily, I know that Brian Sass and Paul LeBuhn of Maple Lane Pest Control, (586) 939-6810, are two of the best critter guys in the business. I made an emergency call and Sass came out the next day.

Questioning Kathy, Sass learned that the critter had stopped making noise the night before and she had heard only a few sounds the following day. Sass searched the attic looking for droppings, holes in the roof or walls, or other telltale signs. Nothing.

Next, he climbed up on the roof and crawled along the entire roof edge inspecting the gutters and soffits for rotten wood or the telltale half-round holes that squirrels chew through gutters and rotting wood to gain access to homes. Nothing.

He inspected every square foot of the roofing. Special attention was given to overhang junctures where different rooflines met, because these difficult-to-fill crevices are often left open by builders.

Brian Sass, Maple Lane Pest Control, inspecting roof gutter and soffit for signs of varmint entry. A small section of rotten wood will provide an entry for a squirrel looking for a warm place for the winter.

Sass went to his truck, took out and baited a catch and release trap. The trap, he explained, was just a security precaution in case a squirrel or raccoon had been able to make its way into the attic undetected. If his analysis was correct, the scented peanuts in the trap would remain undisturbed.

He then carefully inspected every inch of the perimeter of the house. Fat black, red, and gray squirrels glared at him cheekily from surrounding pine trees. Birds grudgingly flapped away from feeders filled with a variety of grains. Chipmunks scolded, then darted away under bushes or escaped into gutter drains scarred by bite marks from dog attacks during previous escapes.

Plenty of critters but no holes.

"The probability is that a couple of chipmunks have gotten bored warehousing nuts and pine cones in your garage and have found a way into the attic through the breezeway. You didn't hear any noise at night because chipmunks go to bed the same time we do," Sass says.

"The good thing about this is that chipmunks live underground and just use buildings to store food. The bad thing is that since they already have their food, they will probably not be interested in the bait in my trap.

"The best way to get rid of these critters is to get a very ornery cat. Most people don't like that kind of terminal solution," he says.

Kathy remembered that in previous years, a very rugged black and white tomcat patrolled the neighborhood. There had been few chipmunks, a much lower bird population, and no scurrying in the walls. Sadly, one day Tom decided that he was tough enough to face down a passing truck and was transported to that great cathouse in the sky.

Chipmunks are not much of a problem. The critters that every homeowner has to look out for during the fall are squirrels, raccoons, possums, skunks and field mice. All these guys want to come in, bed down, raise a family and can cause serious damage.

The average person doesn't spend more than 10 or 15 minutes a day looking at the outside of his house. A squirrel usually doesn't travel more than 300 feet in any direction during its entire life. It has hours to inspect every inch of your house to find the weak spot that will permit it to gain entrance.

Preventative maintenance is the most effective form of critter control. "At least twice a year the homeowner should get up on a ladder and inspect his home very carefully. Any rotten wood has to be replaced. This is especially important in the fascia boards in back of the gutters," Sass explains.

"Squirrels often find this soft wood and chew a small half moon opening through the top of the back of the gutter and the siding. This small hole is absolutely invisible from ground level," Sass says.

"All openings have to be plugged. Builders often leave air vents in brick or small openings where rooflines come into conjunction with the overhang. These openings are invitations for small wildlife. Brick vents have to be blocked with screening and small construction openings should be filled with backer rod or foam," he says.

An unscreened chimney like the one Brian Sass of Maple Lane Pest Control is pointing to is an easy "port of entry" for many birds, squirrels, and raccoons. Raccoons will actually bend back metal on chimneys and fans to make the opening large enough for them to crawl through easily.

Chimney protectors should be attached with screws going directly into the brick work because pressure-attached protectors can be pried off by raccoons. Roof fans should be screen covered because a determined raccoon will actually bend the fan blade up to provide an entrance.

Only by blocking or protecting every conceivable opening in your home's exterior can you be sure you won't be making a frantic call to a pest control specialist this winter.

Now, if we could only find a nice way to get rid of those cute little chipmunks.

OCTOBER 13, 2001

Programmable thermostat can save 10-20 % on heating, cooling

By Glenn Haege /
Special to The Detroit News

The government estimates you can save as much as 10 percent a year on your heating and cooling bills by simply turning the thermostat back 10 to 15 percent for 8 hours during a 24-hour period.

That means that during the heating season, if you turn the heat down when you go to bed at night or leave for work, you save 10 percent. If you remember to turn it down at both times, you could save almost 20 percent on the heating bill.

If you reverse the process during the cooling season and turn the thermostat up when you go to bed at night, and up when you leave for work during the day, you would get similar savings on your cooling bills.

The problem is we usually forget, and the heating or cooling stays on full blast when we go to bed at night and go away during the day.

One of the easiest ways to make sure the temperature is turned up and down at the proper times so that you save money on energy bills is to install and use a programable thermostat.

Even if you are a super-efficient person and remember to turn the thermostat up and down at all the proper times, a programable thermostat, will make those changes more efficiently than you ever could. When you program the thermostat it takes a few days to learn your heating and cooling systems. If you want the temperature to be 73 degrees when you get up at 7:30 in the morning, the thermostat learns how long it takes to go from the night-time setting to the morning setting and then will turn on the furnace and start the blower going so that at exactly 7:30 a.m., when you crawl out from under the covers, the temperature is 73 degrees.

The same procedure happens at night. If you want it to be 65 degrees at 11 p.m., the thermostat will start scaling back the heat from its daytime setting so the household temperature is exactly 65 degrees at 11 p.m.

Most programable thermostats will let you set 4 to 6 different temperature settings during a 24-hour period. You can also have different weekday and weekend settings. Some will let you program each day separately.

Unfortunately, according to Jim Williams of Williams Refrigeration, (888) 268-5445, the new thermostat's greatest strength is also its greatest weakness. A programable thermostat that is just put on the wall and not programed doesn't save anyone a dime.

If you have a programable thermostat installed, you have to make sure the heating contractor sends out a technician who knows how, and is willing, to program the thermostat for you.

You should also have done your homework and have written down the different temperatures that you want to have at different times of the day.

For instance, you sleep with the covers on at night so the temperature can go down to 65 degrees. When you get up, you may want it to be 73. If the house is empty during the day with everyone away at work or school, the temperature could safely be lowered when everyone leaves.

Even if you stay at home, you will probably want the temperature lowered a few degrees after breakfast when you start your daily chores. Then, when you stop your chores and sit down to watch TV or read, or when the family returns, you want the temperature turned up to your favored at-home setting. A good programable thermostat can do all this for you easily.

Not all thermostats are created equal. Prices can range from less than $50 to several hundred dollars or more. Some are very difficult to program. Others, like the new Honeywell, (800) 328-5111, Professional Model Program-mable Thermostat model 8602 are preprogramed, but permit easy reprograming by merely pushing the Wake, Leave, Return or Sleep buttons.

Most thermostats are meant to stand alone and just adjust your home's heating and cooling cycles. Others, like the Honeywell 8600 or the Bryant, (800) 428-4326, Thermo Distat, can be equipped with outside sensors and control heating, cooling and humidifi-cation to provide a total comfort system.

Programable thermostats do not need to be expensive and many, such as the Lux, (800) 468-1317, TX 500, are carried as do-it-yourself items at home centers and hardware stores. All you have to do is turn off the electricity, take off your old thermostat and attach the new one. The pre-programed setting will take over and start saving you money as soon as the electricity is turned back on.

One word of caution about the old mercury thermostat you will be taking down. The small amount of mercury in the thermostat is hazardous waste. You can do a great deal of damage if you just throw it into the garbage. Call your city's sanitation department and ask where you should take the thermostat for disposal. If you live in southern Oakland County, call (248) 288-5153

Two new ideas from the Pink Panther

By Glenn Haege /
Special to The Detroit News

If you drool over home theater or wish to turn your basement into an attractive living/working space, the Pink Panther has got a deal for you.

Several weeks ago, my staff and I visited Owens Corning's Science and Technology Center in Granville, Ohio. The purpose of the trip was to meet many of their key Research and Development people and to learn about some of the new products under development.

Frank O'Brien-Bernini, vice-president of the center, picked us up at the airport and spent the day with us. Much of the information was about projects that are still in the pipeline and not yet ready to be written about here. Two of the most exciting projects, however, are available today and could start improving your quality of life before the snow flies.

Owens Corning has made home theater practical and put quality basement remodeling on the fast track.

Home theater is not just a fancy television set and a couple of extra speakers. To get the proper effect, you need to devote an entire room to sight and sound. Most of us spend a lot more time watching television than we spend in the kitchen or bathroom. When you consider how much time the average family watches TV, having a special room designed to optimize viewing pleasure can make a lot of sense.

Up until now, if you decided to upgrade your audio/video experience, you would go to a high fidelity specialist and start cobbling together a system. If you were lucky, the store might offer an installation service. The system would usually be wired into an existing room. If modification to the room were called for, it would be performed by a builder who would probably know next to nothing about enhancing sight and sound quality.

Owens Corning has revolutionized the buying process. Instead of trying to reinvent the wheel each time, the company provides turn-key rooms called Visionaire FX Personal Entertainment Centers. The rooms can be adapted to a wide range of sizes, but come in 13-by-19 feet and 15-by about 22 feet base sizes. They are designed specifically for the equipment used and seat six people in big theaterlike seats. Prices, which start at less than $29,000, include lighting, SelectSound Reversible Acoustic Panels and Diffusers, sound and video equipment.

If you want to have a home theater designed to your exact specifications and equipment, Owens Corning Acoustic Design Services will undertake the project for you. They can also completely condition the walls, ceilings and floors of their home theaters so that almost no sound escapes the room.

Right down the hall from the elegant home theaters, Traci Aloi, product technical leader and one of the inventors of Owens Corning's Basement Wall Finishing System, showed us the company's new idea in basement remodeling. The new system enables a franchised contractor to completely refinish a basement in as little as seven to 10 days.

Up until now, basement remodeling has used paneling or drywall for walls. Both products are subject to moisture damage and mold growth. The mainstays of Owens Corning's new system are 2-1/2 inch thick, fabric covered, rigid fiberglass panels and specially designed PVC moldings and supports that create moisture-resistant walls with an R-11 insulation value. The panels are easy to assemble and also can be taken down if you need to rewire or want to reconfigure the room.

The rigid fiberglass panels breathe, do not support mold growth and keep out the cold, which makes the basement easier to heat in winter and drier and more comfortable during the summer. The combination of benefits creates affordable, attractive and livable basement rooms.

The Owens Corning Basement Finishing System is not a do-it-yourself project. It has to be installed by company-trained and franchised contractors. In Metro Detroit, the basement system is installed by Fairway Construction, (800) 354-9310, in Southfield, and Home Run Basement Systems, (734) 668-8770, in Ann Arbor.

The basement remodeling and home theater systems are just in their infancy today, but they are light years ahead of their competition. If the ideas sound interesting, give Owens Corning a call at (800) 438-7465, and ask for more information, or visit www.owenscorning.com on the Internet. Learn all you can before you do, then brag about the result.

Get a lock on old man winter by ensuring doors are prepared

By Glenn Haege /
Special to The Detroit News

One of the things we should all do before we run out of the last of the warmer weather, is make sure all the doors are ready for the grim reality that is just ahead. That includes front and back doors, storm doors, sliding glass doors and garage doors.

If you have storm doors, screens have to be removed and replaced with glass. All hinges on front and back doors and storm doors have to be treated to a squirt of 3-in-One oil. Locks should be dusted with graphite. If they don't work effortlessly now, they will be a problem when winter comes.

Locks that seem stiff may be just dirty. Take out the lock. Wipe off all the moving parts and dust with graphite. Then re-assemble. The lock should work fine. If it still catches, make certain that the door is in proper alignment. A couple of hinge screws may have gotten loose. Tighten them and all should be well.

The rollers on sliding glass doors see a lot of difficult action. Make certain that the lower guide is totally clear of dirt and grease. Wipe old grease off rollers with a rag dampened with mineral spirits or rubbing alcohol, then lubricate with 3-in-One oil or Lithium grease.

Now comes the hard part. It is time to lubricate the garage door and door opener. As soon as the weather gets cold,

WD-40

Although Henry Tarnow does not believe in using WD-40 as a lubricant, he says that it makes an excellent cleaner. WD-40 has the ability to cut through old grease and make it easy to remove. Spray the WD-40 everywhere there is old, sticky grease. Then remove the grease with paper toweling.

many garage doors start to moan and groan when they are raised or lowered. That noise is a sign that the doors have been improperly lubricated. That, in turn, could take several years off the life of your door or cause needless service calls.

According to Henry Tarnow, of Tarnow Garage Doors in Farmington Hills, (800) 466-9060, there are two steps to lubricating a garage door. First, all the old grease and gunk that doesn't belong has to be removed; then the hinges and moving parts have to be oiled. Tarnow recommends using 3-in-One oil or a good silicone or teflon spray.

Taking the old gunk off is more important than applying new lubricant. Once it turns cold, old grease becomes very tacky. Instead of lubricating, the old built-up grease pulls at the moving parts and causes premature door failure.

Although Tarnow does not believe in using WD-40 as a lubricant, he says that it makes an excellent cleaner. WD-40 has the ability to cut through old grease and make it easy to remove. Spray the WD-40 everywhere there is old, sticky grease. Then remove the grease with paper toweling.

It is especially important to clean roller guide tracks and other places that should not really be greased. If your garage has an older Stanley Door with a tube-type door opener, spray the tube with WD-40 and remove grease buildup with paper toweling.

Once you have cleaned off the grease, lightly lubricate all moving parts with 3-in-One oil or silicon spray.

There are basically two different types of garage doors - old-fashioned tilt-out doors and sectional doors.

"On old tilt-out doors, be sure to lubricate the pivot points where the arms connect to the wall. There are two door pivots, left and right. Also lubricate the roller where the arm connects to the door and where the spring connects to the arm," Tarnow says.

On sectional doors, Tarnow recommends that you lubricate the overhead torsion springs, the rollers, hinges and anything that moves. Make sure you do not accidentally lubricate the tracks that guide the rollers. Those tracks should be kept clean and dry so that rollers move back and forth effortlessly.

Most sectional doors have hinges mounted on the back of each section that should be lubricated.

"In this market, we also have Taylor sectional doors," Tarnow says. "Typically, these doors have springs on each side of the door. Each one of these springs has two pulleys, one above the spring and one at the top of the track. The pulleys should be lubricated. Taylor doors do not have external hinges between the sections. Squirt some lubricant along the inside edges of each section. The lubricant will work a lot of rust out of the enclosed hinges and help the door move better during the winter."

When it comes to lubricating of door opener systems, take care not to lubricate the track or the tube on the door openers. Lubricating these parts can make them so sticky that movement becomes almost impossible during cold weather.

Check the manual that came with your garage door opener before lubricating the chain or tracks on the door opener. On some models, grease buildup can cause such problems that lubrication is forbidden. On the other hand, some screw drive openers need to be lubricated to function properly.

A little investigation takes the mystery out of lubrication, and opening and closing all your doors will be an open-and-shut case.

You can prepare for roof dams, but there's no absolute prevention

By Glenn Haege /
Special to The Detroit News

It's not even snowing yet, and I'm writing about roof dams. The reason why I'm jumping the gun is because last year many of us went absolutely bonkers from ice and snow on the roof, ice in the gutters, ice damming, roof leaks and associated problems.

Problems caused by ice dams and the associated water damage cost residents of the northern tier of the United States and Canada millions of dollars. My radio show was inundated with ice dam questions, and I wrote a few articles on the subject.

My staff and I kept researching the problem and possible solutions throughout the rest of the year. I visited the Owens Corning Science and Technology Center, where I talked with Frank O'Brien-Bernini, vice-president of Science & Technology, and Merle F. McBride, Ph.D., P.E., senior researcher, on just about everything having to do with insulation. Dr. McBride is highly regarded as one of the top experts on insulation theory in the country.

After all this digging, I can tell you that the best way to make sure your house does not suffer from ice damming this winter is to move to Florida. There is a great deal that you and I can do to make certain that our homes conform to the latest in cold roof or hot roof theories. After that, it's in the lap of the gods.

The reason I am belaboring the point is because homeowners who have spent good money making sure that their home's roof, gutters, attic ventilation and insulation systems are the best they can be are still having problems. Many perfectly good, conscientious roofing, gutter, gutter cover and insulation contractors are getting bad-rapped by homeowners who believe that since the problem isn't solved, the contractor has done something wrong.

This is usually not the case. The culprit, according to O'Brien-Bernini, is the construction of the house's roofline. The problem starts at the extreme tip of the roof, where roofline and soffit converge and the gutter starts. There is not enough room in this small triangle of space to squeeze both the insulation needed to keep heat from rising, and the rafter ventilation required to keep the under side of the deck boards below freezing.

Any time there is snow on the roof and the temperature is above 32 degrees Fahrenheit in the attic, the warm roof deck boards transmit heat to the shingles. This heat melts the underside of the snow on the roof.

Water from melting snow trickles down the roof until it gets to the gutter or anywhere else where the temperature is below freezing. At this point the water turns into ice, and an ice dam begins forming.

Some folks try to outwit Mother Nature by installing electric heat cables, which melt the snow and ice on the lower roofline and inside gutters and down spouts. This is an excellent theory, and it works as long as you can afford the electric bill and nothing goes wrong. If it starts snowing and the electricity is not on, the cables are useless. If the cables cross or get loose, they can short out and create electrical damage. In the event of a really bad storm, should power go out for a few hours, the cables cease to perform.

Some people are discarding the "Cold Roof" theory in favor of the "Hot Roof" theory, which insulates the bottom of the deck boards and separates it entirely from the house proper. It's a good theory, but until it has many years of positive experience, I can't really endorse it. Besides, in the past few weeks I have had calls from people with roofs made out of Structural Insulated Panels (SIPs) who have had problems.

An SIP is a sort of sandwich made from two pieces of plywood and ridged foam insulation. The SIP is the ultimate embodiment of the Hot Roof theory. If even this type of construction can develop problems, I, and everyone else I know, have run out of answers.

So what is the very best that you as a homeowner can do?

■ Cover the floor of the attic with enough insulation so that no heat escapes from the house proper into the attic. The National Building Code calls for R-49 of insulation on the attic floor.

■ Make certain that the soffit has plenty of soffit vents and protect and direct the airflow to the ridge of the roof with attic rafter vents.

■ Maintain an unobstructed ridge vent so that the air can escape from the house after cooling the roof.

Jimmy Kugat of the Xavier Corporation, (734) 462-1033, insists that you can improve airflow by installing turbo vents on the ridge at each end of the house. In theory, this would improve the cooling of the underside of the roof.

■ After all this, finish up by doing what I am planning to do. Go to your local hardware store and get a roof rake and a supply of calcium chloride crystals to take care of the inevitable ice. Then pray for a warm winter.

A little advice and these products will help you maintain your home

By Glenn Haege /
Special to The Detroit News

Here is some clear, concise home product advice that you may be able to use right now.

Ice Melters

If you think that this is going to be a long, cold winter with plenty of ice and snow, now is the time to stock a supply of ice melters. My spies tell me that the manufacturers' reserves of rock salt, calcium chloride and other ice melters were used up last year and have not been replenished. Plus, some manufacturers would rather be sold out than have to carry excess inventory over the summer.

This might be OK if we were talking nonessentials. When it comes to ice storms if you, me and the road commissions don't have sufficient supplies, there will be slipping and sliding everywhere. Some retail distributors are already getting panic calls from smaller counties that can't get the supplies they need.

If we have a bad winter, look out. Oh, by the way, the price has more than doubled.

Weathergard Windows

Weathergard Windows, (800) 377-8886, has just been approved by the National Fenestration Rating Council (NFRC) for the prestigious Energy Star rating. Both of Detroit's big vinyl window manufacturers, Weathergard and Wallside, make good windows. Weathergard is the first to compete head to head with the largest window companies in America and have their windows tested by the NFRC. Their windows are now certified to carry the Energy Star Label.

In addition to the Energy Star Rating, Weathergard announced the change to a new glass for its residential windows. The new glass, made by AFG Industries, is called the Comfort Titanium Low-E system. According to the manufacturer, the use of titanium gives the glass a .3 U-factor. This incredibly low U-factor makes a very energy-efficient window.

Gleme Glass Cleaner

This product has won a great many advocates since I first introduced it to readers. Made specifically for the janitorial trade, Gleme contains a mixture of alcohols and other cleaners that make it very effective and streak free.

When Scrubs, the local retailer that sold Gleme, went out of business I could not find anyone interested in selling the product to the public. No sooner did I announce that I couldn't find anyone than intrepid Detroit News readers began e-mailing me places where Gleme was still available.

All but one sell the product only in case lots. Arthur told me that Amer-I-Clean Equipment & Chemical Supply Co.,

(248) 398-4746, in Oak Park sells Gleme. Barb said to try Tuttle Supply Inc., (734) 283-6630, in Wyandotte. Pat told me that she purchased Gleme at Fastenal, (313) 295-3220, in Taylor.

Phyllis found Gleme on the Internet at www.dudco.com. Mary Ellen and Cecil found it at the Scott Tissue store near the Dayton Mall, three miles south of Dayton, Ohio. And Rick found a web site that sells Gleme by the can: www.cleanandpaper.com.

I've checked and the product is indeed available at all of the above places.

In addition, my old friend, Stuart Borman, one of the owners of the now defunct Scrubs store, says that he is so impressed with the tremendous following for the product that he will be opening a product specific web site, www.cleanwithgleme.com, in the next few weeks.

Duct cleaning

We've had a very cold/warm/wet fall. This is perfect weather for the spread of microbes. Duct work is an excellent breeding ground. The furnace has kept it warm. The excess humidity has kept it moist. If the ducts are littered with dirt, dust, flaked skin, cat, dog and human hair, it's party time! The duct work in many homes is filled with everything dust mites, mold, mildew, and microbes need to feed and propagate.

Add a cold snap that keeps the furnace blower motor running and all the bad guys will be spread throughout the house. Colds, sinus and runny noses will abound. It happens every winter.

Most of us have forced air heat. The rule of thumb is that if you have children and/or cats and dogs (big dogs are the worst) the ductwork should be cleaned every 3 or 4 years. If you don't have kids, cats or dogs, ducts only need to be cleaned once every 7 years.

If you have a new house or are going to get a new furnace, you also need your ductwork cleaned. The ducts in many new homes are filled with saw dust and everything from old newspaper to sandwiches and pop bottles. The blower motor on a new furnace will be a lot more powerful and run for a longer length of time than an old one so more dust will be spread throughout the house.

There are a lot of duct cleaners out there. Some you may want to consider are A-1 Duct Cleaning, (800) 382-8256; Dalton Environmental, (800) 675-2298; Dusty Ducts, (313) 381-7801; Fresh Air Solutions, Inc., (800) 341-4076; Safety King, (888) 382-8776; Sanit-Air, (888) 778-7324; Sterling Environmental, (888) 992-1200; and VentCorp, (248) 347-9300.

What you don't see is worth what you get with Code Plus construction

By Glenn Haege /
Special to The Detroit News

Over the years, I have kept on mumbling about Code Plus construction while most builders go about building homes just like they have for the past 20 or 30 years. Oh, there have been a few upgrades. House wrap was one of them. Like most innovations, the consumer (you and me) demanded it, the builder didn't suggest it.

Readers and listeners who are building new homes come to me at shows and personal appearances and ask how to upgrade construction. Most new home buyers, even those spending $500,000 or more, have no idea what Code Plus means, or the advantages that it could give them over the years. Many get downright angry when they move into their new, old-thinking home and find out what they could have had for the same or just a little more money.

Code Plus has nothing to do with getting 10,000 square feet of extra dry wall and five unnecessary bathrooms. It is not all that closely related to cost. A Code Plus house should not cost more than 15 percent over standard construction. Most of this initial outlay could be recouped by the homeowner in energy savings within five years.

The added quality of life that Code Plus can give is therefore added at little or no cost. All it takes is a forward-looking builder and a buyer who wants the best and is willing to learn enough to demand it.

Code Plus means thinking out of the box and getting more than the bare minimum. To give you an idea about what I mean, I'm going to spend the next few weeks building a word picture of a Code Plus house. We're not going to spend time talking about the things you see and can readily shop for, like flooring or high-end kitchens and baths. I'm going to write about materials and structural components you don't see that can make a big difference.

Code Plus starts at the very beginning and makes itself felt throughout construction.

Basement and walls

The basement would be built of insulated concrete forms (ICF) or precast concrete insulated panels. Both of these systems create walls that are sandwiches made from two layers of rigid foam insulation with a 4- to 8-inch thick filling of concrete. A heavy layer of rigid foam insulation is also placed beneath the concrete slab basement floor. In the southern tier of states, or anywhere with a termite problem, special anti-termite protection would be added.

Since this is my dream house, I am going to use the same ICF system to form all exterior and interior walls. I will waterproof the basement walls with a skin of Consella Dorken Delta-MS, (888) 4DELTA4 (www.deltams.com), dimpled water-proof sheeting.

The result of my Code Plus Construction choices so far is a house that will save the homeowner at least 50 percent on my heating and cooling bills, is whisper-quiet and has a moisture-, mold- and mildew-proof basement.

If your builder insists on using more traditional 2-by-4 stick-built technology, the poured concrete or block basement walls should be insulated to R-8 on the outside and R-11 on the inside of the block. The above ground walls should be insulated to R-13.

If using traditional technology, the basement also should be waterproofed, not damp-proofed, from the outside during construction. I like the Consella Dorken dimpled sheeting, but there are several good film systems available. The important thing is to keep water from ever getting to the concrete walls.

Exterior

The exterior skin of the house can be a tasteful combination of Nova Brick, cultured stone and vinyl siding. In outward appearance it will look no different than any other house in the subdivision, but the homeowner and his family will enjoy the Code Plus features for as long as they live there.

The interlocking Nova Brick needs no mortar and drains naturally if moisture somehow penetrates the skin. The cultured stone is used as tasteful design accents and is maintenance-free. The vinyl siding will look like wood, but will never rot and, if I wash it twice a year, should not need painting for at least 20 years.

Roof

I will roof the house with either concrete tile or metal; and insulate the underside of the roof deck with Icynene, (800) 946-7325. The result will be a fireproof roof that the manufacturers say can withstand 100-mile-an-hour winds, should not need any major repairs for 50 years and is mold- and mildew-proof.

Windows and doors

Windows would be top-of-the-line Marvin, Pella, Andersen or Weather Shield. They will have vinyl- or aluminum-clad exterior frames. The windows will be double-glazed, energy efficient, low-E glass with special UV-resistant tinting on the sides of the house that receive the most sun.

Inside, the floors and doors will be constructed using Owens Corning sound control technology. When combined with the insulated block interior walls, the result will be whisper -quiet. Noise outside the house will not come in. The sound control within the house is so good that Junior could practice with his rock band in one room while Mom or Dad nap undisturbed in the next.

I'll also specify a power-vented air exchange and high-end wiring and heating, cooling and air cleaning systems. There's no space to describe them all now, so I'll cover them over the next few weeks.

Electric and plumbing set-up for a Code Plus house is worth the cost

By Glenn Haege /
Special to The Detroit News

Code Plus is more than just the basic structure of a house. It is also the plumbing, electrical, security and home maintenance systems that keep the house running. These are all things that are not even thought about by the average new home buyer. You expect them to be there.

Given a choice, most builders put in the minimum the building code allows. Code Plus construction pays a lot of attention to these all too easily neglected details. The house is built to run more efficiently and be readily adapted to future needs.

Many homes have 3/4-inch diameter pipes connecting to the city water lines bringing water into the house. Water is a critical need for the proper functioning of toilets, showers and faucets. We'll upgrade to 1-inch diameter pipe. This small increase dramatically increases the amount of water available to the house at any given time.

If water pressure is a problem in our community, we will include an in-line water pressure boosting pump such as the Davey XP and HS series, to improve the flow. Call (866) DAV-PUMP.

In our Code Plus house, we will call for all hot and cold water lines to be copper. In some parts of the country which have water with very low pH and high CO_2, high quality CPVC pipe, such as FlowGuard Gold, would be preferred. In the vast majority of the country, however, copper is the quality standard.

All the water that comes in has to go out. The drain waste vents and pipes will be iron. PVC pipes and fittings are less expensive and easier to install. They are also less substantial and more prone to have problems.

When it comes to electrical, the home will have a minimum of 200 amp service, a larger home may require two 200 amp, 40 circuit panels. Wiring will be Category Five (CATV). This is extra heavy, shielded wiring that will assure that plenty of power will always be available.

Most people can't afford everything they would like their home to have on the day they move in. Pre-engineering a house for advanced systems is relatively inexpensive. Retrofitting the house for new systems after the house has been built is very expensive. Our home will be prewired for sound and broadband computer as well as video and audio monitoring and communication systems.

Electrical systems are only as good as the power being supplied. Even the power companies recommend building

222

homes geared to take occasional blackouts in stride, yet most new homes have no protection. Our Code Plus house will have a natural gas powered automatic standby generator that will sense when power is being limited and take the house off line when necessary. It will go on any time the power goes down and automatically turn itself off when site generated electric power is no longer needed.

Most house fires could be contained with little damage and no loss of life if a sprinkler system is installed. The house will also be prepped for a sprinkler system.

One if the most effective ways to improve air quality is to install a central vacuum system. They make taking care of carpeted, hardwood, tile and vinyl floors a great deal easier. Honeywell thinks they are so important that they even include a central vac system in their advanced technology Home & Building Control Package, (800) 345-6770 Ext. 2033. Other quality central vacuum systems are made by Beam, (800) 369-2326, and VacuFlo, (800) 822-8356.

The electrical systems, of even the best built house, can be zapped by a nearby lightning bolt. To make sure this never happens, whole house surge protectors will be mounted to protect the electric panels. We will also install surge protectors where the telephone and cable lines enter the house.

All these protective systems and back-up systems can not assure that disaster will never happen, but our Code Plus house will assure that we have done everything to protect our homes and our families.

Next week, I will have the third and final installment of this series on what you should look for "behind the scenes" in a Code Plus house. In that article, I will give recommendations on heating and air conditioning systems, filter and air cleaners and water heaters.

Admittedly, this all gets a little complicated. Some of the things I've written about today are a little like Greek to average home buyers. All they want is to buy a home. They are too busy raising families and making the money needed to pay for all this to become construction experts.

An increasing number of professionals hire personal construction managers who have the expertise and will take the time to be on the job every day to make sure that Code Plus quality is not only in the purchase agreement but actually built into the house.

Most builders are very honorable but they can't be everywhere, all the time. They have to rely on job supervisors and lead carpenters who are trying to make deadlines and often hire less than adequately trained personnel. In the final analysis, it is up to the buyers to see what is going on and make certain that they are getting a Code Plus house.

Code Plus heating and cooling appliances help you save in the long run

By Glenn Haege /
Special to The Detroit News

Manufacturers make special "builder's grade products" for every major piece of equipment included in a house. That includes furnaces, central air conditioning units, water heaters, garbage disposers, doors, garage doors, windows, just about everything. "Builder's grade" and "minimal quality" are synonymous.

You deserve better. Code Plus makes sure that you get it. This article is going to cover Code Plus heating, cooling and air cleaning.

The type of heating system you choose is a personal preference. A few hardy pioneers choose solar backed up by generators and electric heat. It is a heating system that is "almost there". Stay tuned.

A much larger percentage chooses geothermal,. which utilizes a heat pump and a closed loop system to let Mother Nature do most of the heating and cooling work. Properly designed, the system can even give you an almost unlimited hot water supply. Geothermal has an expensive initial cost, but saves so much money over the long run that it is an excellent heating and cooling choice for people who would normally have to settle for propane or electric heat. The Water Furnace Company, (800) 222-5667, is a prime manufacturer. Detroit Safety Furnace, (800) 682-1538, distributes Command-Aire, and Foster-Kilby, (800) 632-5706, distributes Florida Heat Pump.

Hydronic heating uses electric lines or water pipes under the floor to heat the house. This type of heating has several advantages: your tootsies always stay warm. Heat starts at ground level and rises slowly, keeping you comfortable. Every room in the house can be heated equally, so there are no cold spots. There are never any drafts caused by a blower motor turning on.

This type of heat is created by a boiler system or extensive use of electricity. The boiler system is excellent, but the electric system is cost-prohibitive. The Lennox Complete Heat furnace water heater system, (972) 497-5000, and the American Water Heater Company Polaris Heating System, (800) 937-1037, are excellent for hydronic heating. They also can be adapted to supply the house with a limitless supply of hot water.

Most of us use natural gas forced-air heating systems. There is now a 90 Plus Efficient furnace design that is far superior to other furnace designs and would be my personal choice for a Code Plus house. The new design has variable speed motors and a modulating burner design. Currently, the new design is found on top-of-the-line Rheem and Ruud Furnaces, [both have the same customer service number:(800) 621-5622], as well as Trane, (888) 872-6335, and American Standard Furnaces distributed by Foster-Kilby.

The modulating burner design means that if it isn't very cold outside and the furnace could heat your house efficiently with only half the burner operating, that's all that goes on. Your furnace burns longer and more efficiently. This is better for your personal comfort and cuts down wear and tear on the furnace.

Most furnaces have one or two speed blower motors. Variable speed motors have a wide range of blower speeds. The blower motor can operate continuously at low speed, eliminating blower motor draft. They are so efficient that they cost no more to run than a 60 or 70 watt light bulb.

I would team up the furnace with central air units made by the same company, so that they would be engineered to work with the furnace blower motor system. Central air units with 12 SEER are most cost efficient in Northern tier states. Since this is new construction, I might be tempted to specify the more efficient 14 SEER system.

A high SEER rating gets more important for southern tier states. I would specify 17.8 SEER rating equipment for use in Florida, Texas, Nevada and Southern California or any state that has high heat and humidity readings over an extended period of time.

Heating and cooling requirements vary in different parts of the house at different times of the day. The Code Plus house should be zoned with ductwork zone controls by companies like Duro Dyne, (800) 966-6446, and Research Products, (608) 257-8801. Each zone should have its own thermostat.

The heating system would also be enhanced with a state of the art Flow-Through humidifier with external sensors that automatically adjust humidity levels according to outside temperatures. Top of the line units are made by Honeywell, (800) 664-6478, April Aire, (608) 257-8801, and Lennox.

The average furnace is protected with an inefficient fiberglass filter. In a Code Plus house this would be upgraded to a thick media filter like the Trion Air Bear, (800) 338-7466.

Inside air is usually far dirtier than the fresh air we breath outside. If enhanced air quality were an issue for medical reasons, I might upgrade to a Dynamic Electronic Air Cleaner, (800) 916-7873, and an Amaircare Whole House By Pass HEPA filter system, (877) 839-3036. These two Canadian companies are making some of the highest quality air filtration and cleaning equipment available today. The By Pass filter in addition to either the thick media filter, or the Dynamic air cleaner, could actually make inside air quality cleaner than outside air.

Over the last three weeks we have outlined some of the many features that should be included in Code Plus construction. If you do your homework and learn about these upgrades, then find a builder willing to include them in your new home, I guaranty that you will be bragging for a long, long time.

Gift ideas help make it easy to shop for that special do-it-yourselfer

By Glenn Haege /
Special to The Detroit News

I've never understood why fruitcake gets a bad wrap from people. They obviously never tasted my Grandma Sternfel's fruitcake. Her cakes were sliced paper-thin so they would last until Easter. Everyone who knew about them, fought for them.

Grandmother has been gone for several years and her fruitcakes are but fond memories. Recently I discovered a fruit-cake that is a close runner up to Grandma's. Collin Street Bakery, (800) 292-7400, makes a fruitcake that is almost as good. It is so fruity and nut filled that 20 percent of its weight are pecans. Their large fruitcake costs $41.95. They are expensive but so good you'll brag about them.

Here are some other ideas to help over-stress your credit card this holiday season.

All the home centers have used their clout to come up with gangbuster gift ideas. If you have a special someone who has been a very good boy or girl this year, Home Depot's Ryobi four-piece Super Combo Cordless Kit priced at $200, is hard to beat. The kit contains a powerful 18-volt cordless drill, reciprocating saw with a general purpose blade, a 5 1/2-inch circular saw with a carbide tipped blade, flashlight and two rechargeable batteries, a diagnostic charger and case.

Should that be a little pricey, Home Depot also has a Black & Decker combination hand saw/jig saw for $60. Designed to take a lot of the work out of sawing, it has a husky 3.4 amp motor and interchangeable saw and jig saw blades.

Both Damman Hardware and Home Depot have the Black & Decker VersaPak Cordless Pivot Driver on special in the $30 range. This 3.6-Volt cordless screwdriver locks in 2 positions, so you can drive screws from almost any angle. It doesn't matter how many tools the handyman or woman on your list has, if they don't have a Pivot Driver, they need one.

Snow rakes can be a lifesaver gift for any homeowner. The problem is we forget to buy then until it snows, and the stores are sold out. Many hardware and home centers have them right now, and they would make a great gift. Frentz and Sons Hardware, (248) 544-8111, in Royal Oak, has the best I've seen. The Garelick aluminum snow rake has wide plastic wheels that protect the roof by keeping the edge of the rake about 1/2 inch away from the shingles. The price is $43. John Frentz told me that he would hold back 100 for my readers. It's first come, first served, so hurry.

Fiskars classic Bucket Boss line turns buckets into very practical tool organizers. This year, the line extends all the way from the Mug Boss desk organizer at $5 to the 5-gallon Bucket Boss. This monster has a total of 56 pockets, 36 of them are outside the bucket and tiered so that all your pliers, hammers, and wrenches are organized and instantly accessible. At $27, it gives you a lot of bag for the buck. The Bucket Boss brand is available at many stores, but this time of year the best way to buy is the company web site, www.bucketboss.com.

Bucket Boss also has some of the best work gloves I have seen. Their Insulated True Grip Gloves at $31 and Deluxe Work Gloves at $24 combine the protection of work gloves with the flexibility and clingyness of a football receiver's glove.

The best gloves I've seen on the local level are IronClad Box Handler Gloves, $24, at Contractors Clothing, (248) 544-7380. The gloves are very flexible and have sticky grip stripes.

If you have a little handyman on your list, Contractors Clothing carries Carhartt Kids overalls ($23) and jackets ($57), sizes 1 year and up. If you actually want to put the tike to work, for $20 Home Depot has a Workforce beginners 20 piece tool set. The set includes a claw hammer, 2 screwdrivers, adjustable wrench, pliers, measuring tape, magnetic pickup and a 1/4-inch ratchet socket set. Everything is packed in a race car-shaped kit.

If you know someone who falls asleep listening to the radio, give him a way to listen without disturbing anyone. C. Crane Co., (800) 522-8863, has a Soft pillow speaker encased in padding for just $19.95.

Should your handyman or woman be a fan of my radio show, C. Crane also has the VersaCorder Tape Recorder, which records up to 4 hours on one side of a regular cassette for $100. They also have a Quarter Speed Cassette Player for $40 that will let your handyman listen to the VersaCorder tapes while jogging or puttering around in the garage.

You can't work all the time, so Brookstone, (248) 643-7055, at Sommerset has some neat ways to relax. There's a gray fleece massaging foot warmer for $60 and a bed rest pillow with a built in massager and reading light for $125.

Taking care of your footsies really must be in because two stores down, Sharper Image, (248) 643-4747, has a heated massaging foot spa with a wireless programmable remote and a two-roller massaging unit for $119.95. If the problem is not aching, but stinky feet, they also have an ionic shoe freshener for $39.95.

Now quick, better get shopping before they run out.

DECEMBER 15, 2001

Tricks and tips will help you survive entertaining holiday party guests

By Glenn Haege /
Special to The Detroit News

The holiday party season is in high gear. The invitations are out. The menu and shopping lists are all made. The gifts are wrapped and stashed until the big day.

Here are some hints to help make sure you get through the party period.

Outside

It doesn't matter that we've had a long fall. The bad weather will probably break the day before your party. Be ready.

Make certain the snow shovels and ice melters are handy, and the snow thrower is prepped and ready to go. Spray a coat of silicone on the bottom and the top edge of the shovel. That way, the snow won't stick and even the thickest, wettest snow will just glide off the blade.

Ice melters are always in short supply when you need them most. They are the last thing you want to be rushing out for on the night of the party.

Rock salt is inexpensive, but ineffective under 20 degrees Fahrenheit. When it is colder than that, you need a calcium chloride product. Some brand names of calcium chloride are Gibraltar DuoFlake, Prestone Driveway Heat and SnoMelt.

Magnesium chloride, potassium chloride and urea are easier on plants and paws. They are basically fertilizers that also melt ice. In our market, Gibraltar distributes magnesium chloride under the name Mag Chloride Pellets. They distribute a sodium chloride, calcium chloride and potassium chloride mix called Ice Devil Blended Deicer. A urea ice melter called Anti Skid by Suretrack Melt Inc., (717) 661-7179, is found in many supermarkets.

If outside windows look dirty, your best bet this time of year is to use automobile windshield washer fluid straight from the container. Apply the undiluted cleaner to the window, then squeegee off and wipe up drips with a towel.

Inside

Windows and mirrors can be cleaned streak-free with a mixture of 2 ounces of liquid household ammonia and 1 teaspoon of liquid hand dishwashing soap in a gallon of water. Wipe on then squeegee off.

During the winter, it is possible to spend hours dusting only to have to re-dust the next day. It's not you, it's the humidity. The week before the party, take special care to keep the humidity in the proper range. Adequate humidity keeps dust to a minimum, stops carpets from static sparks and reduces floor and wood furniture squeaks.

A light coat of Doozy Furniture Polish, (888) 851-8500, will protect leather couches and keep wooden furniture from showing fingerprints.

Since guests tend to congregate in the kitchen, brighten up laminate and solid surface countertops with Hope's Counter Top Polish, (800) 325-4026.

If you are going to use your good silver several times during the holiday season, Flitz International, (800) 558-8611, metal polish shines rapidly and retards tarnishing.

In the bathroom, The Works Tub and Tile Cleaner by Lime-O-Sol, (800) 448-5281, cuts through soap scum and eliminates watermarks better than anything I know.

The powder room is going to be over-stressed during the party. A couple weeks before the event, use a bacteriological/enzyme active drain cleaner in all sinks. Make certain that the commodes are free flowing.

Three hours before the guests arrive, dial the furnace down at least 3 degrees and click the fan control on the thermostat from Auto to On. Dial the water heater up to Hot. The extra cooking and people will deplete the hot water supply at the same time they add heat to the house. Every person adds 700 British Thermal Units (BTUs) of heat. Twenty extra people can easily add 4 or 5 degrees to the inside temperature, no matter how cold it is outside.

Finally, make certain that you are ready for the inevitable emergency with my emergency spill kit. A can of inexpensive foaming shaving cream, a bottle of club soda, and a couple of boxes of bargain white facial tissue can blot away almost any party problem.

When a spill happens, remain calm. Press an inch-thick wad of tissue on the spill. Do not rub. Facial tissue is very absorbent and will wick up the moisture. When the tissue is wet, replace it. If the stain is on a carpet, stand on the last wad of tissue with the sole of your foot, so that you absorb moisture from the carpet padding.

Should any stain remain, sprinkle on club soda and let it foam away the stain. After letting the soda work for a couple of minutes, absorb the remains with facial tissue. If necessary, repeat the process.

If the spill is something like gravy or beans, use facial tissue to lift up the ingredients. Use a grasping motion, do not rub. Repeat as necessary. When the bulk is gone, gently work shaving foam into the carpet or fabric fibers. Let the shaving cream work for a couple of minutes, then remove with facial tissue. When the last of the stain has been removed, sprinkle on club soda and blot up residue with tissue.

If you have a really bad stain like red wine or cranberry juice, you can get rid of any remaining stain the next day with Motsenbocker's Lift Off #1, Food, Beverage & Protein Stain Remover, (800) 346-1633, or SpotShot, (877) 477-6874.

Have a great party. Save this article until after your New Year's celebration.

DECEMBER 22, 2001

Safety is a key ingredient to making sure your holidays are happy

By Glenn Haege /
Special to The Detroit News

'Tis the season to be jolly, but there are a lot of people out there who want more than that. Retailers want to be jolly and make a lot of money selling you stuff. Restaurateurs and caterers want to be jolly and make a lot of money catering parties. Charities such as the Salvation Army and the Red Cross want to be jolly and raise a lot of money, so they can do good works.

All these things are commendable, but there are also not-so-nice people who want to be jolly and snatch and grab your purse, break in and steal your valuables and Christmas presents, swindle you with fake charities and steal your ID. The very sickest of these would get an extra giggle out of also beating you up or raping you.

These predators are very active during the holiday season because people of goodwill will let their guard down. We are so busy that we overlook obvious security measures. Let's pause for a moment to make sure we are doing the basics to keep our homes, families and persons safe.

One of the potentially most devastating crimes is the theft of one's identity. Ian Lyngklip of the Consumer Law Group, (248) 746-3790, says that it is surprisingly easy for a person to steal your identity. Many of us receive preapproved credit offers and even unsolicited credit cards in the mail. While you are out Christmas shopping or partying, the identity thief can easily steal mail from your mailbox. He could then send in a change of address form and go on a big Christmas buying spree. You could rack up huge bills without even knowing about it.

You might not know this happened until you were dunned by a collection agency or had a loan rejected because of bad credit.

Your credit also can be stolen using carbons from credit card charges, phone records, utility bills, employment and health records, ID badges or anything that incorporates your identity and your Social Security number, according to Lyngklip.

One of the best ways to keep this from happening is to empty your mailbox as soon as the mail is delivered. Where permissible, have mail stuffed through a chute in the door, so it is not available to outsiders.

Receipts or carbon copies of credit card forms or any other sensitive document should be torn into very small pieces before being discarded. If you don't already have one, a personal shredder is almost a necessity. It can make all of your discarded mail unreadable.

230

Breaking and entry is an even more common crime. Many people make it easy for thieves by hiding house keys in the mailbox or leaving a spare key over the doorway or under a mat. When you go out for the evening, leaving a set of keys with the parking attendant that includes your house key and car keys is like asking to be robbed. If the key ring also has your name and address, it is an engraved invitation.

I am not saying that the vast majority of parking lot attendants are not very honest individuals. I am saying that the keys they collect are usually not safeguarded adequately. Key rings are easily stolen and neither you nor the attendant might know about it until you come out for your car and found the keys missing.

Quite often, it does not even take a key. A lot of otherwise smart people will leave the door open while they rush over to the neighbors for a minute, or leave a key under the mat when they go to bed, so that a visiting relative can come in without having to wake up the household.

This thoughtfulness can allow your house to be cleaned out while you sleep. It also sets you up for a nighttime attack by someone who is not content with just taking your possessions. According to Interactive Technologies' web site, www.getsafe.com, 38 percent of all assaults and 60 percent of all rapes take place during a home invasion.

It is your job as a homeowner to do everything possible to make sure these things do not happen. Here are a few suggestions:

1. Be alert. If someone is loitering around your neighborhood, report them to the police.

2. Keep the lights on and make certain that the house has a lived in look during the holidays.

3. Make sure all doors, sliding doors and windows are locked. Dead-bolt locks for doors and metal rods or wooden dowels blocking sliding doors are a must.

4. Shred all receipts and unsolicited credit cards before throwing them away.

Lyngklip suggests that you also buy a consumer report from each of the three major credit reporting companies every six months to make certain that no one has been playing fast and loose with your reputation. The three companies are Trans Union, (800) 888-4213; Equifax Information Services, (800) 685-1111; and Experian, (888) 397-3742. The cost of each report is $8.50. The information you receive may be priceless. Oh, by the way, have a happy holiday, you've earned it.

DECEMBER 29, 2001

Despite all the reports of economic gloom and doom, building business is up

By Glenn Haege /
Special to The Detroit News

It is very easy to be nervous. We got sucker punched on September 11th and everything went down from there. Television reports tell us that the economy is going nowhere, bankruptcies abound, and unemployment is up. Is anybody safe?

During this period of doom and gloom, America's Master Handyman (me) has been almost alone saying that the Home Improvement/Home Building segment was hanging in there.

I am a pretty confident individual, but even I eventually began to have second thoughts. With all these naysayers, could the Handyman be wrong?

I felt a little better when I read the headline in the Nov. 19 edition of Nations Building. The headline read, "Housing Industry a Source of Strength. Downturn could be smallest ever."

Obviously, the nation's builders and the Handymen were out of the editorial loop. I started calling around to see if business was way down in the home improvement segment.

The first person I called was Howard Kuretzky, president of Kurtis Kitchen, (734) 522-7600. Kurtis is the second largest purchaser of KraftMaid Cabinets in the country. KraftMaid is the nation's largest maker of semi-custom cabinetry. Obviously, Kurtis should be singing the blues.

Handyman: "So Howard, how much do you expect business to be down next year?"

Kuretzky: "Are you crazy? We are projecting a 15 to 20 percent sales increase."

Handyman: "I hear people are cutting back. I suppose the size of your jobs is way down."

Kuretzky: "Glenn, we have had more big jobs this year than any year in our history. That trend is continuing. I don't know who is feeding you bad information. We expect 2002 to be a banner year."

I tried Mike McCoy, president of Coy Construction, (248) 363-1050. Coy made a name for itself by becoming one of the largest deck builders. Since then, they have become the nation's largest basement remodeler. With the business downturn, I knew that McCoy, his brother, and their crews must be desperate.

Handyman: "Mike, how many crews are you laying off? How much business do you expect to lose next year?"

McCoy: "My brother and I are expecting to grow at least 10 or 15 percent next year. As far as the crews go, we are doing everything we can to hold on to our people. If you know any good craftsmen, we'd like to talk to them."

Handyman: "Aren't you the least bit concerned?"

McCoy: "We had a 20 percent increase in business in 1999; a 20 percent increase in 2000; and a 15 percent increase this year. If it turns out that we only increase business by 10 percent next year, I will definitely start worrying."

Handyman: "Why do you think business is hanging in there?"

McCoy: "Simple mathematics. When people understand that by remodeling the basement they can add living space for $100 less per square foot than by adding on, they can't wait to buy."

Add McCoy to the list of misguided souls. I tried to call Eric Brakke at Four Seasons, (248) 352-4250, but the lines were so jammed, I couldn't get through. Joe Aiello at Pine Building, (888) 500-7463, was too busy to return my calls.

I almost struck pay dirt when I called David McGraw, president of Kimball & Russell, (248) 624-7000. Kimball & Russell is a big Andersen Window distributor. Since this is a national, mass marketed product, I knew McGraw had to be hurting.

Handyman: "So David, how much do you expect to lose next year?"

McGraw: "I can't give you an answer. Andersen just bought out a large custom window manufacturer in Ontario, so we will be able to offer builders a wider variety of custom sizes than ever before. That alone will create a big increase in sales. But I honestly can't tell you how much."

It was pretty much the same when I called Brad Upton at Dillman & Upton, (248) 651-9411, the hardware/lumber yard in Rochester.

Upton: "We're rebuilding our custom display area (again) this winter because of the large increase in Kitchen and Bath business. All I can tell you is that business is holding strong.

"You have to understand, some lumber prices are at a 5-year low. Drywall prices are also down and there is good availability. This makes it a very good time to buy."

In desperation to find someone pessimistic, I called David Heffner, Vice-President, Sales Manager of Consumer Lending at Standard Federal Bank, (877) 732-8240. Heffner wasn't much help.

Heffner: "Your readers can get the best home equity financing deals in 15 years. We can finance up to 80 percent of a home's value at between Prime less 0.5 percent to Prime plus 0.5 percent. If they need to borrow 100 percent of a home's value, we have a program at only 3 percent over prime. Your listeners can learn more by calling, or by visiting one of our offices or on the web at www.standardfederal.com.

"With money this cheap, it doesn't make sense to put off needed home improvements, so we expect to see big growth in home equity loans next year."

Next time you watch doom and gloom on your nightly newscast, remember the rate on home equity loans is at a 15-year low, lumber prices are down, availability is good, and the contractors are busy. The year 2002 will be a very good year for the home improvement industry. I hope you join us and have a very happy and prosperous new year.

Subject Index

Anti Skid, 121, 228
antiallergen disposable
  vacuum bag, 127
antimicrobial cloths, 137
Apex Supply, 62
Applegate Insulation, 155
Appliances, 12-13
April Aire, 225
  350, 7-8
  360, 7-8
  Model 760A, 9
Arborists, 147
Architectural Stone, 29, 32
architectural metal panels, 149
Arens, Egmont, 15
Armor-All, 43, 156-157
Armstrong, 167
Armstrong's Robbins
  Premium Hardwood Flooring, 189
Arrow Fresh & Clean Neutraquat, 37
Art
  Dishwasher, 177
  Fridge, 177
Arthritis Foundation, 58
asbestos, 81
ASHI, 194
Ashtiani, Amir, 196
Ask Glenn Column, 76
Aspergillus, 88-89
asphalt roofs, 21
Associated Landscape
  Contractors of America, 147
Association of Professional
  Landscape Designers, 146
attic insulation, 93, 118
Audia Woodworking &
  Fine Furniture Inc, 60-61
Audia, Sam, Sr. 60-61
automatic humidity control, 8-9
automatic standby generator, 223
Axoma Spa, 41

B

Back up electric power 348-349
B&G Equipment Co., 199
basement water damage, 89

baby-safe house, 100-101
bagless vacuums, 112
Barbara, 36
barrier-free, shower, 40
basement, 220
  escape window, 85
  laminate flooring, 200
  remodel, 123
  waterproofing, 220
  windows, 84-85
  flooded, 76
  new home, 90-91
basements,87
Bath Brite,44
bathroom cleaning, 151
bathtub deep cleaning, 44-45,
batts, insulation, 154
  fiberglass, 118
Bauder, Lillian, 64
Beam, 223
Beaver Distributors, 52
bedroom & bath products, 17
Behr, 39, 47, 174-75
  Plus 10 Solid Color Stain, 51
  Premium Plus, 51
  Wood Cleaner Brightener
    Conditioner, 47, 173
Bekaert ECD Solar Systems LLC, 149
beltless drive vacuum cleaner, 19
Benchmark, 44, 66, 71
  Legend, 60
  benefits of Code Plus
    construction, 221
Benjamin Moore, 96, 158, 159, 160
  Alkyd Porch & Floor Enamel, 158,
    159, 160
  MoorGard, 51
Benz, Melitta, 15
Berndes Cookware, 132
Better Homes and Gardens, 141
  New Complete Guide to Home
    Repair, 193
Beverage Warehouse, 54
Bicycle Stand, two place, 136
Biewer Lumber, 39
Big Builder Rankings, 180-81

I

J

K

Newell Rubbermaid, 16
Newhome Bath & Mirror, Inc., 179
NFRC, 218
Nice N Easy, 50
Nichols, Wayne, 76-77
Nirvana Safe Haven, 145
noise, outside, 66
non-ammoniated window
  washing solution, 202
North Carolina Department of
  Health and Human Services, 112
Northstar, 176
Novabrik, 148, 221
Novi Expo Center, 22, 138
Nu-Way Supply, 22, 139
Nu-Wool, 155

O

O Cedar Static Sweeper, 37
Oakland Community College, 65
Oakridge National Laboratory, 155
O'Brien, Bob, 28
O'Brien-Bernini, Frank, 212-213, 216
Office Depot, 156
old
  finish, 174
  House Journal, 110
  House Magazine, 110
Olympic, 39
  Deck Cleaner, 38
Olympic Maximum
  Waterproofing Sealant, 38-39
  Overcoat, 207
Once 'n Done, 53
One-piece toilet, paper holder, sink,
  storage cabinet and towel bar, 178
Oralgiene USA Inc, 17
OSI caulk, 187
Otres Inc., 19
  Kitchen Sanitizer, 19
outdoor furniture cleaning formula, 43
oven, convection, 16
overheated wiring, 102
Owens Corning, 63, 67, 92,
  118-119, 154, 155, 207
  acoustic design services, 212-213

insulation, 184
  Science and Technology Center, 216
  Sound Control Technology, 221
  WeatherLock, 119
Owens Corning's
  Basement Wall Finishing
  System, 213
  Science and Technology Center,
  212-213
Oxygen bleach, 173
Oxyne, 127
Oxysolv Rust Remover, 57
Ozone, 127

P

Padouk hardwood, 189
Paint
  N' Paper, 129
  Shaver/Remover, 50-51
  old, removal, 50-51
painting
  steel entrance door, 57
  varnished door, 56
Panasonic, 19
  HEPA Filtered Power Wave, 113
pantyhose compresses, 115
Paoletti, Renee, 14
Paper Tiger, 97
Parker, Terence, 149
party
  dress, cleaning, 107
  survival guide, 228-229
Patio Gourmet, 27
Patricia, 136
PC8900 Perfect Climate Control, 8-9
Pease, 59
  Industries, 58
Pella, 221
  Window, 13
Pendergast, J.C., Inc., 54
Penicillium, 88-89
Penofin, 39, 174-75
  Ultra, 169
  Red label, 38
  Weather Blaster, 47, 168, 173
perfect holiday gift, 100-101

S

W

Walker Crawford, 129
Walkway Saver, 136
wall
  insulation, 221
  paper, removing, 96-97
  Street Journal, 74
  switch,
    15-amp, 190
    mercury 190
    Wizard, 97, 203
Waller, Candise, 28, 30
walls, cleaning, 96, 150
Wallside window, 218
Wal-Mart, 80, 134
Walters, Dick, 165-167, 188-89
Walton, Fred, 15
Wash Caddy, 156-157
washing machine, compact, 18
Water
  coil hose, 199
  damage, 88-89, 186
  Furnace Company, 224
  leaks, 89
  pressure balancing, 41
  Spike, Jelled, 199
  wasted, 192-93
Waterproofing Contractors,
  certified, 77
WD-40, 215
weather resistant bulbs, 102
Weather Shield, 13, 67, 221
Weathergard window, 218
Web Tablet, 142
Weber, 27
WebPad Internet Appliance, 142
Weintraub, Wayne, 138-139
Weiser Lock, 13
West Nile Virus, 74
wheelbarrow, fold-away, 79
wheelchair friendly shower, 40
Whirlpool, 142
  appliances, 12-13
Whitney Design, 18

Wilk, Bob, 109
Willard Bishop Consulting, 14
William Zinsser, 97
Williams
  Jim, 6-7, 20, 54, 163-64, 210
  Panel Brick, 23, 27
  Refrigeration, 20, 144-145, 163,
    164, 210
  and Heating, 6
Wilsonart, 28, 30, 32
Windex, 202
Windjammer Clear
  Removable Sealant, 92
Window
  cleaning, 151
  inside, 228
  film, laminated, 204-205
  impact resistant, 13
  tint, 204-205
  washing solution,
  inside, 42
  non-ammoniated, 202
  outside, 42
  well
  drain, 201
  System,85
  wells, 84-85
windows
  and doors, 221
  basement, 84-85
  double-pane, 67
  foggy, 20
Windsor Peak Press, 111
Winfield, Jamie, 158, 159, 160
winter
  freeze/thaw cycles, 149
  projects, 123
Winters, Joysa, 144
Wiring, 91
  overheated, 102
Wisok, Kay, 29
Wm. Zinsser, 56
  1-2-3, 69

More clear, concise How-To Advice
From America's Master Handyman

Fix It Fast & Easy! In over 19 years on the air Glenn Haege has answered over 60,000 listeners questions. His answers to over 100 of the most asked "How To" questions are included in this book.

166 pages $14.95

Upgrading Your House, Fix It Fast & Easy! 2 In depth information on all major remodeling jobs: kitchens, baths, dormers, basements, heating, cooling, plumbing, electrical, windows, roofing, siding, and more

416 pages $19.95

Take the Pain out of Painting – Interiors Everything you need to know to have a professional looking paint job, plus a 40 page section on faux finishing and the industry's only comprehensive stain kill guide.

264 pages $14.97

Take the Pain out of Painting – Exteriors In depth explanations on painting every exterior surface from wood and aluminum siding to shingles, concrete block and log homes; plus when to paint, when to stain and how to prepare the surface for a great looking, long lasting job.

224 pages $12.95

Haege's Homestyle Articles, The Detroit News, 1995-99 The first five years of Glenn Haege's highly popular "Handyman" articles cover almost every home improvement subject from air quality, cleaning, heating and cooling to deck care, painting, roofing, electrical problems, and flooded basements. Also includes special reports and a comprehensive listing of the most requested phone numbers and web sites.

598 pages $24.95

Ask your favorite book seller for these titles or order direct:
By Phone: Call (888) 426-3981

By Fax: (248) 589-8554

By e-mail: Go to www.masterhandyman.com and click on Book Store

By Mail: Use the handy form on the next page and mail to:
Master Handyman Press, Inc.
P.O. Box 1498
Royal Oak, MI 48068-1498

Master Handyman Press, Inc.
Quick Order Form

Please send me the following books by Glenn Haege:

Haege's Homestyle Articles, 1995-99, 598 pages $24.95, $ _____

Haege's Homestyle Articles, 2000-01, 260 pages $14.95, $ _____

Fix It Fast & Easy!, 166 pages $14.95, $ _____

Upgrading Your House, Fix It Fast & Easy! 2, 416 pages
$19.95, $ _____

Take the Pain out of Painting – Interiors, 264 pages $14.97, $ _____

Take the Pain out of Painting – Exteriors, 224 pages $12.95, $ _____

Send to:

Name: _____

Address _____

City: _____ State: _____ Zip: _____

Telephone: _____

E-mail address: _____
Sales tax:
  Please add 6% Sales tax for all books shipped to Michigan Addresses.

Shipping:
  US: $4 for the first book and $2 for each additional.
  International: $9 for the first book and $5 for each additional.

Payment:
  Check, Money Order or Credit card:
    Visa, MasterCard, Amex, Discover

Card number: _____

Name on card: _____ Expiration Date: ___/___

Authorization signature: _____

Call (888) 426-3981 or send to:
  Master Handyman Press, Inc.
  P.O. Box 1498
  Royal Oak, MI 48068-1498

This last page
is a tribute to
Gordon Earnest Sommer,
Production Manager,
Web Master,
husband, father,
grandfather,
friend.
March 4, 1939 - February 6, 2002.

-30-